Vampira and Her Daughters

ALSO BY ROBERT MICHAEL "BOBB" COTTER
AND FROM MCFARLAND

*The Women of Hammer Horror: A Biographical
Dictionary and Filmography* (2013)

*Caroline Munro, First Lady of Fantasy:
A Complete Annotated Record
of Film and Television Appearances* (2012)

Ingrid Pitt, Queen of Horror: The Complete Career (2010)

*A History of the Doc Savage Adventures
in Pulps, Paperbacks, Comics, Fanzines,
Radio and Film* (2009; paperback 2016)

*The Great Monster Magazines:
A Critical Study of the Black and White Publications
of the 1950s, 1960s and 1970s* (2008)

*The Mexican Masked Wrestler and Monster
Filmography* (2005; paperback 2008)

Vampira and Her Daughters

Women Horror Movie Hosts from the 1950s into the Internet Era

ROBERT MICHAEL "BOBB" COTTER

Foreword by Penny Dreadful

McFarland & Company, Inc., Publishers
Jefferson, North Carolina

LIBRARY OF CONGRESS CATALOGUING-IN-PUBLICATION DATA

Names: Cotter, Bobb, author.
Title: Vampira and her daughters : women horror movie hosts from the 1950s into the internet era / Robert Michael "Bobb" Cotter ; foreword by Penny Dreadful.
Description: Jefferson, North Carolina : McFarland & Company, Inc., Publishers, 2017 | Includes bibliographical references and index.
Identifiers: LCCN 2016055697| ISBN 9781476664347 (softcover : acid free paper) ∞
Subjects: LCSH: Television broadcasting of horror films—United States. | Women television personalities—United States—Biography-Dictionaries. | Horror films—History and criticism. | Horror television programs—History and criticism.
Classification: LCC PN1992.8.F5 C68 2017 | DDC 016.79145750973—dc23
LC record available at https://lccn.loc.gov/2016055697

BRITISH LIBRARY CATALOGUING DATA ARE AVAILABLE

ISBN (print) 978-1-4766-6434-7 ∞
ISBN (ebook) 978-1-4766-2656-7

© 2017 Robert Michael "Bobb" Cotter. All rights reserved

No part of this book may be reproduced or transmitted in any form or by any means, electronic or mechanical, including photocopying or recording, or by any information storage and retrieval system, without permission in writing from the publisher.

On the front cover: Maila Nurmi as host of *The Vampira Show* on KABC-TV in Los Angeles, 1954–1955

Printed in the United States of America

*McFarland & Company, Inc., Publishers
Box 611, Jefferson, North Carolina 28640
www.mcfarlandpub.com*

Dedicated to Dad, Mom, Brownie, Ingrid Pitt, "Chilly Billy" Cardille, Zacherle, Christopher Lee, Elena Watson, Yvonne Craig, Richard "Dick Nitelinger" Golembiewski, Lemmy, David Bowie and Jeff Rice (R.I.P.); George "E-Gor" Chastain (Webmonster of "E-Gor's Chamber of TV Horror Hosts"), Paul C. Riggie (The Reception), my wonderful wife Cheryl, Lucky the Wonder Dog and, on the drums, Mr. Bun E. Carlos

With special thanks to Roberta Solomon, Penny Dreadful, Misty Brew, Timexx, Dennis Druktenis and the late, great *Scary Monsters* magazine, Terence Sanford, Eide's Entertainment, Paul Counelis, Carmela Hayslett (Roxsy Tyler), Nicole Brooks (Sally the Zombie Cheerleader), Marlena (Midnite) Metzger, Jo Rowan (Stella Lugosi), Janet Decay, Reyna Young (Miss Misery), Kris Selman, Kathy Brown (Suspira Sheridan), Dixie Dellamorto, Mr. Lobo, Darryl Mayeski (*Screem* magazine), Halloween Jack, Halloween Jacqueline

Table of Contents

Foreword by Penny Dreadful 1

Preface 3

Biographical Dictionary and Filmography 7

Bibliography 161

Index 163

Foreword
by Penny Dreadful

The Horror Host … your friend … your fiend. The Horror Host—there to guide you through fanged nightmares and unnatural terrors.

Where do horror hosts come from? Some say we are all the unholy spawn of the Bride of Frankenstein and Lou Costello. I'm not allowed to talk about that, though. I hope nobody burns me at the stake for mentioning it. Generally speaking, the first person who told scary stories around the campfire was a horror host. They took their listeners by the metaphorical (crawling) hand and led them through the world of shadows. Later, the Ghost Masters of the live Spook Shows served as "proto" horror hosts. Dr. Silkini, Dr. Scream and Dr. Jekyll all got their doctorates in Unspeakable Horror.

The first "proper" (improper?) horror hosts, however, appeared on the radio. Shows like *The Witch's Tale*, *The Hermit's Cave* and *Inner Sanctum* were introduced by individuals who could very much be described as full-on horror hosts. The Hermit, Old Nancy the Witch of Salem, Raymond and others welcomed listeners into their lairs and described that evening's tale of the macabre. Raymond's sardonic sense of humor may have even helped pave the way for later hosts. Shortly thereafter, the lurid EC comic books *Tales from the Crypt*, *Vault of Horror* and *Haunt of Fear* had their own set of horror hosts. The Crypt Keeper, the Old Witch and the Vault Keeper took gleeful delight in showing readers all manner of grotesque things. These comic book hosts continued to shape and inform the format.

As far as television, Vampira is generally recognized as the very first television horror host. Her show debuted on the Los Angeles scarewaves in 1954. Others say a fellow named the Swami hosted a show on Chicago TV before Vampira hosted hers. Regardless of who came first, Vampira clearly became a huge hit. She is typically considered the "mother" of horror hosts and of the TV horror host format. Horror hosts became "a thing" in her wake, with television stations creating their own macabre hosts once the "Shock Theater" package of horror and mystery films became available in 1957. Perhaps the best horror host is the legendary Zacherley (first called Roland). With his manic, mad experiments and infectious laugh, he still reigns as "King of the Horror Hosts." The most anarchistic was Ghoulardi, and his fans are legion. Today the most famous is Elvira, whose show catapulted her to international stardom.

Some horror hosts had a dark sense of humor (Simon), while some were completely serious (Gorgon). Others were just plain funny (Stella). Some were monsters (Shock Armstrong), some were regular, very witty people (Bob Wilkins). Even though the television landscape has changed dramatically since the 1950s, the horror host has not. Like the proverbial zombie, we keep coming back from the grave. Svengoolie, Dr. Gangrene, Ghoul-a-Go-Go, Dr. Dreck, Mr. Lobo, Wolfman Mac, Count Gore de Vol, Dr. Sarcofiguy and many more lurk in the eerie glow of your TV or computer screens. Just like the EC Comics' horror hosts, we take such gleeful delight in showing you that which is forbidden and appalling ... but in a nice way. You see, the horror host has always been a pal to children. We're the friendly creepies who help you through that scary movie. The horror host is sometimes scary, sometimes funny and always weird. We come in many flavors, just like Life-Savers ... or maybe we're more like Death-Savers. Either way, horror hosts are simply hex-cellent, and I do hope you'll enjoy this tome of terror.

Penny Dreadful (Danielle Gelehrter), one of the longest-serving of the Modern Age of Horror Hosts, is most famous for her Shilling Shockers. *No longer doing* Shilling Shockers *as such, she maintains the persona, and continues to appear in annual Halloween specials. The recently released ninth season of* Shilling Shockers *was its last, but the show may one day be reincarnated under a different name.*

Preface

> "There's a whole new breed of women that feel they're just as smart, just as courageous as men—and they are. They don't like to be over-protected, and they don't like to have their initiative taken away from them."
> —*It Came from Beneath the Sea* (1955)

In the beginning, there was television. Not the multi-headed, trillion-channel, specialized, compartmentalized beast that we know today; at first, the fare offered was limited to what the major networks and corporations chose to give us and to what local stations could invent. Happily, the two converged in what would come to be regarded as a pivotal chapter in pop culture history with many of its participants going on to become pop culture icons. Vampira (Maila Nurmi) was not only the first of what would later become known and loved as "Horror Hosts"; in fact, Nurmi was doing Vampira a good two or three years before the legendary "Shock Theater" was packaged for syndication and the Golden Age of Horror Hosts began. And the first, the original, was a woman. And, no offense to Zacherley, whom I love and respect, but the most-recognized Horror Host is a woman: Elvira, Mistress of the Dark.

Nobody knows exactly who had the brainstorm of "Hey, let's have a host for the monster movies on TV," but, in truth, the idea of a presenter that bookended gruesome events with humor in order to assure audiences (especially children) that this was only a movie (or radio broadcast, or a play, or a comic book) was very old. In that sense, Vampira was upholding a well-established tradition, only for a new medium. She had everything it took ... except for the right movies. Most of the movies she presented were creaky old mysteries like *The Thirteenth Guest*. She didn't have the "Shock Theater" package to back her up (although that legendary package contained its own fair share of cinema-in-need-of-an-oil-can). But, before this becomes the entry on Vampira, suffice to say that Horror Host-dom probably still would have happened, but it would probably have looked and talked a whole lot different. And it became its own tradition, which is still being practiced to this very day.

As a history, mine may disappoint some readers, because for some horror hosts, there is a near-complete lack of information. I share that disappointment. Research was not a problem with the bigger names, but many times, a horror host was a local or regional phenomenon, and a lot of times, all we have in the way of information are the memories of those who were associated with the show or station, or the odd promotional piece. Add to that the fact that many of the hosts were not professional actors; he or she was the TV station's weather person or another type of employee, and got pulled into the whole routine. So it's not like you can go to Wikipedia or the IMDb and look 'em all up and have done with it. I did the best I could, with a lot of help from my friends. That being said, there were still three hostesses for whom information is so elusive that all that remains are their names: Madame Ghoulery, Rhonda (not Shear) and Wilhelmina.

One of my friends came up with the concept for this book. At the 2015 summer Monster Bash convention, which, fittingly enough, is held in Mars, Pennsylvania, I was lamenting the fact that I couldn't do an Elvira book. Enter George Chastain, better known as E-Gor, who perpetrates the Mother of all horror host websites, "E-Gor's Chamber of TV Horror Hosts." He suggested that, since my last three books had been about women, why don't I do a book on female Horror Hosts? After some discussion with him and Doctor Riggie, Jr., we agreed that would make for a great book. You hold the result in your hands.

While I love horror hosts in general (else I wouldn't be writing a book about them), and the contributions they've made to pop culture, it seems like, from Vampira on, their style has been one of jokes and sarcasm. Are they, in a way, just as responsible as the evil Medved brothers for the "Bad Movie" cultists? Now, admittedly, a great percentage of the movies *were* low-budget fare that perhaps deserved the acid that was thrown in their faces, but quite a few were not; the host would make fun of it regardless. Whether it was *Cat-Women of the Moon* or *Frankenstein*, the song remained the same. I get that, at the time, horror hosts provided a humorous respite from the scary films (although, in retrospect, it's difficult to see even *Frankenstein* scaring anybody that much), but those were different times, so we can allow for that. But, regardless of the quality, did horror hosts help or hurt how the public perceives horror films in general? Just askin'...

And another thing: There's been much debate about whether the "new wave" of horror hosts is "legit." Some would argue that the only real hosts are the ones who were actually on TV, had jobs with the stations, etc., and the new folks viewable via public access and YouTube and websites are just wannabe hosts; they somehow aren't carrying on the tradition. I disagree. From the earliest days of television through about the '80s, they had something called local programming. Network affiliates throughout the country might have *The CBS Evening News* with Walter Cronkite, and the usual spate of major-network shows and sports, but other than that, they were pretty much left to fend for themselves in terms of how they filled the rest of the air time. Now it's all different; practically all the stations are possessions of mega-corporations, and they all run the same thing at the same time on the same channels, be they in Tarzana, California, or West Mifflin, Pennsylvania. There is virtually no local programming, except for the news and other odd bits. So where is a horror host to go? I would argue that the public access, YouTube and website hosts are the modern versions of local, independent stations. Not only that, but the new breed of hosts are hosts because they want to be; stations no longer pick someone out of the secretarial pool or the host of, say, *Gardening Today* and tell them, bang, you're a horror host. The do-it-yourself spirit lives in the new hosts. The new hosts have deviated from the norm of force-fed mainstream culture, and looked to both the past and the future to keep the fire burning.

One *more* thing—and this is in regard to the original horror host characters who had "wives" (either real or imagined). It is entirely possible that I'm over-thinking this, but I still feel that it needs to be addressed in some manner. Here goes: Domestic abuse and spousal assault have been around much longer than movies, and it continues today,

Preface

even though by now, we as a people should have risen above it (as we should many other things that unfortunately still exist). The point is, again, did some horror hosts help or merely reinforce the prevailing attitudes of the times? I think of two hosts in particular: Marvin and Zacherley. Marvin's (Terry Bennett) co-host was "Dear," played by Joy Bennett. Her face was never seen, and Marvin perpetrated all sorts of heinous acts on her—and apparently with no serious effect. No matter how Marvin brutalized "Dear," she was always back after the next commercial break, none the worse for the wear, cartoon-like, as if she was Wile E. Coyote getting up and dusting herself off after an A-Bomb explosion. "Isobel," or "My Dear," was Zach's on-air "wife," and unlike "Dear," she wasn't even a real character. Zach kept her in a coffin, which very often he ran a large iron pole through, or some similar indignity; when she "spoke," it was in an ape's voice that had been monkeyed around with. Now, don't get me wrong, I love Zach and Marvin. Still, I can't help but feel that it begs the question brought up earlier. It was all supposed to be "ironic" and in good fun, but seeing as how the overwhelming audience was comprised of male children, how many of the kids received unconscious reinforcement that it was an acceptable way to view and treat women? To be hidden from the world, either figuratively or literally, subject to whatever violent whim that seized their mates; without speech or speaking unintelligible gibberish. That's another reason that the female hosts were so important: from Vampira, dangerous for both her sexuality and her independence, to Moona Lisa, through Crematia and Stella, down to Elvira and Penny Dreadful, female horror hosts have been symbols of female empowerment. True, many of them have been physically beautiful women (though not all, and some have not even been women), and they have used that to attract viewers, but, over time, this became less of a studio demand (especially as local programming began its death throes) and more a decision of the women themselves. Moreover, the women own the characters so, in terms of marketing and income, any money that they generate goes, not to some station that continues to pay the host a flat fee, but to the women. Cassandra Peterson is a gorgeous woman, sure, but she's also very shrewd, and she has made Elvira not just a household word but a brand, a franchise that, in Vampira's time, would have been inconceivable. So, unfortunately, there's still a "glass ceiling" for women, but the female horror hosts have certainly done their part to shatter it. I love the sound of breaking glass.

The following is a dictionary of horror hosts arranged by character name, except when the host went by her real name for the show. The only other thing I'll say by way of introduction is to answer a couple of questions: Bobb, why are your last few books been so female-centric? Well, that's simple enough: Even though women have made important strides in the genre, I feel that their contributions are still, in some cases, criminally under-appreciated, so the more exposure they get for their efforts, the better. As to whether I've been in the Borgo Pass the last few years … I had a stroke in November 2012. I like to think I've pretty much recovered, and that I haven't lost the ability to inform and entertain, but only time and the book you hold will tell. I just wanted to take this opportunity to thank everyone for all their love and support and encouragement during these sometimes still-troubled times.

Biographical Dictionary and Filmography

Aunt Gertie
REAL NAME: Dick Von Hoene (1941–2004)
BIRTHPLACE: Cincinnati, Ohio
HOST: *Scream-In* (1969–1972), WXIX Channel 19, Cincinnati, Ohio
BIOGRAPHY: Not to be confused with that *other*, the original "Cool Ghoul," Zacherley (or, for that matter, that *other, other* "Cool Ghoul," George Cavender), Dick Von Hoene was *the* Cool Ghoul for the godless barbarian residents of Cincinnati, Ohio, for three hilarious years on *Scream-In*, a much funnier show than the show that inspired its title (*Rowan & Martin's Laugh-In*). Von Hoene attended the University of Cincinnati and graduated with a B.A. in history and M.A. in theater, which was to serve him well in the role of the Cool Ghoul. He introduced the character on the local radio show *Bob Smith's Monster Mash*, playing him in a series of comedy sketches written for friend and co-worker Larry Smith. Smith, a puppeteer, created Hattie the Witch, who visited *Scream-In* a number of times, and even had a hosting gig of her own a time or two. One of Cincinnati's best-loved celebrities, the Cool Ghoul made numerous personal appearances. Although *Scream-In* proper only had a three-and-a-half-year run, Von Hoene frequently revived the character; he even interviewed himself on an episode of *Northern Kentucky Magazine*, the public affairs show he was hosting at the time of his death. He was an old hand at working with himself; he would appear on *Scream-In* as two different characters at the same time, and one of those was Aunt Gertie.

Sandra Bernhard (1955–)
BIRTHPLACE: Flint, Michigan
HOST: *Reel Wild Cinema* (1994–1996), USA Network
BIOGRAPHY: I believe Sandra Bernhard can best be described metaphorically. She hails from Michigan, and like the music of those other Michigan-based pre–Punk punks such as the MC5 and Iggy and the Stooges, she is raw, abrasive, confrontational and oddly beautiful. She's been on the cutting edge of stand-up comedy for about 40 years; she has a long, diverse list of acting credits; and she's a musician (pop, jazz and blues) and author (*May I Kiss You on the Lips, Miss Sandra?*). Bernhard had this to say about her origins in the stage show *Without You, I'm Nothing, with You, I'm Not Much Better*: "My father was a proctologist and my mother was an abstract artist, so that's how I view the world."

Bernhard attended Saguaro High School in Arizona. Upon graduation, she lived and volunteered in a collective community in Israel for a year. She then moved to L.A.; while waiting for her big break, she worked as a manicurist, doing nails as well as comedy. Bernhard became a fixture of the L.A. stand-up scene, which in 1977 led her to become one of the supporting actors on *The Richard Pryor Show*. The big break came six years later with her role in *The King of Comedy*. In 1985, she staged a solo show called *I'm Your Woman*. Nineteen eighty-eight brought *Without You, I'm Nothing...*, which later became both a film and an album. Rumors began to circulate of a romantic relationship with Madonna, and she made a cameo in Madonna's fake documentary, the woeful *Truth or Dare* (U.K. title: *In Bed with Madonna*). From 1991 to 1997, she was a semi-regular on the sitcom *Roseanne* and made history of sorts in the process: She was one of the first actresses on American network TV to play an openly gay character. Nineteen ninety-one was also the year she appeared in the jaw-droppingly bad Bruce Willis movie *Hudson Hawk*; everybody mugs outrageously, and Bernhard and Richard Grant as Minerva and Darwin Mayflower are at the top of the list, seemingly playing a very, *very* twisted version of Morticia and Gomez Addams.

Sandra Bernhard, host of *Reel Wild Cinema*, 1994.

Produced by Mike Vraney of Dead Kennedys and Something Weird Video fame, *Reel Wild Cinema* began a two-year run in 1994, It featured edited versions of all types of Grade B (and Grade Z) movies and cult films with (as Bernhard put it) "all the bad parts cut out, so you can just enjoy the bad parts." The movies were so massively edited that she was often able to fit three or more films in an episode! Watching the show was like watching those old 8mm Castle Films they used to sell in the back pages of *Famous Monsters* (except that Castle Films never offered anything like *Strip-O-Rama* or *Moonshine Mountain*—at least, not in *FM*), and with the added bonus of a right-on, reel wild hostess. Most were exactly the sort of films near and dear to the hearts of fans of TV horror hosts: low-budget American, Mexican and Japanese horrors of every description. Like some other hosts, Sandra also featured guests such as David Friedman, Roger Corman, Mamie Van Doren, Tura Satana and Fred Olen Ray. The show always paired its movies up with some kind of theme: "Lunatics on the Loose" (*Curse of the Aztec Mummy*, *The Monster of Camp Sunshine* and *Bloody Pit of Horror*), "Supernatural Sirens" (*La Llorona*, *Santo vs. the Vampire Women* and *Girl in a Cage*), "Psycho-a-Go-Go" (*Hot-Blooded Women*, *The Sex-Killer*, *Blood Feast*, *Mondo Bizarro* and *The Lonely Sex*) and "Southern Sleaze" (*Moonshine Mountain*, *Jenny: Wife-Child*, *2000 Maniacs*, *Hip, Hot and 21*, *The Moonshiners* and *Girl with an Itch*).

Since *Reel Wild Cinema* didn't show only horror movies, Bernhard's set was a departure from the usual dark, spooky, haunted mansion; hers was instead a brightly lit, ultra-retro apartment, the very vision of Populuxe, with boomerang-shaped coffee table and the like. Bernhard's introductions to the film clips were typical of her take-no-prisoners style. This is from the "Southern Sleaze" episode:

> Tonight we're gonna raise the Confederate flag, grab a flask o' moonshine, an' touch our brother in inappropriate places! We're goin' to Dixie! That's right, so let's hunker down with some good ol' Southern sleaze, only on USA's *Reel Wild Cinema*. Whew! Hello, I'm Sandra Bernhard, no relation to the trailer-park trash you'll see here tonight; that's right, *Reel Wild Cinema*'s goin' down south, an' I like the sound o' that! But in the south, I'd probably end up livin' out one o' those women-in-prison films; you know, the ones where the female warden always has a hot tub in her office? Our first feature tonight was made by Herschell Gordon Lewis, 1964's *Moonshine Mountain* ... be sure to check out the slightly overweight Courtney Love lookalike warblin' through an authentic bluegrass tune. She appears, as I was, to be hypnotized by the bellybutton of a flabby moonshiner. Yee haw!

Later in the same show, she asks, "Did it dawn on anybody but me that Albert Peckinpah was so old that Jenny was probably his wife *and* child? So far, we've had drooling hicks, killer moonshine, and zany incest; only thing left is some cruel torture. Stick around for *2000 Maniacs*..."

But, ultimately, it all comes down to Vampira, doesn't it? In 2007, she debuted a stage show called *Plan B from Outer Space*, and the circle was completed when Bernhard's new breed of horror host teamed with the original, Vampira, in the 1999 movie *I Woke Up Early the Day I Died*. For Bernhard, it was just one of her many movie roles, and for Maila Nurmi, it was her last.

Other Genre Credits—FILM: *The Apocalypse*, EGM Film International, 1997 (J.T. Wayne); *I Woke Up Early the Day I Died*, Muse, 1999 (Sandy Sands); TELEVISION: *Alfred Hitchcock Presents*: "The Night Caller," 1985 (Karen); *Deadly Nightmares*: "O.D. Feelin,'" 1986 (Rat); *Tales from the Crypt*: "Top Billing," 1991 (Sheila Winters); *A.J.'s Time Travelers*: "Cleopatra," 1995 (Cleopatra); *Highlander*: "Dramatic License," 1996 (Carol Marsh); *Spider-Man—The Animated Series*: "Partners in Danger," Chapter 5, "Partners," 1997 (Voice of Sarah Baker); *Superman—The Animated Series*: "Mxyzpixilated," 1997 (Voice of Gsptlnsz); *Hercules*: 44 episodes, 1998–1999 (Cassandra); *Hercules: From Zero to Hero* (animated), 1999 (Voice of Cassandra)

Blaidonella

REAL NAME: unknown

HOST: *Creature Features* (1972), KTVW, Channel 13, Seattle, Washington

BIOGRAPHY: Sometimes when you research a horror host, all you get is a photograph or TV ad. After days of trawling the Internet, print resources, calling the station, yadda yadda yadda, you come up empty. But here are a few raw facts and a little supposition. KTVW started its on-air life as KMO-TV in 1953, and was owned by Carl Haymond. After a year or so, due to a poor signal and other factors, Haymond was forced to declare bankruptcy and sold the station to J. Elroy McCaw's Gotham Broadcasting, who changed the station's call letters to KTVW. (It's now KCPQ, a member of the Fox monolith.) McCaw died in 1969, and in 1971, the station was sold to Blaidon Mutual Investors Corporation. No doubt, this is where the "Blaidonella" name came from (they also had an afternoon cartoon show hosted by a low-budget superhero called "Flash Blaidon"). But there is no record of *Creature Features* having been part of Channel 13's on-air offerings. There *was* a horror movie show on the station from 1972 to 1976, *Dr. ZinGRR's Astro* (or *Astral*, depending on the source) *Projections*; Dr. ZinGRR was played by DJ Robert O. Smith. The show had a supporting cast, but Blaidonella is not among the characters listed. Is it possible that *Creature Features* morphed into *Dr. ZinGRR*? Maybe the *Creature Features* film package became too expensive to rent; perhaps the lovely actress who portrayed Blaidonella left the station or simply didn't wish to carry on playing the "Fairy Princess" (as shown in the ad, clothed entirely in a white gown and headpiece, quite the departure from the usual black-clad graveyard sirens). Whatever the case, it seems as though Blaidonella has slipped between the cracks of time.

Bubbles

REAL NAME: Doreen Zawislak (Ryder) (1970–)

HOST: *Creature Features/Scream-In/Mad Theater/Horror Theater* (1970–1979), WPHL-TV, Channel 17, Philadelphia, Pennsylvania

BIOGRAPHY: Although the name "Bubbles" seems like an exotic dancer's *nom de stage*, Doreen Zawislak was the farthest thing from the Variations-on-a-Vampira-Theme or the Morticia Addams–like look that most of

Most of what we know about Blaidonella comes to us from this 1972 advertisement"(courtesy George "E-Gor" Chastain).

the female species of horror host seemed to favor; in fact, she was just a child. Moreover, she was literally only a few months old when she made her TV debut with her father, the legendary Dr. Shock (Joseph Zawislak). Dr. Shock's Channel 17 show was unabashedly based on another host, the even-more-legendary Zacherley, and, with Zach's approval, he began haunting the Philadelphia airwaves with *Creature Features*. After a few broadcasts, the name of the show was changed to the more "happening" *Scream-In*; after a few more, it was cancelled. But then the station took note of the ratings and quickly resuscitated the show, albeit with a few changes.

The biggest change was Bubbles. Insomuch as the show's biggest fans were kids, Channel 17 decided that it should be more kid-friendly, and what better way than to have an actual infant, sitting on her daddy's lap, on the show? Fortunately for the station, Joe's wife Sylvia had their fifth child, Doreen, on February 1, 1970, and a star was born—a star named after the show's sponsor, Bubbles Booth Soda. Her first appearance on the newly refurbished *Scream-In* came on July 11, 1970, when she was seven months old. According to the show's storyline, she had been left on the doctor's doorstep by the good Witch Hazel. Hazel was trying to save the little girl from the beautiful but deadly (and never-seen) "Gretchen Berserk," who apparently was part-witch and part-actress. Gretchen "possessed" Bubbles in order to become more famous, so perhaps she was more actress than witch (fill in your own joke here). In an interview with John Skerchock, published in *Scary Monsters* #27, she shared some of her Monster Memories of the show and her dad: "Those were wonderful times for me. I loved going to the studio. Everyone was so nice to me. They really treated me like a star. My sisters were a little jealous of me. Every week I got a new dress to wear on the show from one of our sponsors." Her sister Deb confirmed this: "Yeah, it used to make us mad that she got the treatment."

Bubbles and her father, Doctor Shock, at the height of their fame, circa 1972 (courtesy Paul Riggie).

But that was soon forgotten in the wake of a shared Halloween hardship (for, naturally, the Dr. Shock household was a destination spot for Philadelphia area trick-or-treaters): "I remember my sisters taking me trick-or-treating," said Bubbles. "We'd have to hurry up and go through the neighborhood and get home, because every year Mom would run out of candy and have to use ours. I don't know how old I was before I got to taste my first piece of Halloween candy!"

But life was not all a bed of nails for Bubbles. In a stunt that would have gone viral on the Internet today, and would have caused public and social media outrage...

> My scariest moment with Dr. Shock was when Dad put me in this basket and started putting swords through the basket. We rehearsed this before, but it was still scary. That was at a public appearance somewhere. Dad was always in parades. As Bubbles, I had to be with him. It was neat having all those people waving at you and calling out your name. But one time I felt terrified because we were sitting high on this float, and I'm scared of heights. Dad's telling me, "Wave at your fans. Don't be shy." And here I am, scared I'm going to fall off. One of my fondest memories of Dad was when we were at a public appearance. The people were all around us. Dad had just come out with a record album, *Monster Mash with Dr. Shock* [Argus Records, 1978]. It was a big hit and people were asking for his autograph. Well, Dad let me sign my name, too. It made me feel good to know that I was important to him.

The years 1973 and 1974 saw the winds of change blow through Channel 17. The new station manager didn't want *Scream-In* on Saturday nights any more; from here on out, it would only be shown in the afternoons. The new station manager also thought that there was too much time devoted to Dr. Shock and his wacky routines, so he cut back on the doctor's time; henceforth, he only appeared for six to twelve minutes per show. To complete his hat trick, the station manager changed the name of the show. *Scream-In* was no more, replaced by *Mad Theatre* and *Horror Theatre*, because the sales department discovered that if they sold Dr. Shock as two shows instead of one, they could cut twice as many deals, or some sort of marketing jiggery-pokery. But the biggest change occurred in Dr. Shock himself: Joseph Zawislak was a sick man. Viewers began to notice that, over the years, he was losing weight, but this could possibly be from the exhausting schedule he maintained. His real health problems began when he was riding horses with his brother; Zawislak broke his arm and was replaced for three weeks with a clown. But he was no sooner back on the air, when he suffered his first heart attack. He took new health precautions, but he was fighting a losing battle; he passed away on September 28, 1979, at age 42. Doreen said:

> Our whole world came to an end. I was only nine years old, and already I was missing a big piece out of my life. My dad meant a lot to a lot of people. It's been 20 years since my father passed away ... those times were wonderful for me, but because I was so young when my dad's show was on, everything is like a blur. ...I was close to my Dad. I know he'd want to be remembered. I plan to do all I can to see that he *is* remembered.

Don't worry about that, Doreen. As long as there are Monster Kids and Horror Hosts, Dr. Shock and Bubbles will never be forgotten.

Bunny Galore
REAL NAME: Martin Ramsdin
BIRTHPLACE: London, England
HOST: *Bunny Galore's Movie Nightmares* (2012–) Information TV; Showcase TV; Showcase 2; U.K.

BIOGRAPHY: "No one knows how old aging actress Bunny Galore is, but rumours abound that she was the first Neolithic pin-up" (*The List*)

Bunny Galore is the alter-ego of British performer Martin Ramsdin. She's mainly a burlesque and pantomime artist; she's been working the circuit for 17 years and counting. She's also been a horror host for the last few years. She discovered the horror-host genre via *Elvira's Movie Macabre*. Suitably intrigued, Ms. Galore made her online debut in with a "pilot" called *Movie Nightmares*. The next year, she pitched it to a British television station. They were suitably intrigued, and she's been at it ever since. The horrors that she shows are mostly public domain (*House on Haunted Hill*, *White Zombie* and *Carnival of Souls*, which featured a guest appearance by fellow horror host Mr. Lobo), but she also shows stuff like *At War with the Army* and *The Last Time I Saw Paris* ... which I guess qualify as nightmares. Her sidekick is a man of ... well, at least three faces: the Vicar, Zog the Alien and Jan in the Pan.

Although Bunny Galore is a late bloomer, her shows are always cheeky, naughty, a wink and a nod, but well-informed. She's entirely charming and, above all, fun, and proves that horror-hosting is not solely the province of the young. Carry on, Bunny!

Caroline Schlitt (1963–)

HOST: *USA Up All Night* (1989–1990), USA Network (cable)

BIOGRAPHY: The daughter of writer-producer Robert Schlitt (*Matlock* and *The Father Dowling Mysteries*), Schlitt attended Northwestern University's National High School Institute's Theater Arts Division in 1980. She had a brief career as an actress and a writer in the late '80s and early '90s, including appearances on (surprise!) *Matlock* and *The Father Dowling Mysteries*. She is best-remembered as the short-lived first host of *USA Up All Night*; she lasted six months before a new sheriff came to town, Rhonda Shear. Schlitt retired from the business when she got married, and lives in either Atlanta or Northern California.

Cherry Payne

HOST: *Midnight Hour* (2004–?), Public Access Channel 22, Haverhill, Massachusetts

BIOGRAPHY: This tidbit comes from the now-defunct MonsterFashion website:

DATELINE MONSTERVILLE—MonsterFashion Films is proud to announce ... the new MonsterFashion television show *Midnight Hour*! The show will be hosted by MonsterFashion king Matt Sanborn and his beautiful co-host, Cherry Payne. Six episodes are in the can. Sanborn and Payne will introduce and talk about the movies and give some no little fact and actual insight into these great and not-so-great movies. The movies to be shown: *At Midnight I Will Possess Your Soul*, *The Brain That Wouldn't Die*, *The Unholy Three*, *Horror Express*, *Night of the Living Dead* and *Nosferatu*.

It's probably no good chasin' Sanborn or Cherry. Their website is defunct, so it's a pretty safe bet to assume that they are, too.

Cosmosina

REAL NAME: Unknown

HOST: *Science Fiction Theater* (1963), KOGO-TV, Channel 10, San Diego, California

BIOGRAPHY: Cosmosina is perhaps *the* most elusive of the early female horror hosts. There is no known video recording of Cosmosina. There are also no recordings of

Tarantula Ghoul, but at least with Taranch, we know her real name, there are the recordings of the records she made, and there are a few surviving print pieces featuring her. We don't know Cosmosina's real name, she never made any records, no video survives, and there is only one surviving print ad for her show. It's mistakenly been reported or suggested that Moona Lisa (Lisa Clark), who replaced her on *Science-Fiction Theater*, also played Cosmosina, but Jeff Clark, Lisa's husband, refuted this in James Fetters' must-have history of Southern California horror hosts, *Creatures of the Night We Loved So Well* (Sabre Enterprises LLC, 2011). Clark recalled that the woman who played Cosmosina was working in a Tecate, California, health spa when she was spotted by a KOGO executive, who asked her if she would like to be on TV. When the show became a hit (stop me if you've heard this one before), the actress asked for a raise and was promptly replaced by Moona. Try as Mr. Clark might, he couldn't remember the actress' name. She hosted the show for two months before being replaced.

Countess Lutzika

REAL NAME: not available
BIOGRAPHY: not available
HOST: *Tales from the Tomb* (mid–1970s), Evansville, Indiana

Countess Vampula

REAL NAME: not available
HOST: *Monsterpiece Theatre* (with the Bowman Body; 1983–1984), WNVC, Channel 56, Fairfax, Virginia
BIOGRAPHY: All the information we have on this particular co-host is what Bill Bowman, the Bowman Body, provided in the *Virginia Creepers* documentary: "*Monsterpiece Theatre*, there was another person on there, and she was the Countess; she was this young lady and she did a very good job. ...Her personality would change when she put the costume on, and she stayed that person until she took the costume off.

No record of the actress who portrayed the Countess can be found, though we have bits of dialogue from the show, such as this:

Countess Lutzika, from the mid–1970s (courtesy George "E-Gor" Chastain).

BB: "Countess.... Countess, I've got some bad news for you."
CV: "What is it?"
BB: "Mike from the library called; it seems your services are no longer required."
CV: "My services no longer required? What is this?"
BB: "Booted.... Fired.... Cutsville.... It was something about eating the customers' fingers."
CV: "Well.... I got hungry."
BB: "I see..."

Countess Von Stauffenberger

REAL NAME: Eleanor Herman
HOST: *Creature Feature* (with Count Gore de Vol, 1973–1987), WDCA Channel 20, Washington, D.C.

Count Gore De Vol recounted the Countess's amazing origin in the *American Scary* documentary:

> Stu (the director) comes in, he says, "You're not gonna believe what's out front." ...He said it was the most fantastic oil portrait you've ever seen ... and if you think that's good, you ought to see the buxom blonde that comes with it. I said, "Okay, we'll have her do the presentation and then we'll play it by ear." And I said, by the way, "How old is she? Because I don't wanna have any problems on the show with minors and stuff," and he goes, "Oh, no, she's 22 or 23 years old." So we're waiting and we're chitchatting, and she mentions that she's in junior high school! So I got to see Eleanor again, she's all grown up now ... and we started keeping in touch, and then occasionally, I would say, "Hey, come on the show," and we'd have her on as the Mummy, and of course there was a lot of double entendres in that...

Crematia Mortem

REAL NAME: Roberta Solomon
HOST: *Creature Feature* (1981–1988), KSHB, Channel 41, Kansas City, Missouri
BIRTHPLACE: Kansas City, Missouri
BIOGRAPHY: One of the most satisfying things about this author jazz is the quality of people you get to meet. Ingrid Pitt was a diamond. Veronica Carlson, who says I'm like a member of the family now, is another. A third such example of glittering humanity is Roberta Solomon, a.k.a. Crematia Mortem. My first exposure to Crematia was very similar to the circumstances under which I first encountered Elvira: on tour with my band, playing in a bar with a TV set in Missouri. The only difference was, I never found out who she was, because the band was getting ready to go on stage. But my eyes sure were glued to that corset!

Not having the national exposure that Elvira had, Crematia soon faded into the back roads by the rivers of my memories, and I didn't discover who she was until years later. When I started this project, I found that I could contact her directly; and then after summoning up the courage to do so, I phoned. I had to leave a message and for some reason I was worried that she wouldn't return my call. Imagine my surprise and delight when I answered the call from an unfamiliar area code, and after a tentative "Hello," the caller replied, "Is this Robert? This is Crematia!" After we got more proper introductions out of the way, she was more than willing to talk about Crematia. She said she still gets requests for photos, t-shirts and such and that she was looking to add a store to her website to sell such items (I'm gonna hold you to that, Roberta!). She is amazed and honored to have so many people remember her as Crematia, so she consented to the following interview, done for this book, via email, in the summer of 2015:

BC: *Tell us something about your early career, and how you got into television. Whose suggestion was it that you become the character, or how did the character come about?*

RS: My background is in theater and music performance, but I was a semester away from a Theater Degree at UMKC (University of Missouri–Kansas City) when it hit me that I didn't want a stage career. I'd turned down a role in a revival of *Hair* because I didn't want to tour, and around the same time, I had an epiphany onstage in the middle of a show, that I was supposed to be doing something else. So, instead of finishing my degree, I took a bunch of classes the next year that piqued my interest: art history, etymology, early English literature, that kind of thing.

At the time, one of my best friends was a student announcer at KCUR, the campus radio station. They played classical music during the day, did local newscasts on the hour, and aired jazz and blues at night and on the weekends. They were looking for a couple of new announcers, and my friend suggested that I apply for the job. "All you have to do is pronounce the foreign composer's names correctly," he said. "They'll teach you how to do everything else."

An original Crematia Mortem postcard from KSHB-TV, 1982 (courtesy Roberta Solomon).

I landed the job, and spent the next few months training to be a radio announcer. My first air shift was Christmas Eve, and I knew the minute I opened the mike that I'd found the thing I was meant to do. So I changed my degree to communications studies, with an emphasis on Broadcast Performance.

I worked at the radio station as much as I could and started waiting tables to make some extra money. I'd been on the air at KCUR for about eight months when I was "discovered" by a radio salesman from another station in town who happened to sit at my table. He'd heard me on the air, told me that the easy listening station he worked for was looking to hire an announcer for their seven-to-midnight shift, and suggested I apply for the job. The following week, I threw a demo together, went in for an interview, and won the job.

The station was an AM-FM combo, and there were always interesting people coming in at night, to appear on the talk show across the hall and visit with Walt Bodine, the legendary host. One of his industry friends who popped in regularly was Rob Forsythe, the creative director at KSHB. We became friends, and one evening he suggested that I apply for a weekend TV host position that had opened up. Channel 41 at the time was airing a show called *All Night Live*, hosted by Ed Muscare. It had huge numbers during the week, and they decided to expand it to the weekend. I auditioned for and won that job, and hosted the Saturday version of *All Night Live* for about a year, using the name Sally Roberts.

After about a year, the director of the show told me that they loved what I was doing, but wanted my comedy elements to match the monster movies we were showing. They wondered if I might be open to being a horror host. I was like ... "Sure!" That was it.

I think we had about $500 to dress the set ... and me. The director and I went to garage sales and thrift stores to scrounge together some set decorations. We bought a wicker chair, a stuffed bird, a crappy couch, and we hung some cobwebs in the corner of the studio. I went out and bought a black negligee and a long black wig from Wild Woody's, one of those weird local stores where you could find just about anything: groceries, guns and wigs. I'd already decided that my character's name should be Crematia. My AM talk show friend Walt Bodine gave her the last name Mortem. On the night of my last show as Sally Roberts, I told the audience I'd been fired. I said, "I have no idea of what's going to happen with this show next week, but I'm sure it's just going to be horrifying. As to your new host, all I know is that she's been hanging around a long time, she's old, and they dug her up somewhere."

The next week, the show opened with Bach's Toccata and Fugue in D Minor, lots of screams and howls, and a tight shot of the stuffed bird. And then Crematia came walking out of the shadows. The show was on the air for eight years.

BC: *You lasted longer in your original run than many horror hosts. To what do you attribute your longevity?*

RS: I did the *Creature Feature* during a wonderful transitional time in television. In the early '80s, cable was starting to grow, but most of the big cable companies were still in their infancy. People still watched movies on their local TV station, and late night was considered no man's land. It was a great place for a local character to develop a rabid fan base, and since KSHB was a superstation, carried on cable to eight states, we had a bigger audience than most horror hosts in other markets. But I also think that the approach we took to make Crematia "family-friendly" (a term that hadn't even been coined then) allowed us to grow the audience beyond the core horror-nerd fans. I was quite aware that there were lots of little kids in the audience. It was a cool thing to do on a Saturday night; families would make popcorn, stay up late, snuggle together on the couch and watch monster movies together. We got letters from grandparents, babysitters, big brothers and sisters, saying, "It's our weekend ritual to watch Crematia, and we appreciate the fact that she's funny and silly, but not embarrassing." Viewers felt safe watching the show. They trusted that we might flirt with impropriety; we were rude at times, but never got offensive.

Crematia was sexy, she appeared on TV every week in a corset! But we never led with sex, and the character I created was totally clueless about it. I described Crematia as "kind of like your weird aunt who loves you very, very much, but embarrasses you by leaving lipstick on your cheek when she kisses you." I have to say, the show was also delightfully funny, and it was funny for years. We had no budget, but we had some great comedic minds working on the *Creature Feature*. Steve Fritts, the director, was a maniac. Rob Forsythe, KSHB's creative director, is one of the funniest guys I know. The three of us would spend several days each week putting the show together, finding where the jokes were. We'd test out ideas with each other and then actually script the show. When we had guests, we wrote the script for them. Even today, I laugh out loud at some of the stuff we came up with. The show lasted as long as it did because the audience loved Crematia, the movies we aired were wonderful, and it was very, very funny.

BC: *What are some of your fondest memories?*
RS: I was involved in literacy programs while I was doing the show, and every year right before Halloween, we'd hold a Scary Story Contest. The grand prize was a night on the town in a limo with Crematia. The winner was allowed to bring a friend and a parent or guardian, and came to KSHB for a Happy Meal dinner from McDonald's with Crematia and the Creature Feature crew. They'd get a station tour, some *Creature Feature* swag, and then we'd all pile into the limo and visit a couple of haunted houses, where the winner was ushered to the front of the line and announced to the crowd. We always picked a kid to win. Since this was in the '80s, cellphones weren't around yet, but the limo had a phone and we would allow him to make one call. I remember one red-headed kid who was just delightful. He called his mom with his head sticking out of the moon roof, the wind whipping his hair, yelling down Ward Parkway, "*This is the greatest night of my life!*"

BC: *Are there any especially funny or dysfunctional memories of the show?*
RS: Viewers were always coming up with weird creations that they wanted me to feature on the show. One kid made this giant monster costume out of papier mâché, and brought it down to the station in a truck. He had to stand on stilts inside of it. The thing was so weird, we did a whole episode around it.

Crematia was always looking for her perfect man; in this episode, the setup was that she would see this giant monster across the room, and be instantly smitten. The monster would then walk toward her and lovingly offer her a dead flower. But when the kid on the stilts inside of the monster costume started towards her, his giant papier mâché foot caught on the edge of the rug. He fell like a tree, in slow motion, to the floor. As sappy, lovestruck music played, and with the cameras running, he landed with a *whoosh* in a big puff of dust. There was this deathly silence, and then his tiny voice from out of the costume pleading, "Can somebody help me?" I was mortified because I thought we'd had our first workplace injury. The kid was fine, and we actually wound up using the video in the show. We said, "He was head over heels in love!" There were some weirdos watching the show for sure. One guy made these creature statues out of chicken bones and wire, like some sort of strange taxidermy. They were quite fantastic, and for a while we featured them on the show. But then I started to worry that he might be killing animals for his odd art project, so we told him to stop sending them.

(Author's note: Roberta mentioned that the station showed the wrestling matches put on at a local wrestling hall. I thought this was pretty cool, as I'd gotten my first exposure to horror movies and horror hosts when "Chilly Billy" Cardille hosted the *Studio Wrestling* program on Pittsburgh's Channel 11. Cardille always ran promos for what was going to be on *Chiller Theater* that night.)

BC: *Tell us about the wrestling connection.*
RS: KSHB aired the local wrestling matches that happened each week at Memorial Hall in Kansas City, and each week, the wrestlers on the circuit would tape their pre-match challenges at the station, as I was taping my show in the other studio. We'd hang out in the halls together, the guys in their wrestling costumes and me in my corset. I got to know Ric Flair, George "The Animal" Steele, Rowdy Roddy Piper, Bulldog Bob Brown, the Iron Sheik, Rufus Ruffhouse Jones and most of the guys who were traveling the Midwestern circuit. They were delightful.

BC: *What brought Crematia to an end?*
RS: KSHB became a Fox affiliate a couple of years before I stopped doing the show. At first, the fledgling network didn't carry much programming, so our show wasn't affected. But as Fox grew, they began offering more late-night and weekend shows, and the *Creature Feature* kept getting pushed back later and later, from 10:30 to midnight, and even later. Because of that, the audience changed. Kids couldn't watch the show any more, because they couldn't stay up that late. I really loved having younger kids watching the show, and some of the magic disappeared for me when there were fewer of them watching. By then, I'd done the show for eight years, so it was time to leave.

BC: *What are you most proud of in your current line of work?*
RS: I love doing voiceovers and am so proud to have made a living at it for 20 years, without living in Los Angeles or New York. It's an endlessly fascinating career, and I've worked in pretty much every area of the industry. I was really proud to be part of an Emmy-winning documentary a few years back (*Decoding Immortality* won an Emmy for Best Science and Technology Programming in 2012), and working with creative people just gets me high. Things are glacially starting to change, and more and more women's voices are being heard, but I'm proud to be among the first women to voice movie trailers (*The Expendables, On My Way, Space Station 76* and *Tiny Giants*, an IMAX film produced by the BBC).

BC: *How did your career as a voice actress come about?*
RS: I've been doing freelance work almost as long as I've had a career. Not long after I started in radio, I began voicing commercials and corporate projects outside the station. In the late '80s, I joined with several other successful voice artists to create our own agency, Voices Inc., and when I left radio in the '90s, I put a studio in my home and stepped into voice work full time. My career in voiceovers has morphed and changed over time, and I'm just incredibly grateful every time I step into the booth.

Darcinia, the Duchess of Darkness

REAL NAME: not available
HOST: *Dungeon of Dramas* (c. 1982), KGSW-TV Channel 14, Albuquerque, New Mexico
BIOGRAPHY: There's not much to report here. Like many other horror hostesses,

literally only a few seconds of footage survive, and I have no personal or professional information for Darcinia, only a scattering of memories from fans. Here's one from the "Cheese Magnet" site, offered up by "Brian": "In Albuquerque, we were stuck with Dicky the Bomber's *Bedtime Bombs* and Darcinia, Duchess of Darkness; on Channel 14, I think it was. Darcinia loved to do this laugh she was convinced sounded evil—it wasn't." Author Scott Phillips weighed in with this: "There was Dr. Distortion, and the successor to Darcinia, the short-lived Feverita ... this clip [a YouTube video called "Horror Hosts"] features a short segment of Darcinia. Not much, though. What kills me is that I had several of Darcinia's shows (movies plus host segments) on Beta, but tossed all that stuff about 12 years ago.... Argh!" Argh, indeed! He also remembered that her show ran in the early '80s.

The Daughter of the Ghoul

REAL NAME: Janet Jay, a.k.a. Janet Decay

HOST: *The Daughter of the Ghoul Show* (2013–2014), WCTV, BAT-TV, Cox Cable and Time-Warner Cable, Cleveland, Ohio, *The Mummy and the Monkey* (2015–), ScreamZine, Bizarre TV (Roku)

BIOGRAPHY: It's pretty much all in the interview which follows, which Janet was kind enough to grant me in 2015. She and Grimm have a funny show, and they're really nice people to boot.

BC: *Please tell us as much of your background as you care to.*

JD: Growing up in the Cleveland area, Euclid to be specific, my younger brother and I were raised on Nintendo, late-night movie TV hosts and Lake Effect snow. We weren't "made" until the 1980s, so we missed the greatness of Ghoulardi, but during that time you could still catch "The Ghoul" and "Big Chuck and Li'l John" on late nights, and Mom would pop us some kernels over the stove. If I was lucky, and Mom and her boyfriend could afford the Cablevision bill, I could tune in to the old Universal monsters on AMC and catch a glimpse of the gorgeous Elvira on TV. Growing up in the 1980s and 1990s was the tail end of the *TV Guide* days, before the Internet and reality TV took over everything. Our family would flip through those pages, circling the shows we wanted to watch and tune in during the listed time slots. In a sense, it brought families closer together; we couldn't TiVo or DVR anything. I originally wanted to go to art school, the Cleveland Institute of Art, but couldn't muster up enough finances to cover the high cost of college, so I've been working full-time ever since and paying my own way, while acting and modeling on the side. It's always been a dream of mine to do something with art, something creative and fun.

BC: *Do you like horror and science fiction movies?*

JD: Absolutely! Those genres have the best creativity. To quote someone who was like a dad to me, "A horror film is like a pizza, even when it's bad it's still pretty damn good!" I've seen many horror and science fiction films and there's a million more that are on my list to watch.

BC: *How did you come to be a horror host?*

JD: It all started around 2006 or 2007 when I started making costumes and wearing them to comic book and Anime [Japanese animation] conventions. My mother taught

The Daughter of the Ghoul

me how to sew when I was a kid, and being a nerd girl, I thought it would be fun. Back around that time, social media was still new, and I had a Myspace account, so when you put up photos dressed in Spandex as Catwoman, I guess it creates attention. Local actors and directors in Northeast Ohio would message me and ask if I wanted to be a zombie extra or a vampire extra for their film projects. So I started getting into acting. The bug bit me and I was itching for more. I've worked with various independent studios as an actress. The roles I play vary from a zombie or vampire extra to a ditzy lab assistant to a tough police officer. After working for local film studios, a director based out of Akron, Robert Kotabish, told me that someone was looking to cast a hostess for the *Daughter of the Ghoul Show*, and I auditioned the very next day! Daniel Kristancic from DMK Productions cast me to help host his public access cable program in 2013, and I've been a hostess ever since.

BC: *What are the names of some of the films you've been in?*

JD: I've starred in *Revenge of the Spacemen*, directed by Jay Summers. He also helped me build my sarcophagus, along with Terrance Ryan, a Cleveland special effects artist. I've also starred in various films from RAK Films. Robert Kotabish is a long-time friend and supporter. As I said, he helped me get into horror hosting by telling me about the *Daughter of the Ghoul* casting call. I've worked with other directors, but these two deserve mention due to how kind and supportive they've been during my life.

BC: *Is the name of your show* The Daughter of the Ghoul Show *or* The Mummy and the Monkey?

JD: So many people are confused by this. I hosted *The Daughter of the Ghoul Show* from 2013 to 2014, and in 2015 when I was told *Daughter of the Ghoul* was cancelled, I then joined forces with my fiancé James Harmon—a.k.a. Grimm Gorri—to host *The Mummy and the Monkey*. So far, so good, and we're building momentum. Recently we were picked up by ScreamZine and Bizarre TV on Roku. We've attended many events and venues as guests. Grimm Gorri—the Monkey—and Janet Decay—the Mummy—bring you two shows in one! We each have our own segments and skits along with a featured video or movie. A storyline between our characters cements the two shows within a show. *The Daughter of the Ghoul Show* is run by Daniel Kristancic from DMK Productions. He started it in 2011 and had other girls help host until I joined the team in 2013. He focuses mostly on public access channels and it varies by city and provider. In early 2015 he told me that the show was cancelled, so I started my own production with Grimm. We now have Weird Room Productions, and we write, edit, direct and shoot *The Mummy and the Monkey Show*. We're on Roku, YouTube and Time-Warner cable in Wadsworth, Brunswick and Dayton, Ohio. In New York, Channel 98 in Syracuse, and Chicago's public access station.

BC: *When I first contacted you, you alluded to "the whole story behind the show." Please tell us that "secret history."*

JD: Shortly after Daniel Kristancic—or "Danny K"—told me the show was cancelled, he started working on new shows without me or without a hostess. For reasons unknown, any form of communication was stonewalled, but as they say, when one door closes, another one opens. We've had many great horror movie hosts in Cleveland, but never a female. We're adding something fresh and new for the next generation while trying to keep that fun tradition going here. Our ultimate goal would be to have a syndicated network show screen on a weekly basis.

BC: *You're carrying on the tradition of great Cleveland horror hosts that started with Ghoulardi and the Ghoul. Are you a "direct descendant," like Son of Ghoul?*

JD: Let's clear that up by stating that Son of Ghoul is not a "direct descendant" of the Ghoul, Ron Sweed. Son of Ghoul, Kevin Scarpino, won a Ghoul Look-Alike contest in the 1980s and was given the title Son of Ghoul by Ron Sweed. Kevin has his own show in Akron, Ohio, and nearly 30 years later, it's still going strong. When I hosted *The Daughter of the Ghoul Show*, I hosted it as my character Janet Decay, and they've had several other hosts and hostesses, so it's really just a title, like *The Tonight Show*. Some of the Son of Ghoul info can be fact-checked online.

BC: *What's your day job?*

JD: I worked in retail for 13 years, and now work in the automotive industry as a service writer. I try to keep the two worlds separate, although people I work with seem to enjoy *The Mummy and the Monkey Show*.

BC: *Was the character created by you?*

JD: Lakewood and Akron, Ohio, host charity zombie walks, and I would go out with my friends in costume with our donations of non-perishable food in hand. Everyone was covered in fake blood and gore, and I kept wondering what I could do to be different and stand out. So what's an "old school" original zombie? A mummy! In 2010, Janet Decay was ... born? Dug up? She's evolved since then. The original makeup was more dark and messy, and her hair looked like a rat's nest. These days, Decay is more of a "perky" Goth, more outgoing and friendly. I like her to be sexy, and creepy-cute, but without being trashy or smutty; your friendly "ghoul next door" type, the kind you can take home to "Mummy." Her left eye is white, and I wear a contact lens as homage to the Ghoul and Son of Ghoul's funky glasses with the one lens removed. Decay's bandages and outfits were designed and hand-made by me.

BC: *Do you write the show?*

JD: Yes, but not solo. My fiancé helps write and we make a great team. We will bounce ideas back and forth to create scripts and skits. Some of it is ad-libbed, but for each episode and segment, we have a guideline, a script outline. My partner-in-crime James Harmon is great with storyboarding and putting props together. He went to the Art Institute of Pittsburgh. We try to keep *The Mummy and the Monkey* more on the PG side, to keep that Cleveland tradition of watching a horror movie host show with your family. If you like fart jokes, cheesy skits and a mummy lady flaunting her midriff, you might dig it!

BC: *I love your look—so different than the standard black gown. How did you decide on that? And as for Grimm—gotta love a guy in a gorilla suit!*

JD: The classic "little black dress" never goes out of style, but this little ghoul needed to dig up some different rags and start a whole new fashion statement. The Universal and Hammer Mummy movies, along with avant-garde art styles and designs, gave me the inspiration I needed to create my own look. Most of my drawings are an odd combination of anime-fashion design, and I drew out my costumes for Janet Decay in 2010. Since then, her makeup and wardrobe has evolved. I've had fans give me little ankh

The Daughter of the Ghoul

"Yummy, Mummy!" (2014) (courtesy Janet Decay).

charms and other jewelry pieces for my collection. The character of Decay: she was a silent film actress in the 1920s in Cleveland who turned into a real-life mummy! The film studio that she acted for had ancient Egyptian relics that they thought were mere stage props, [and they] cursed her for all eternity. And as for Grimm Gorri, he resembles more of a chimp than a gorilla, and little kids just point and shout "monkey," so close enough, I guess. He's Cleveland's late-night missing link that's always been around town. Within *The Mummy and the Monkey Show*, Grimm Gorri hosts his "Eerie Cinematery" segment. He has a little demon sidekick called Cliff and it is fun to see what monkey business they're up to. Some speculate that the King Kong type of ape that was on *Big Chuck and Li'l John* may be a relative of Grimm Gorri.

    BC: *Do you have any horror host role models?*

    JD: *Yes*! The local great legends that were on TV in Ohio: Hoolihan and Big Chuck, Big Chuck and Li'l John, Ghoulardi, the Ghoul, Son of Ghoul, Super Host and A. Ghastly Ghoul. And from other regions, Elvira—of corpse!—Vampira, Count Gore De Vol and Zacherley. Honestly, *every* horror host is our role model. We love other hosts, and the more, the scarier! Every region needs their own movie host, and to quote Count Gore De Vol, "There's plenty of room in the coffin for everyone!"

BC: *What are some of your fondest memories of your show?*

JD: I would have to say *The Mummy and the Monkey's Pumpkin Spice Halloween Special*. We filmed it live at a Halloween festival in Akron, and it premiered on the Kreepy Kastle online channel. Doing the shoot and even the editing process was a ton of work in such little time, about a week. We had a deadline and wanted it out to sell at Ghoulardifest, a *huge* convention devoted to Cleveland TV memories and horror movies.

BC: *Have you had any moments where, say, Grimm stepped on your bandages and you had a wardrobe malfunction, or he found his suit attacked by moths, or just something that was supposed to happen and didn't, or vice versa?*

JD: When we were shooting the *Cleveland Horror Hosts Conquer the Cons Special*, Belgor the alien's nose kept falling off during the shoot, and we had to re-do those scenes multiple times. During the credits, you see his nose fall off in the blooper reel. Sometimes Grimm's glasses go crooked or his hair needs adjusting before we shoot. Surprisingly, no wardrobe malfunctions with Decay. Her outfit is pinned and kept together pretty good, despite the lack of cloth!

BC: *Which do you prefer, TV or the Internet?*

JD: *Both*! I look forward to the day when the line is blurred between the two. You see it more now with Roku, and smart phones and tablets. Now a Friday night movie can be a Tuesday afternoon if it fits your schedule. The TV is the Internet, and Internet is the TV.

BC: *How long do you see yourself doing the show?*

JD: For all eternity. Mummies last a long time, and Grimm Gorries never die, they just smell that way.

Other Genre Credits—Films: Killerdatewww (short), 2009 (Best Friend); *Post-Mortem*, Fleet Street Productions, 2010 (Victim); *Never Escape*, Mancinetti Pictures, 2010 (Screaming Girl); *Easter Casket*, Dustin Mills Productions, 2013 (Prima); *Serial Nightmares*, Ghatt Productions, 2013 (Flower); *Revenge of the Spider* (short), Radiograph Pictures, 2013 (Flo); *RAK Force*, RAK Films, 2013 (Robot); *Blood Stars*, RAK Films, 2014 (Ms. Relaxo); *Snuffet*, Dustin Mills Productions, 2014 (Melissa Schweine); *Revenge of the Spacemen*, Radiograph Pictures, 2014 (Janet); *Spider-Man and the Rise of Darkness* (animated), Brady25 Films, 2014 (Voices: Madame Web/Mistress Death); *Raw Focus*, Mouse Nest Productions, 2015 (Roe); *Night of the Living Dead—Rebirth*, Mouse Nest Productions, 2015 (Waitress Ghoul); Television: *Superhero 101*: 2013 (Silver Bullet); *The League of Science*: "Sesame Street," 2012 (Frida Frankenstein); *Random Marvel* (animated): "Fantastic Foursome," 2009 (voice of Invisible Woman), "The Phantom Signal," 2011 (voice of Wasp), "Take A.I.M.," 2012 (voices of Invisible Woman/Wasp), "Wolverine Buster," 2012 (voice of Invisible Woman); *Batman—Abyss* (animated): "Terror Has a Face," 2013 (voice of Poison Ivy); *IndieHorror.TV's Anniversary Party* (Movie), IndieHorror.TV, 2013 (Hostess Janet Decay)

Dear

Real Name: Joy Ann Page (Bennett)

Host: *Shock Theatre* (December 1957–August 1959), WBKB-TV, Channel 7, Chicago, Illinois

Dear

BIOGRAPHY: Born Joy Ann Page, Joy Bennett was an integral part of Terry Bennett's ventriloquist act from the time he met her while performing it in Florida in 1950. In 1953, they got married in New York, and then toured Canada for a year with the act. In 1954, they moved to Chicago. At WBKB-TV, Terry got a job as a writer, producer, on-air promotion director and program development coordinator. In 1957, the station acquired the "Shock" package of vintage horror and mystery films and the management thought that someone should host them; in fact, an interdepartmental memo revealed that management hoped that the host would be more popular than the movies, with viewers tuning in to see what the host would get up to. Bennett created the legendary "Marvin," and he and Joy went on to become two of the most-loved horror hosts in history. They were so popular that management decided to expand the show by a half-hour to give them more opportunity to carry on. During this half-hour, "The Shocktale

Joy ("Dear") and Terry Bennett, circa 1957 (courtesy George "E-Gor" Chastain).

Party," they were joined by fellow cast members "Shorty" (Bruce Newton), "Orville" (Ronnie Born) and "The Deadbeats," the house band that, naturally, played "music to die for."

Regarding Joy's character, Don (*The Great Movie Serials*) Glut wrote, "You would only see her from the back at first, and every time they would cut to Marvin, he would always be doing something terrible to his wife, and then of course, by the next commercial break, she would be back to normal and everything was fine." In *Scary Monsters* #82 (2012), he continued with his memories of the show: "Marvin ... wasn't just a beatnik; he was a totally mad, horror-crazed fiend who, while sometimes cackling insanely, got supreme delight from murdering, maiming and/or dismembering the other character introduced on *Shock Theatre*'s opening night, a sexy young woman whose face was not seen, referred to originally as simply 'Dear'...."

After two years, *Shock Theater* had run its course. Terry and Joy still hosted a children's show, and they adopted a baby boy. In 1962, they moved to New York City. Joy Bennett remembered for the Chicago Television History website, "[W]e left Chicago because our shows had come to an end. An era was passing—and Terry was offered a fairly lucrative position at WPIX, Channel 11, on 42nd Street in New York. And family was there. We bought a house in New Rochelle and Terry became a producer."

From 1962 to 1967, Terry Bennett produced many local shows and finally became an on-air personality, although he did not reprise his "Marvin" role. But things had once again begun to change, according to Joy: "By 1967, the era of live shows utilizing staff musicians had come to an end. [Terry] was primarily a performer, a ventriloquist, an actor and writer. In those days, there were few avenues open, and he turned to advertising and freelance. Commercials had become big business!"

Terry found steady employment again when he became the advertising manager of a company called Castro Convertibles; he took a similar position with Chock Full o' Nuts Coffee. But the New York nut was growing too tough to crack, so the Bennetts moved a final time, to Tampa, Florida. Joy talked about the final years: "Terry did a six-hour talk show using his many different voices as if they were real guests appearing on the show. He appeared as an M.C. on many telethon telecasts, and even had a newscast show. He engaged in freelance advertising and conceived B.K. the Lion for the Burger King chains, doing most of the publicity stunts himself."

Terry Bennett passed away on October 12, 1977. He was 47 years old. Joy, who never remarried, still lives in Tampa with her family.

Die Wilde Hilde (The Wild Hilda)

REAL NAME: Unknown

HOST: *Hilde's Wilde Horror Show* (June 1992–September 1993), RTL Network, Germany

BIOGRAPHY: "Wild Hilda" hosted a year's worth of classic and recent horror films on the RTL Network in Germany. There's little video footage of her, but what survives shows a fairly elaborate set and a gorgeous woman who looks like a cross between a *Rocky Horror Picture Show* character and Elvira: dyed hair, what can only be described as a bat-themed Basque outfit, low-cut and revealing, and topped off by a garter belt, a pair of nylon stockings and high heels. She closely patterned her character and delivery of lines on Elvira: flippant dialogue and naughty, silly jokes centered on her cleavage. She was mildly entertaining, certainly sexy, but the original is still the best.

Dixie Dellamorto

REAL NAME: not available (1987–)
BIRTHPLACE: Westchester, Pennsylvania
HOST (with Mr. Lobo): *Cinema Insomnia with Mr. Lobo* (2010–)
BIOGRAPHY: Dixie Dellamorto was born on June 4. Her father was a sheet-metal worker and a musician and her mom an artist who also did leather-crafting. Dixie says that "she wouldn't be the weirdo I am today if not for them." In fact, she inherited her

Dixie Dellamorto as Ro-Mana, presented by Mr. Lobo in 2012 (courtesy Paul Riggie).

mother's collection of *Creepy*, *Eerie*, *Vampirella* and *Heavy Metal* magazines, all of which were tremendous influences. She studied animation at the Art Institute of Philadelphia. She says she still pores over those old *Creepy* magazines as if they were sacred texts, and still watches *Night Gallery* almost daily (or nightly, as the case may be). She is also a lifelong fan of Pee-wee Herman, Devo and the Cramps. She has designed award-winning fantasy costumes, as well as paintings for various publications (including the first and so far only issue of her magazine, *Horror Hosts and Creature Features,* 2011), art shows, DVD covers, posters, films, TV shows and other promotions. The first issue of *Horror Hosts* was a good effort, containing features on Al "Grandpa Munster" Lewis (Dixie interviewed Karen Lewis, Al's wife for the last 25 years of his life), Count Gore De Vol, the Bowman Body and Bob Wilkins, plus all sorts of "lifestyle" articles like "Touch of Trash: Fearless Fashion," "Terrible Tips and Horrible Hints," "Music for Monsters" and "Creepy Crafters." As she says in the editorial, "This isn't your mother's horror magazine!" She was inspired to become a horror host, in part, by the *Ghoul-a Go-Go* show from New York; she did several paintings on the subject and then became friends with the cast. Then horror host Mr. Lobo spotted her art and she became his "partner-in-slime," first becoming an assistant producer for Mr. Lobo's show *Cinema Insomnia*. She moved to California in 2010 and was co-producer, editor and stage director for a live edition of the show at the Guild Theater in Sacramento.

Dixie is still a major creative force behind *Cinema Insomnia*, as well as in front of the camera, where she often appears as characters in costumes she created, the most popular being "Ro-Mana," a female version of *Robot Monster*. Dixie appeared, uncredited, in 2011's *A Hard Day's Nightmare* in costume, and designed an on-screen ad for that year's Blobfest in Phoenixville, Pennsylvania. She continues to do paintings and graphic design, as well as help Mr. Lobo design and build their own channel and distribution network, OSI 74—Outer Space International (osi74.com). In January 2012, on Friday the 13th, appropriately enough, Dixie married Mr. Lobo at a small ceremony, with the reception held at John's Incredible Pizza. She was kind enough to grant me this wonderful interview in February 2016:

BC: *What is your name?*
DD: It is Arthur, King of the Britons.

BC: *What is your quest?*
DD: I seek the Holy Grail.

BC: *What is the air-speed velocity of an unladen swallow?*
DD: What do you mean—an African or a European swallow?

BC: *I don't know.... Augh!*
DD: Don't get me started on Monty Python quotes! But seriously, my name is Dixie. Probably the most interesting thing about me is that I'm married to Mr. Lobo. When I'm not nagging, shopping, menstruating and other wifely duties, I'm a creative producer, artist and designer. I was raised by a television and some dusty old comic books. Growing up in a nurturing and supportive environment resulted in my becoming a professional weirdo.

BC: *Presumably you like horror and science fiction movies.*

DD: Almost exclusively. I started watching horror films at a very young age. Vincent Price was my first favorite actor. I remember begging my parents to rent *House on Haunted Hill* over and over again from our local mom'n'pop video store. I love paranormal films, and Italian horror is very near and dear to my heart. I watch many movies a week. Typically they're on in the background while I work.

BC: *How did you come to be a horror host?*
DD: I was an aspiring horror host when I met Mr. Lobo. In my early twenties, I lived in Philadelphia and my roommate and I created *Human Sushi Variety Hour.* It was a half-hour show inspired by '50s horror movies and *Pee-wee's Playhouse* featuring Dixie Dellamorto, an undead housewife with a beehive and a beatnik werewolf named Fred.... That was more or less a pipedream.... I had some character sketches and a theme song. I also did some art for New York TV hosts *Ghoul-a-Go-Go.* By the time I befriended Mr. Lobo, I was already over my dream of being a horror host myself and was more committed to being a behind-the-scenes kind of guy. I also play a lot of side characters.

BC: *When was your first show?*
DD: In 2010, I was the co-producer, editor and stage director for a live *Cinema Insomnia* show at the Guild Theater in Sacramento.... I didn't appear in the show but it was the first show I was heavily involved with.

BC: *Have you done any other acting?*
DD: Not really ... mostly extra work. I died in *Plan 9* [the remake of the Ed Wood classic *Plan 9 from Outer Space*]. I did a little more in a movie called *Midnight Show* where I play a sadistic ape from Hell called Gore-illa. I was also a psycho-killer groupie in a rock opera called *A Hard Day's Nightmare.* I also appeared on another Horror Host show called *Monster Madhouse* with Karlos Borloff a couple of times as a cavegirl named Miss Cretaceous; as Mumsy, a psycho homemaker with rubber gloves; and as myself.

BC: *What is your day job?*
DD: I'm a graphic designer. I mostly work on flyers and event posters; I'm currently working for the Sacramento Horror Film Festival. I have done many book illustrations for *Creature Feature* host and critic John Stanley.

BC: *Was the character created by you? Did you create Ro-Mana? Did the* Doctor Who *companion named Romana factor into it?*
DD: I play several characters on *Cinema Insomnia*. Probably the most notable character is Ro-Mana. Yes, her name was inspired by a combination of things—Ro-Man [*Robot Monster*] and Romana from *Doctor Who.* She was born out of necessity because Mr. Lobo needed a sidekick who could talk and move, since his regular co-host is a houseplant. Mr. Lobo and I came up with a female *Robot Monster* character together and I designed her costume and tailored it to be form-fitting. Mr. Lobo and I built her helmet with some help from Gary [*Rocket Patrol*] Hughes, and Bob Burns assures me it's even nicer than the original. *Ha!* Another notable character I play is called Mumsy, who I mentioned was originally a psycho killer I played in *Hard Day's Nightmare*. She was inspired by my love of Italian Giallo movies and black glove killers—only my killer wears Playtex rubber gloves. In the *Cinema Insomnia Haunted House Special* I play

another gorilla-type character called Kogarella in honor of Bob and Kathy Burns who gave me some wonderful advice.

BC: *Who are your inspirations? Who were/are your favorite hosts?*

DD: I grew up with Elvira, Freddy Krueger, and *MST3K* but as an adult I fell in love with the New York-based show *Ghoul-a-Go-Go*. They inspired me to create a lot of art and I was lucky to befriend those fine fellows. I love them to death.

BC: *Who writes the show?*

DD: Mr. Lobo is the head writer. He takes a lot of inspiration from real life so I sometimes contribute to the show without even realizing it. I do throw in gags and story ideas.

BC: *What are some of your fondest memories of the show?*

DD: Working with John Dimes, Jerry Moore and Dick Dyszel on our *Haunted House* special a few years ago and working with the legendary Horror Host John Stanley of *Creature Features Movie Guide* fame.... Honestly, there are too many good memories to name and we're making more every day.

BC: *How did the idea for the (really cool) magazine come about? Will there be a second issue?*

DD: I had the idea for *Horror Hosts and Creature Features* for a while, even before I met Mr. Lobo. I had heard a few people talking about wanting to do it and I waited for it to happen, because it's the kind of magazine that I wanted to read—but it never did. Corpse S. Chris and I had discussed the idea and eventually Lobo and I poured our hearts into the first issue. It was well-received and we had a blast doing it.... But we had several setbacks, the main downer being that not long after the first issue went public, we had a run in with NBC/Universal who was fierce in their protection of *The Munsters* at the time due to their lame attempt to reboot the franchise. I'm not sure if there will be another issue in the foreseeable future since it was an expensive and time-consuming endeavor. And now with the creation of OSI74 there is very little time for it.... It was all rather heartbreaking, to be very honest.

BC: *Talk about your new channel.*

DD: It's a collective inspired by classic UHF, early cable and home video and the new home for *Cinema Insomnia*. OSI74 is an "off world" production colony and distribution network which specializes in bringing you unusual, experimental and entertaining programs from many different creative worlds. It's the sum total of a lot of hard work and passion. We've got 17 creative producers making content and we've really built a family. There are many hosted film shows—Ormond Grimsby's *Monster Creature Feature*, *Ghoul-a-Go-Go*, *Monster Madhouse* and more. You can watch some of our streaming programming on our website www.osi74.com and you can see everything on our Roku channel OSI74.

BC: *What is your favorite Devo album? I remember seeing them on the Freedom of Choice tour. They put on a great show.*

DD: Lobo and I are huge fans of Devo. They were one of the things that brought us together. We saw them in 2012 and they are still fantastic. My favorite album is *Duty Now for the Future* and I literally like every song Devo has ever recorded.... How many bands can you say that about? Especially one who's had a career spanning decades.

BC: *Tell us about Cosmonauti (great name!).*

DD: Jessie Seeherman is a model and comedian friend who I cast for the part of a sexy "Cyber Clone" who is rebuilding Utopia on the Red Planet with the help of her commanding officer, a dog named Col. Spudnik who digs up Cold War science fiction films. It was a side character from an old episode of *Cinema Insomnia* that Mr. Lobo and I expanded to create a sci-fi show for our Secret Sunday lineup on the channel. I designed Cosmonauti's costume and Col. Spudnik's costume and built sets and props for the show with Mr. Lobo.

BC: *What's the biggest difference between the old hosts and the new?*

DD: No one is an expert and there is no right or wrong way to become a Horror Host. However, Mr. Lobo has many different categories and theories for hosts. He's worked with Bob Wilkins and John Stanley from *Creature Features*, the Ghoul, Svengoolie and Count Gore De Vol. He considers those guys Silver Age horror hosts [1965–1985]. Many are still active today in various ways. Vampira and Zacherley were in the Golden Age [1954–1964], of course. Many Golden Age hosts were local stage actors hired by the local TV stations to present a package of movies that they licensed. Sometimes they already worked at the station as a staff announcer, news anchor or engineer—this was more common in the Silver Age. It was a job in every sense of the word. In the 1980s, Elvira was the first local TV host to go national in syndication.

Now we're in the Bronze or Aluminum Foil Age [*laughs*] but the biggest difference we can see is that being a horror host today is being *an artist*. It's like being a musician or a painter. You recognize the job as an art form and you are self-motivated and usually self-distributed. In the late 1980s and into the '90s many shows thrived on public access … the greatest success being *Mystery Science Theatre 3000* which was later picked up by huge cable networks like Sci-Fi [SyFy] and Comedy Channel. Now you will find many shows on the Internet and streaming channels like OSI74. Also, the pool of films is limited as the rights to many films are expensive [so you need] a major network picking up the tab. Part of why we decided to create our own channel and pool our resources is to help procure a better variety of films and fine-tune our shows for a new audience. I'm not sure if that answers your question…

BC: *What does the future hold for Dixie?*

DD: The future is now! Our new channel OSI is exploding as we have just hit 450,000 plays on the channel and it is growing every day—we will be on more and more streaming platforms in the future. We will be making more episodes of *Cinema Insomnia* and *Utopia Fantastika* as well as helping out with other shows on the network like *Sleazy Pictures After Dark* with Sleazy P. Martini, *Midnight Frights* with Spottswoode, *Monster Madhouse*, *Monster Creature Feature* and more. We will be developing other new shows with a retro feel—like game shows and sitcoms and hosted kid shows. Designing graphics, posters, merchandise, animations and branding for the channel and our associates has been a really great challenge as an artist and producer. We are also going to be doing more live events with films and we hope it never ends…. All systems go!

Other Genre Credits—FILMS: *A Hard Day's Nightmare*, Milliken Films, 2011 (Psycho-Killer Groupie); *Plan 9*, Darkstone Entertainment, 2015 (Victim); *Midnight Show*, Shuttlecock Films, 2016 (Gore-illa)

Elvira

REAL NAME: Cassandra Peterson (1951–)
BIRTHPLACE: Manhattan, Kansas
HOST: *Elvira's Movie Macabre* (September 28, 1981—July 13, 1985), KHJ-TV, Channel 9, Los Angeles, California (39 episodes syndicated by Contel); *3-D TV*: (Special, May 1985), KHJ-TV, Channel 9, Los Angeles, California; *Macabre TV: Elvira's Halloween Special* (October 31, 1984), MTV; *Elvira in Salem Halloween Special* (October 31, 1986), MTV; *Elvira's Premiere Party* (Special, September 1988), MTV; *Elvira's Thriller Theatre* (1989), Channel 10, Australia; *Halloween Havoc* (October 1989, 1990, 1991), Turner Television Pay-Per-View; *Heavy Metal Heaven* (six episodes, November 1989), BBC, England; *Joe Bob Briggs' Drive-In Theatre* (co-host, along with Zacherley, Ghoulardi and John Stanley; October 21, 1991), Showtime; *Halloween Movie Shlock-a thon* (October 30–31, 1993), TBS; *Halloween Bash* (November 17, 1994), Fox; *Attack of the Killer "B"-Movies* (September 14, 1995), NBC; *Elvira's Movie Macabre Halloween Special* (October 1997), KCAL-TV, Los Angeles, California; *Monstermania* (1999), AMC; *Bride of Monstermania* (1999), AMC; *Attack of the 50-Foot Monstermania* (1999), AMC; *13 Nights of Elvira* (2014), Brainstorm Media via Hulu

BIOGRAPHY: As I wrote in the introduction, a lot of the history of horror hosts is based on memories, particularly of those hosts who had only local exposure. This may be odd in the case of an international icon like Elvira, but my very first memory of her is a very local, personal one: I was on tour with my band, Th' Inbred, in 1987, and we were playing a show in a bar in Jackson, Mississippi. We had just gotten finished with our set. Much like my first exposure to Crematia Mortem, the bar TV just happened to be showing *Elvira's Movie Macabre*, and Elvira just happened to be on at that moment doing a bumper, and I remember thinking, "Damn, that woman's got some fine legs!" And then it hit me: Elvira was the First Horror Hostess of Punk. The black dress and hair, the spiky beehive hairdo, the studded leather wristbands, her attitude; she was the complete package. Sure, she had her antecedents, all the way back to Vampira, of course (we'll get into that a little later), but, you know, Elvira was now! Elvira, from the look and sound of her, was one of us! I only saw a little bit more of the movie and her (I was engaged in my other chief profession at the time, chasing females), but she left a lasting impression. Little did I know what a phenomenon she was becoming, getting, er, bigger, every day, and that I was one day destined to meet and talk with her, at least three times so far; she gave me the idea for this book. I started out with the idea of doing a biography of Cassandra/Elvira, but when I spoke to her in April 2015, she said that she was already working on one herself. Expressing my surprise that there hadn't yet been a book about her, she said, "Yeah, I know…. I'm just always so busy." And then she suggested, "Hey, you could always write one of those unauthorized biographies," but I demurred, thinking that a publisher would never go for it. The rest isn't history, but it is in the introduction.

Cassandra Peterson was born in Manhattan, Kansas, the daughter of an insurance salesman and a mother who ran a costume shop. She and her parents lived on a farm just outside of Manhattan, in Randolph, Kansas; at the age of seven, they moved to Colorado Springs, where she lived until she was 17. And she was a horror fan. She was in second grade when a cousin, on the sly, took her to see *House on Haunted Hill*, and she became hooked, both on horror movies and Vincent Price, who remains her favorite genre star. Her favorite television shows growing up were *The Twilight Zone* and *The Addams Family*; she even built the legendary Aurora monster models. It didn't exactly make her popular with her peer group, and she was bullied a lot as a child. So the process of hardening the carapace began to take place; she describes herself as rebellious and cocky during her teen years (although she admits it was a false bravado). She also says she ... er, developed practically overnight. This led to a series of jobs go-go dancing at local clubs, starting at age 14. But she still had many rivers to cross, literally.

At age 17, she left home to become a Las Vegas showgirl. While appearing in a show called *Viva Les Girls* she met and very briefly dated Elvis Presley. Impressed by her talent, he encouraged her to strike out on her own. Also while in Vegas, she had a small, uncredited role as a showgirl in the James Bond film *Diamonds Are Forever*, in one of the many actual shows filmed as a backdrop to the main action. To complete the Vegas adventure trifecta, she was working in a nude revue when she met Tom Jones. In a 2008 interview with *Blender Magazine*, she revealed that she lost her virginity to Jones, which, after it was over, literally had her in stitches—only it wasn't laughter, it was pain, due to the randy Welshman's aggressive lovemaking technique. She said, "I thought, well, if I'm gonna do this, it might as well be with Tom Jones ... it was painful and horrible." Besides leaving her in need of medical care, which was bad enough, he left her with something even worse, a broken heart. Cassandra thought they were going to run away and get married, but when she went backstage the next night to see what she thought was her new paramour, he was with two of his background singers, with whom he was busy rehearsing the Horizontal Bop. "I was disgusted," said Cassandra. It's not unexpected that her infatuation ended then and there.

Acting on the advice from Elvis, Cassandra moved to Italy and became the singer for the rock band I Latins Ochanats & the Snails. During her time in Italy, she met famed director Federico Fellini, which led to a small part in his film *Roma*. Soon after that, she decided to move to Hollywood. Back in the U.S., she toured with the musical-comedy group Mamma's Boys and, like Maila Nurmi before her, posed for men's magazines like *High Society* and *Modern Man*. She also took acting classes and in 1979 joined a famous L.A. improv comedy group, The Groundlings. It was then that the seeds of the Elvira character were sown; she developed a character based on the stereotypical "Valley Girl," which KHJ director Larry Thomas saw her perform when he attended one of the Groundlings shows. Thomas was looking for a horror host to replace Sinister Seymour, and wanted Cassandra to try out for it, but she was on her honeymoon at the time, and refused to cut it short for what she thought would be a fruitless audition. When she returned, the station still hadn't filled the role, so she went to read for it. They reportedly gave her an awful script, which she figuratively threw away and used the experience she had gained at improv. The stations execs loved it and she got the job. The only bump in the road came from Maila Nurmi. The thing that KHJ neglected to tell Cassandra was that they weren't just looking for a horror host to replace Seymour; they wanted to revive Vampira. Nurmi had been in talks with KHJ to do just that, but when negotiations broke down, Nurmi took Vampira and walked. She also sued, claiming that the character of Elvira too closely resembled her own creation. The results of that trial are detailed in the Vampira entry.

Not being able to use the name Vampira, the station was temporarily flummoxed. From a *Femme Fatales* interview:

> We had everyone—and by everyone, I mean the sound guys, the lighting guys and whoever happened to be in the station at the time—throw different names into a coffee can, and we picked one of them out. Someone had written down "Elvira." And to this day, we still never have been able to find out who put the name in.... I have always had this feeling that someone used that name because of the song "Elvira" by the Oak Ridge Boys. So I got stuck with that name, a name I really *hated* at first.

Her original KHJ show was on for four years; as Joe Bob Briggs sagely observed in *American Scary*, the show wasn't on that long; she really didn't get hugely popular until after *Movie Macabre* ended and she started doing commercials, promotions and merchandising. She is right under your nose with her own brand of perfume, you can play Elvira pinball and slot machines, and you can dress like her in an officially licensed costume and complete the outfit with an Elvira purse. When you're ready to go, you can get in your car and catch a whiff of an Elvira-scented rearview mirror-hanger, and pop in one of one of her many CDs. After a day of impersonating her, you can go home and build a model of her, or

Elvira—what a stocking-stuffer! A publicity photo from the mid–1990s.

admire your Elvira figurine. Then you can have some Elvira wine in your Elvira glassware. Or, if you're a suds-doggie, then you can pop the top on a can of Elvira's Night Brew. You can read *Elvira: Transylvania 90210* (obviously, a parody of *Beverly Hills 90210*) by Cassandra and John Paragon, or *Bad Dog, Andy*, a children's book, also by the Peterson-Paragon team. A project that very surprisingly never got off the ground was her idea for a line of Elvira lingerie; maybe she should talk to Rhonda Shear. There's also a great deal of unauthorized material out there, which she won't sign. Unlike Maila Nurmi, Cassandra was able to parlay Elvira into a financial bonanza. She became a pop culture icon—something that Vampira became too, but in Cassandra's case, the recognition came and the dividends started to pay much sooner. She has also been constant as well as consistent, remaining in the public eye until the present day whereas, sad to say, Maila labored for years in obscurity, until she was rediscovered by the punk rock generation. It was only then that Maila Nurmi began to receive her due.

But this isn't to say that the character of Elvira is merely a cash cow for Cassandra; it has given her a platform from which she can do the most good for her most cherished charities and passions, including being a spokeswoman for PETA. It has meant female empowerment not just for her, but for females the world over. The horror genre (and, by extension, horror hosting) has become very much an equal-opportunity genre. Women are no longer portrayed simply, mostly as victims (and if they are, it is more often than not a woman director who is putting them through their paces). You can see for yourself how many women cite her as an influence in this book. And whereas fan conventions used to be totally male-dominated, there is also a much more even mix; Elvira showed that, hey, it's not necessarily different for girls.

Elvira has been the subject of two comic book series. The first, DC's *Elvira's House of Mystery* (1986–1987) ran for 11 issues, plus a Christmas Special, also from 1987. The second was much more successful: Claypool Comics' *Elvira, Mistress of the Dark* (1993–2007) had a run of 166 issues, plus two trade paperback collections. The quality of the work done on both series was uneven. The first issue of *Elvira's House of Mystery* certainly looked promising, a 64-page Halloween Special with a cover by Brian Bolland (*Judge Dredd, Wonder Woman*). But the insides were a letdown: a combination of uninspired scripting and artwork that failed to exploit the considerable possibilities for horror and "Good Girl Art," in the style of Torchy, Phantom Lady and Sheena. There were a couple more great *Elvira's House of Mystery* covers: Issue #5, by Mark Beachum, featured a nicely executed piece with Elvira in bondage on a swing, and the last issue, another giant-sized Halloween Spectacular, featured a classic cover by Dave Stevens (*The Rocketeer*), with Elvira riding a broomstick against the backdrop of a moon that's full and bright. The published cover, as discovered years later, had been ever-so-slightly altered; in his original drawing, Dave had playfully, but not obviously, placed the broomstick as if to appear in between Elvira's legs. The ever-conservative DC had their art department touch it up so that she appeared to be riding "side-saddle." Dave also did a wonderful "punk" cover for *Twisted Tales* #1 (Eclipse Comics, 1987) that in fan circles is known as simply "the Elvira cover," because of the female subject's uncanny resemblance to a certain Mistress of the Dark. Claypool dispensed with cover artists altogether; every issue of *Elvira, Mistress of the Dark* (even the trade paperbacks) had an Elvira photo cover. Even though the writing talent included folks such as Kurt Busiek and Fred Hembeck, again, the art was only serviceable, and although the work marginally reflected the "Good Girl" sensibility a little better from panel to panel, it was not the stuff that dreams were made of.

The *Movie Macabre* series has been packaged and re-packaged on single- and double-feature DVDs. The films she hosts are mostly public domain, but there are a few oddball gems to be found, including *Werewolf of Washington, Count Dracula's Great Love, Blue Sunshine* and *The Satanic Rites of Dracula*. Let's face it, if you must own a copy of, say, *Night of the Living Dead*, then you might as well own one that's got Elvira hosting. And then, of course, there are her two feature films proper, *Elvira, Mistress of the Dark* and *Elvira's Haunted Hills*. The former came about because the then-president of NBC asked her to do a show tentatively titled *Ghoul School*, with Elvira as the teacher of a class that was literally full of little monsters. Cassandra said that she wanted to do a movie first, then a series. The film took about three years, but it finally happened; *Ghoul School* didn't. The film had a $12,000,000 budget; *Elvira's Haunted Hills*, one million. She professes to like both, with the first one, somewhat naturally, getting the edge. She says that *Mistress of the Dark* was like a dream come true and is proud of the fact that it was inspirational for so many women—although she says she didn't mean it to be. In her eyes, it was her version of *The Wizard of Oz*!

Elvira, Mistress of the Dark starts off with a clip from the cult classic *It Conquered the World*, the movie on *Movie Macabre*, and her opening bit is classic Elvira: "Hello, darlings, it's me, Elvira, the gal with the enormous ... ratings. Can anybody tell me what that movie was about? I'll tell ya what it was about; it was about an hour and a half too long! And don't forget, next week, it's *The Head with Two Things*.... I mean, *The Thing with Two Heads* ... and until then, this is Elvira, the gal who put the boob back into boob tube ... unpleasant dreams." And then the weather calendar falls over her, and the stagehands start moving her couch off the set while she's still on it.

The basic plot is this: Elvira quits her show because the new station owner has been promised a night in the sack with her. Elvira is opening in Vegas. That is, she *thinks* she's opening in Vegas, until her agent informs her that she has to put up money for her show, which Elvira naturally doesn't have. Then she receives news that her great-aunt has died ("Great aunt? I didn't even know I had a good one!"). Expecting a large inheritance, she travels to Falwell, Massachusetts, where she learns that her great-aunt has left all her money to her servants, and all that Elvira will get is her great-aunt's house, her poodle and her cookbook. Elvira's Uncle Vincent really wants to get his hands on that cookbook, because it contains untold secrets of dark powers: the *Necronomicon* if it was written by Julia Child. Of course you know this means war.

From there on out, it's a full-on frontal assault against self-righteous, hypocritical morality, pitting Elvira against both Uncle Vincent and the "good people" of Falwell, led by the impossibly prudish Chastity Pariah. "We've got this town council that lives in mortal fear that somebody, somewhere, is havin' a good time." And that's exactly what they make of Elvira; she can't get a job. Her only friends are the poodle, the teens in the town and Bob Redding, played to dim-bulb perfection by Daniel Greene. The kids are united (especially three young men with a camera in a scene which pays tribute to *Animal House*) and help her rebuild her house, only to be threatened with expulsion from school if they associate with Elvira. Bob just happens to run the movie house (which only shows G-rated movies), and since she can't find any other work, she decides to stage a live midnight spook show. Bob agrees to stage it and the kids, despite the threat of expulsion, attend. But Elvira's big finale is ruined by Bob's jealous girlfriend, who replaces Elvira's glitter with tar and feathers.

After whipping up a recipe she got from the Cookbook from Hell, Elvira serves it to Bob, who takes off the lid and uncovers a snarling demon that bears a passing resemblance to *The Beast from 20,000 Fathoms*. Soon they discover the secret of the cookbook and Elvira's mother, who really *was* a "Mistress of the Dark." At a pot-luck picnic, Elvira sneaks in a love potion casserole. The picnic soon turns into a (G-rated) orgy. The town council, spurred on by Uncle Vincent (who still wants that cookbook), decides to burn

Elvira 37

Elvira at the stake for being a witch. The crowd chants in murderous frenzy while Girl Scouts toast marshmallows over the flames. Elvira, with the aid of her mother's ring, conjures up a storm to douse the flames. Uncle Vincent, who now has the cookbook, starts some inclement weather of his own. He turns three council members into real pigs, and then confronts Elvira in a graveyard. He chases her into the house, but Elvira destroys him with the ring. While she sits on the steps of her decimated house, the townspeople converge on it—to say they're sorry, and welcome her as one of their own. But then a lawyer arrives and tells her that as the sole living relative, she's inherited Vincent's fortune, and it's time for a show-stopping (literally) production in Vegas. Elvira is surrounded by male dancers dressed as demons and she in a jaw-dropping spider-themed bra, plus a garter belt and seamed stockings. She even ends the film with her signature catchphrase: "Unpleasant Dreams."

Elvira, Mistress of the Dark is a really fun movie. The dialogue is smart and sharp ("A guaranteed standing ovulation!") and the jokes are delivered at a rat-a-tat pace which never lags. (In her car, Elvira almost collides with Bob, who asks "How's your head?" Elvira immediately zings back, "Well, I haven't had any complaints yet.") Middle-class social mores and right-wing, religious conservatives are easy targets, admittedly, but the film never comes off as preachy, and the townspeople are ultimately shown to truly be "good people." The film affectionately spoofs many film clichés, and not just horror; in the final confrontation between Elvira and her uncle, she comes out dressed as Rambo, and her weaponry is accordingly large. Fun, fun, fun, and she even got her T-Bird back to stay.

Elvira reclines in her most famous pose in the most timeless of her photos.

Thirteen years later came *Elvira's Haunted Hills*, an homage to AIP Vincent Price Poe films, particularly *House of Usher* and *Pit and the Pendulum*. In fact, the film is dedicated to the late, legendary star, who was a friend to Cassandra and to the film's director Sam Irvin. Price and Irvin corresponded through the mail for many years, and when Irvin made his first film (*Guilty as Charged*, 1991), he got a congratulatory missive from Vincent. The tone of *Elvira's Haunted Hills* is much different than the first film; there is still smart dialogue, but the humor in the second is much more outright slapstick and sight gags. It takes place in "Carpathia, 1851." It doesn't make her a less endearing comic figure, or smart, sexy woman, but it somehow makes her less of a master of her domain. She is also somewhat less distinctive; rather than existing in a world that exists only for her to stick her finger in its eye, it is a world populated by oddball characters, and so she is one among many. That it got made at all is a testament to all involved, Cassandra said in a 2001 *Femme Fatales* interview:

> Making it was difficult. Selling it has been difficult, too! I wrote the first script for another Elvira movie right after the first one right after *Mistress of the Dark* was released. I sold it to a company. They went bankrupt and took the script down with them, so I was back at square one and decided to go into negotiations with Roger Corman on *Elvira and the Vampire Women*. We never got to shoot that one either, but we'd taken the time to write the entire script and do the budget. As much as I love Roger, I would've wound up making $1.50 an hour with the contract he wanted me to sign. He would have retained all the rights and made all the money from it. He's been very successful doing things that way all his life, so I respect him for that! But I might as well go get a job waiting tables if it came down to that kind of money.

Elvira's Haunted Hills is not without its merits, and again starts out promisingly: The credits are run over an AIP-like shifting colored-sand background, and then cuts to the sight of Elvira being buried alive behind a brick wall. But then she and her maid wake up to the sound of their landlord at the inn, demanding his rent. After some Monkees- or *Munsters*-like fast-motion from Elvira and Zou Zou (Mary Jo Smith, who also had Groundling grounding), the film gets in its first movie-parody scene when the landlord breaks through the door with an ax, proclaiming "Here's Johann!" It seems whatever century she's in, Elvira has problems with cash flow, and she's on her way to Paris to do a show to rectify that. In fact, she's on her way there literally on the back of Zou-Zou. But soon a carriage picks them up, and it stops for the night at Hellsubus Castle, where, it seems, Elvira is a dead ringer for the sinister Lord Hellsubus' wife, Elura (which she should be, since they're both played by Cassandra). Smith is a great foil for Cassandra, the rotund Costello to Elvira's Abbott. True, she is the butt (pun fully intended) of a lot of jokes, but she also gives as good as she gets. To Cassandra's credit (she co-wrote the film, as she did the first one), Elvira doesn't hog all the funny lines between them.

That night, Zou Zou is frightened by strange noises coming from the dungeon, so Elvira investigates. In the library of Lord Hellsubus, she finds the stable-master, a Fabio-type (Gabriel Andronache), reading the lord's books and polishing his pistol. His polishing pace gets much quicker when he sees Elvira, and of course it's made to look like he's masturbating, to which Elvira cracks, "Better be careful; that thing might go off in your hand." In a parody of Harlequin Romances and foreign films, the stable-master lips move one way, but the dubbed dialogue, obviously, moves another.

The Usher–like Lord Hellsubus was played by one of the stars of *The Rocky Horror Picture Show*, Richard O'Brien, and to say there was friction between Cassandra and

O'Brien would be putting it mildly. The role was initially slated for Richard Chamberlain, who ended up committing himself to another project, although that didn't prove fatal to Chamberlain and Cassandra's friendship. But O'Brien had an idea how the movie should be, and naturally, Cassandra had her own, and since it was her movie, well, we know how that story works out. In the end, though, they smoothed out their differences and she has nothing but praise for O'Brien.

The rest of the cast and film are painted in broad strokes; Mary Scheer plays Hellsubus' second wife, who obviously has something to hide. She is in league (and in bed) with an unctuous doctor (Scott Atkinson), who does a poor job of concealing his lust for Elvira. Heather Hopper is an extremely nervous member of the family who is given to fits of catalepsy. O'Brien comically chases Elvira around a cemetery, and she stumbles upon Scheer and Atkinson plotting and embracing, which naturally leads to dire consequences; in this case with a parodic predicament involving that Pit and that Pendulum. Naturally, this provides an opportunity for a bondage scene, with Elvira, naturally, straining most fetchingly against her ropes. In this case, the pendulum comes much closer to Elvira than most other similar situations, until the razor-sharp pendulum cuts the elevated ropes that bind her cleavage. Her life saved, her attention can now be directed towards the immediate problem: She broke a nail.

Elvira has become such an enduring and endearing pop culture icon that she has even earned a parody of the character on *The Simpsons*. The hilarious spoof, as usual containing more than one level of reference, is called "Boobarella," and she titillates Springfield with lines like, "We'll return to the movie after these commercial breaks, but first, *look at my boobs!*" Elvira may have transcended horror-hosting almost completely; she's associated with Halloween obviously, but that's not the same thing. Her image has become so pervasive, with bigger advertising campaigns for bigger corporations and all sorts of appearances as Elvira on much bigger television stations, it's my opinion that many people, particularly newer fans, just know her as Elvira and have little or no idea that she was ever a host. Oh, sure, real fans know, but I'd be willing to wager that if you inquired of the average person, who Elvira is, and what she did before she shilled for Coors and was a pinball machine, you'd receive a blank stare and a shrug of the shoulders. Possibly a mumbled "I dunno ... uh, she was sexy?"

Other Genre Credits—FILMS: *Diamonds Are Forever*, Eon Productions, 1971 (Showgirl; uncredited); *Jekyll and Hyde: Together Again*, Paramount, 1982 (Busty Nurse); *Pee-wee's Big Adventure*, Warner Brothers, 1985 (Biker Mama); *Allan Quatermain and the Lost City of Gold*, Golan-Globus Productions, 1986 (Sorais); *Elvira, Mistress of the Dark*, New World Pictures, 1988 (Elvira); *The Ketchup Vampires* (short), Kidpix, 1992 (Elvira); *Superstition* (short), Iwerks Entertainment, 1997 (Elvira); *Encounter in the Third Dimension* (short), nWave Pictures, 1999 (Elvira); *Elvira's Haunted Hills*, Media Pro Pictures, 2001 (Elvira); *Scares and Dares* (short), 2001 (Elvira); *Her Morbid Desires*, Irena Belle Films, 2008 (Elvira); *Zombie Killer* (short), Special Entertainment, 2008 (Vampira, voice only); *The Scream*, Scream Productions, 2009 (Elvira); *The Haunted World of El Superbeasto* (animated), Carbunkle Cartoons, 2009 (voice of Amber); *All About Evil*, Backlash Films, 2010 (Linda); *Vault of the Macabre*, 2014 (Elvira/Narrator); TELEVISION: *Fantasy Island*: three episodes (1978, 1983); *Space Ghost Coast-to-Coast*: "Switcheroo," 1996 (Elvira); *Teenage Mutant Ninja Turtles* (animated), four episodes

(2013, 2015—voice of Mrs. Campbell); NON-GENRE TV APPEARANCES AS ELVIRA: *CHiPs*: "Rock Devil Rock," 1982, "Things That Go Creep in the Night," 1983; *The Richard Simmons Show* (1983), *Last of the Great Survivors* (1984), *Get Out of My Room* (1985), *WrestleMania 2* (1986), *Parker Lewis Can't Lose* (1992), *The Girls Next Door* (2006), *The Search for the Next Elvira* (2007), *The Marilyn Denis Show* (2011)

DISCOGRAPHY:

Elvira and the Vi-Tones 3-D TV—"3-D TV (Three Dimensional)" b/w "Elvira's Theme," Rhino Records, 1982

Elvira presents Vinyl Macabre—Oldies but Ghoulies (Vol. 1), Rhino Records, 1983

Track Listing:

1. Mark Pierson, "Elvira's Theme" (Intro)
2. Bobby "Boris" Pickett, "The Monster Mash"
3. Jumpin' Gene Simmons, "Haunted House"
4. Comateens, "The Munsters"
5. The Bollock Brothers, "Horror Movies"
6. Sheb Wooley, "Purple People Eater"
7. The Shaggs, "It's Halloween"
8. Neil Norman and his Cosmic Orchestra, "Twilight Zone"
9. Jim Parker, "The Vegas Vampire"
10. The Challengers, "Out of Limits"
11. Dickie Goodman, "Horror Movies"
12. Red Lipstique, "Drac's Back"
13. Mark Pierson, "Elvira's Theme" (Outro)

Elvira presents Haunted Hits, Rhino Records, 1987

Track Listing:

1. Bobby "Boris" Pickett, "The Monster Mash"
2. Jumpin' Gene Simmons, "Haunted House"
3. Ray Parker Jr., "Ghostbusters"
4. The Marketts, "Out of Limits"
5. The Five Blobs, "The Blob"
6. Dave Edmunds, "Creature from the Black Lagoon"
7. Sheb Wooley, "Purple People Eater"
8. Vic Mizzy, "The Addams Family Theme"
9. Alice Cooper, "Welcome to my Nightmare"
10. Neil Norman and his Cosmic Orchestra, "Twilight Zone"
11. Oingo Boingo, "Dead Man's Party"
12. Lambert, Hendricks and Ross, "Halloween Spooks"
13. Skyhooks, "Horror Movie"
14. Screamin' Jay Hawkins, "I Put a Spell on You"
15. The Cramps, "I Was a Teenage Werewolf"
16. LaVern Baker, "Voodoo-Voodoo"
17. Elvira, "Full Moon"

The cassette version of *Haunted Hits* contained six additional tracks not found on the album:

1. Lewis Lee, "Attack of the Killer Tomatoes"
2. Screamin' Jay Hawkins, "Little Demon"
3. The Tubes, "Attack of the 50-Foot Woman"
4. Big T Tyler, "King Kong"
5. The Jayhawks, "The Creature"
6. The Ran-Dells, "Martian Hop"

Elvira presents Monster Hits, Rhino Records, 1994

Track Listing:

1. Elvira, Introduction
2. Elvira, "Monsta' Rap"
3. Screamin' Jay Hawkins, "Little Demon"
4. Alice Cooper, "Feed my Frankenstein"
5. Bobby "Boris" Pickett, "The Monster Mash"
6. D.J. Jazzy Jeff & the Fresh Prince, "Nightmare on my Street"
7. Joey Gaynor, "The Addams Family Theme"
8. Elvira, "Here Comes the Bride (of Frankenstein)"
9. Elvira, Outro

Elvira presents Revenge of the Monster Hits, Rhino Records, 1995

Track Listing:

1. Elvira, Introduction
2. Elvira, "Haunted House"
3. Charles Sheffield, "It's Your Voodoo Working"
4. The Tubes, "Attack of the 50-Foot Woman"
5. Warren Zevon, "Werewolves of London"
6. Bobby "Boris" Pickett, "Monster's Holiday"
7. Oingo Boingo, "Weird Science"
8. Elvira, "Zombie Stomp"
9. Elvira, Outro

Elvira/Leslie and the LY'S—"Zombie Killer," Hefty Hideaway Records, 2008

Elvira's Gravest Hits, Shout! Factory, 2010

Track Listing:

1. Elvira, "Elvira's Theme"
2. Lori Chacko, "Once Bitten, Twice Shy"
3. Elvira, "3-D TV"
4. Elvira, "Full Moon"
5. Elvira, "Monsta' Rap"
6. Elvira, "Zombie Stomp"
7. Elvira, "Haunted House"
8. Elvira, "Here Comes the Bride (of Frankenstein)"
9. Elvira, "Here I Am"

10. Elvira, "Le Music Hall"
11. Leslie and the LY'S, "Zombie Killer"
12. Ghoultown, "Mistress of the Dark"
13. Lori Chacko, "Once Bitten, Twice Shy" (Alternate Version)

Elvira, Mistress of the Dark—"2 Big Pumpkins" b/w "13 Nights of Halloween," TMR, 2013

Elvira's Heavy Metal Halloween, Somerset Records, 2014

Track Listing:

1. *The Exorcist* (Main Theme)
2. *Frankenstein*
3. Bach, "Toccata and Fugue"
4. Beethoven, "Moonlight Sonata"
5. "Funeral March of a Marionette Gounod" (*Alfred Hitchcock Presents* Theme)
6. "Godzilla"
7. "Phantom of the Opera"
8. Grieg, "In the Hall of the Mountain King"
9. Orff, "O Fortuna" (*Carmina Burana*)
10. *Halloween* (Main Theme)

Esmeralda

REAL NAME: John Voight

HOST: *Gravesend Manor* (1957–1962; also 1964), WOI-TV, Channel 5, Ames-Des Moines, Iowa; *Son of Gravesend Manor* (mid–1970s), WOI-TV, Channel 5, Ames-Des Moines, Iowa

BIOGRAPHY: Esmeralda was one of the characters featured on the *Gravesend Manor* and *Son of Gravesend Manor* shows, which were hosted by Malcolm the Butler (Ed Weiss) and the Duke of Desmans (Jim "Red" Varnum), along with their flunky, "Claude" (Ron Scott). "Somewhere along the line, someone decided that Claude needed a girlfriend," recalled John Voight (no, not *that* one), who played Esmeralda. "I said, 'Well, I'll do it.' So I thought, 'Well, I'm young enough—or I was then—but I'll do just a little bit of.... I'll do some pratfalls." And in the scant minutes of surviving outtake footage, that's just what he does—swinging in on a rope from "upstairs" and doing a first-class belly-flop, his skirt flying up and exposing his behind.

Evilun

REAL NAME: Ruth Sprayberry

HOST: *Terror!* (early 1960s), KSLA-TV, Channel 12, Shreveport, Louisiana

BIOGRAPHY: Local actress Ruth Sprayberry did a short but popular stint as Evilun, hosting the *Terror* package of films for KSLA-TV in Shreveport, Louisiana, which aired at 10:15 on Saturday nights in the early '60s. One of the promotional items she gave away was a card; the front featured a photo of Evilun, along with a skull with a rose in its teeth, and said "I'm so happy you watch *Terror*! It's comforting to know there are so many of you sickies out there. Put my picture next to your heart—if you have one—Evilun." On the back of the card, it certified the recipient as a "Terrorist in bad standing and a personal friend of mine—Evilun." No video or audio footage survives, and the photos that exist show Sprayberry to be a very attractive woman, with long black hair and a gown to match. The threadbare set features the expected shabby walls, a long table and a wicker chair.

Evilun was no stranger to celebrity guest appearances; a clipping from a local newspaper shows her alongside Lon Chaney, Jr. The caption reads:

> Horror movies are getting a bit old-hat on TV, and what's needed these days is something to jazz up a shock-movie show a bit. Such a restorative was found recently by KSLA-TV, Shreveport, La., for its *Terror on Saturday Nights with Evilun* series, a feature show hosted by a Charles Addams-ish monstress of ceremonies. She offered a small prize to the program fan who designed her "worst" monster. In four weeks, there were some 5,000 entries submitted. Payoff exploitation came when the station booked a large exhibit hall, showed off the "folk art," and imported movie monster Lon Chaney to help Evilun judge the winner.

Other photos from the period include another with Lon, possibly from the same personal appearance; one of her with "The Terror Crew," which consisted of a man and a woman in ghoulish makeup; judging a local costume contest, and even, judging from the picture, a float in a parade which proclaimed her to be running for president (no doubt on the Fright-Whig ticket). The following info on Evilun was sent to the excellent "Holly's Horrorland" blog, maintained by that collector and creator of creepy curiosities, Holly Horrorshow, somewhere in Virginia:

> Evilun was portrayed by a very talented local actress named Ruth Sprayberry. She was active in the community theaters of Shreveport, and was a very kind and gracious person. I watched *Terror* every weekend during junior high. The movies were usually not awful, but weren't the best, either—films like *I Bury the Living*, and *Cry of the Werewolf*. Evilun had a small, creepy set, with lots of dry-ice fog and candles in ornate candelabras. She had a very direct, unnerving presence, made the usual wisecracks, and seemed to be having a grand time with it all. The *Terror* program ran for a few years.

Feverita
REAL NAME: not available
BIOGRAPHY: see the entry for Darcinia, Duchess of Darkness
HOST: KGSW-TV Channel 14, Albuquerque, New Mexico

Georgette, the Fudge-Maker
REAL NAME: Bonnie Sue Barney
HOST: *Chiller Theater* (with Chilly Billy Cardille; 1976–1984), WIIC-TV, Channel 11, Pittsburgh, Pennsylvania
BIOGRAPHY: Chilly Billy is the undisputed king of Pittsburgh horror hosts; he was to Pittsburgh TV what the Pittsburgh Steelers are to pro football. The person who's been able to put up with me the longest, my friend Paul Riggie, had the honor and pleasure of interviewing Chilly at the Monster Bash circa 2000, and he said that Georgette, the Fudge-Maker "married a golf pro, and they live in Florida. I haven't seen her in about 15 years. I'm curious—I'm sure she looks great … but she was terrific, they were [all] just nice people. She was Miss Pennsylvania, y'know.... I got her for the younger guys…" Of which I was one, and he certainly had fine taste.

But in looking over a list of the past winners of the Miss Pennsylvania pageant, I could find no reference to Bonnie Sue Barney as being one. Perhaps she was one of the finalists. He elaborated just a bit more in an interview with Sandy Clark for the book edition of *American Scary*: "Then, over the years, I had two other cast members, two girls, the first of which was Georgette, the Fudge-Maker; she was very attractive, very nice, and very young, and she [unlike Terminal Stare] talked. We dressed her as a farmer—Georgette the farmer, and she made fudge. Eventually, she came out with her own fudge! She made good money, too."

Ghoulda

REAL NAME: Geri Chronowit Roberts
HOST: *Shock Theater* (1958–1959), WRVA Channel 12, Richmond, Virginia
BIOGRAPHY: A deep, and deeply feminine (yet somehow eerie and unsettling) voice comes out of the television: "We pause now for station identification ... this is WRVA Television, Coffin 12 Richmond, Virginia..." This was the voice of Geri Roberts, a.k.a. former Richmond, Virginia, horror hostess Ghoulda. She hosted Richmond's version of *Shock Theatre* but, like Hazel Witch, not much survives of the show: no video footage, only a few still photographs, a newspaper clipping and some snippets of audio. The producers of the excellent documentary on Virginia horror hosts, *Virginia Creepers*, scored a short phone interview with her:

> I tried to make her glamorous at first, and they didn't want her glamorous, they wanted her ugly, so we worked from there until we uglied her up enough, and that took quite a long time. We used face putty and a lot of weird coloring, and it took me a couple of hours.... I used to fool around with a maniacal cackle, and I think that might have been the inspiration for it... [She does the maniacal cackle].

Super Ghoulda fan Richard Webb added this information:

> Those of us who were of my age had heard for the past ten years or so of our lives how scary *Dracula* was or how scary *Frankenstein* was, or the Wolf Man or the Mummy films were, and we were finally getting a chance to see these for ourselves. They were unavailable until then, you couldn't go down to the video library and rent it; moreover, we couldn't even watch them at our own time we wanted to watch. They matter to me—she matters to me—because she was part of my misspent youth, and she was a good, fun part of it. She had the little skeleton, which was Lucifer, her dead son.... Darling was her invisible husband, and he was in a rocking chair, which I guess through wires, managed to keep on rocking during each break ... there was Uncle David, who was an off-camera werewolf...

The following is one of the few minutes of Ghoulda audio: "Many of the old legends about lycanthropy have been dispelled by a group of non-believers ... but we know about werewolves, don't we, darlings? Hahahahahahaha! [A wolf howls] No, Uncle David, you can't run loose tonight! There's some raw, bloody

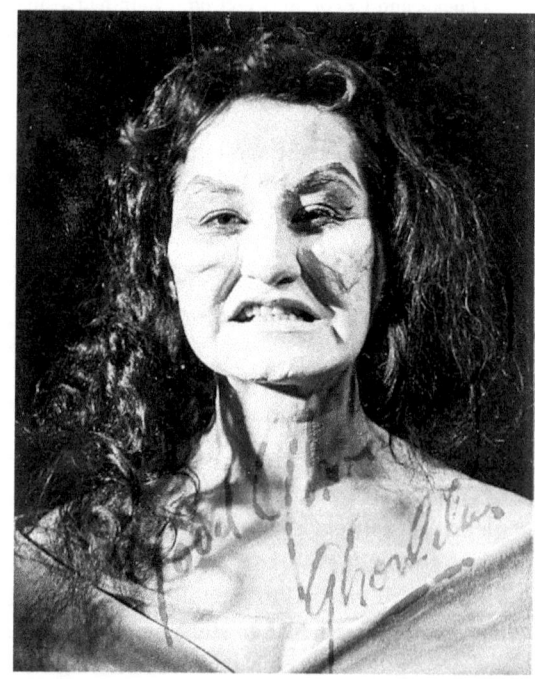

There's a very smart, beautiful woman underneath that ghastly make-up, circa 1959 (courtesy George "E-Gor" Chastain).

meat for you!" Regarding the *House of Frankenstein* scene where the Wolf Man and the Monster are discovered encased in ice, Ghoulda comments, "You'll notice that the Monster and the Wolf Man outdo Sonja Henie when it comes to ice shows.... Skaters are only surface performers, you know, but our boys learn the business from the inside out..."

Webb stated, "She was not just a fixture, she was there watching, she was there enjoying, and that was the thing we got from her, was that we were enjoying them with her, and she was enjoying them with us; that's a big point that I had never really thought about until right now." Geri Roberts had this to say on the phone during her interview with Webb: "That excitement that you feel with live theater is, in a way, something you feel with live TV. It's something akin to what you get stepping on a stage, you know, 'This is it and it's gotta be right...' There's something about that, you only get one crack at it to do it right."

Webb recalled his and his sister's surprise and disappointment when they tuned into *Shock Theater* and found that Ghoulda had abdicated her position:

> My sister sent her a letter to get to get this SPEVA badge... We got that badge, and she wrote us a nice letter... Within a month or so, she was gone... The newsman said, "Ghoulda fans will have to be disappointed tonight because Ghoulda ran off and got married this weekend. She was a graduate student in theater at RPI, and she's left us. Tonight we have *Destiny*," and as soon as *Destiny* came on, we knew who it was, it was Channel 12's version of *American Bandstand*, and the host ... after Ghoulda, he was nothing. He didn't have any of the humor, any of the spontaneity.... I don't know, she wasn't on that much, but she was glorious.

Ghoulda has the last word (as well she should): "Have you ever seen such devotion, hmmm? Hahahahahahahaha!"

Webb also contributed the photographs of Ghoulda, the SPEVA badge, and the only known newspaper clipping to the documentary, which has a photo of Roberts in character at a local function. The caption reads: "Ghoulda, vampire-of-ceremonies of *Shock*, ghostly and ghastly package on WRVA Television every Saturday night at 11:10, makes a "live" appearance at a Richmond Area Community Chest luncheon and rally. Ghoulda presents to Mr. H. Atwood Hitch, Campaign General, an identification of her own pet charity, the Society for the Promulgation and Encouragement of Vampires in America. She receives a Red Feather for her Community Chest work."

Ghoulia/Goolya

REAL NAME: Shirley Vloedman Selman, a.k.a Joni Criss (died in 1970)
BIRTHPLACE: Tucson, Arizona
HOST: *Classic Nightmares* (1958–1959), KGUN-TV, Channel 9, Tucson, Arizona
BIOGRAPHY: This whole entry started, like many of the others, with just a few memories. In an email to E-Gor, Tucson's Jim Morton had this to say: "When I was a kid in Tucson, the local scary movie was called *Classic Nightmares*. It started at midnight on Fridays, and the first movie shown was *Frankenstein* (this would have been sometime between 1956 or 1958; I don't remember exactly). The host was a Vampira-style woman called Ghoulia. She was very urbane, and my folks found her more amusing than I did. The tone of the humor was definitely more adult than what I've seen by Vampira." Kris Selman, the daughter of Ghoulia, added this: "Sitting on vacation in Tucson, Arizona, playing on my computer, I Googled Ghoulia and came up with your site [E-Gor's Cham-

ber...]. The Ghoulia that Jim Morton wrote about was my mother, Shirl Vloedman Selman. She may have been using a different professional name at the time. We lived here in Tucson and she did the Ghoulia show. She had a coffin that she arose from on Fridays and a large stuffed lizard that she used as a prop. During that time, 1956–1958, she also did a children's show, *Aunt Coral and Uncle Shoe*. The song 'Getting to Know You,' from *The King and I*, was the theme."

That was then; this is now ... or at least now as of January 2016. Kris Selman sent a December 2015 email to E-Gor, which he forwarded to me, with an ad that proved to be both historically important and maddeningly mysterious. The ad showed the only known (at the time) image of Kris's mother—except that her name was now spelled Goolya, and proclaimed "Goolya's Back!" It was also for a different station. Had Shirl Selman taken the character to another station and changed the name slightly for legal or some other reasons? In E-Gor's reply, he told her about yours truly and his newest project, graciously requesting both an image for himself and for the book. The ice having been broken, I then got in touch with Kris, asking for both her memories and about that ad—if her mother had played the role for two different stations, about the name change, etc. She sent a most pleasant reply (part of which follows), and the only other known image of her mother as the character.

> She was an exceptional woman—larger than life. From my childhood memory it seemed everyone in the room would still when she entered....
>
> During the time we lived in Tucson, Mother worked for a TV station (don't know which one). She did commercials, co-hosted a children's show, *Aunt Coral and Uncle Shoe*, and hosted the late-night show. She opened the children's show with the song "Getting to Know You" from *The King and I*. I think "Uncle Shoe" was Bert Lahr's brother (?). All I have from memory of Ghoulia is that she rose out of a coffin at the beginning of the show and that she had a Gila monster (large lizard) that she wore on her shoulder.
>
> I found the Goolya ad on a random Google search. I do have one photo of Mom as Ghoulia. ...I can also come up with a time frame for those years.
>
> I wish so much that I could answer your questions. My mother died early in life, in 1970. She was very charming. She would have played the role of Ghoulia so well. I can't imagine anyone better. Mom could be very dramatic and engaging. I have searched for any video, but I don't believe that is available.
>
> Thank you for your interest. This was a good time in Mom's life. The memories make me smile.

In a follow-up email, she made a few clarifications:

1. Herb Lahr is Bert Lahr's son. His obit mentions Uncle Shoe and Aunt Coral.
2. I believe the *Classic Nightmares* Goolya started [in] Jan[uary] 1958 on Channel 9 KGUN. (I'm thinking it was always spelled Goolya, but I'm not sure.) I think it was on sporadically through mid–1959.
3. Mom, Shirley (Vloedman) Selman had done acting, radio commercials, modeling, and night club work in NYC before I was born in 1953. Her stage name was Joni Criss.

Kris included more photos and two local newspaper clippings which offer information. The first, "Show Girl Intends to Run for Presidency" (writer unidentified), finds her still in the Big Apple:

> Beautiful Joni Criss, whose 6-feet 5-inches give her billing as "The World's Tallest Showgirl," said she intends to run for the presidency of the United States by 1970.
>
> She said she's been preparing for the job for some time and should be ready to launch her political career "within the next four or five years." "I have the basic requirements—brains, beauty and ambition—and now I'm going to make the grade," she said.

Ghoulia/Goolya 47

One of the few known photos of Ghoulia/Goolya, from 1959 (courtesy Kris Selman).

    Miss Criss was fairly accurate in the appraisal of herself, particularly concerning her beauty. Although she is very tall, she is effectively proportioned (bust thirty-eight, waist twenty-eight, hips thirty-eight).
    As for her mentality, she boasts a long list of scholastic honors, including a Phi Beta Kappa Key from Indiana University. "I majored in government and political science, and I expect to get my Master's Degree in these fields from Columbia University soon."
    Miss Criss, who is twenty-one, said she chose show business as a stepping stone to politics because "it has more to offer the politically-minded individual than any other field in existence." "Show business,"

she said, "offers a chance to build a name; to learn how to speak in public; to meet people, lots of people, and important people. And at the same time, I am able to earn a good living."

She said she wanted to become president "to show men that women are as good in public office—or any high office—as they are." A woman, she said, would make a better president than a man. "Men are too soft and sentimental," she said. "They're babies. They can be knocked flat very easily by an aggressive woman."

She said she thought she would be a success in politics as "I'd be attractive to men, and too big for the women to worry about." Miss Criss, who is doing nightclub engagements, said she has had four movie offers and a stage offer recently, but spurned them because she wanted "more experience as a solo act."

She said that after she gains prominence in one or two top acting roles, she would return to Indiana and run for the State Senate. "That will take me four or five years, but from then on, it will be all politics for me," she said.

The second article, which is undated and from an unidentified paper, is by Hugh Harelson and is titled "6-Foot-1 Gal Sees Altitude as an Asset (She's Eye-Catching)":

Being a 6-foot blonde "is the greatest asset in the world," says a University of Arizona coed. Shirley Selman stands a statuesque 6 feet 1. She looks taller, especially around "pint-sized" 6-foot men. "Men have a complex!" she laughed. "I'm a drama student and I like nothing better than to have the center of the stage, whether it's a play or everyday life."

Her eye-snaring appearance, she says, has helped land jobs on Broadway and television. Before enrolling at the university last year, she was an understudy for a lead role in Broadway's *Gentlemen Prefer Blondes*.

Shirley, 29, has captured Tucson television roles, too. Her Sunday-morning audience, for a children's show, would be horrified if they recognized her Friday nights. She appears as a vampire type during commercials for a late evening horror show.

Shirley has to look up to her father. He's 6 feet 6. But her mother is only 5–5. Shirley said she stopped growing at 17. Now she's watching her young daughter grow—"taller and taller." Her husband? "He's as tall as I am—in his boots," said Shirley.

Ghoulita

REAL NAME: Lietta Harvey

HOST: *Jeepers' Creepers Theater* (1963), KCOP-TV, Channel 13, Los Angeles, California

BIRTHPLACE: San Francisco, California

BIOGRAPHY: Ghoulita was not your stereotypical female horror host. Whereas most of them wore makeup and wigs to both disguise and accentuate their facial features, their costumes were mostly variations on Vampira, designed to accentuate their other features. Instead, Ghoulita looked like Zombo from *The Munsters* if he was a female. She literally looked a fright! Long white, curled hair; bomb-crater teeth, with a costume made out of a curtain, Ghoulita was the anti–Vampira. Not the stuff that secret, naughty fantasies are made of, unless you're some kind of weirdo. Bob Burns (see Miss Shock) created the Ghoulita makeup and did special effects for the show. He appeared as an ape in the episode in which Ghoulita showed *Black Friday*. (Bob had previously appeared on the show as the Mad Mummy when Jeepers showed *The Mummy's Curse*.) If only the viewers knew that underneath that hideous countenance was a gorgeous woman, she definitely would have been the stuff that more dreams were made of.

Jeepers' Creepers Theater (not to mention Jeepers himself) was the brainchild of Bob Guy (Jeepers) and Jim Sullivan, the station's film director; Sullivan also wrote the show and produced it. He was a graduate of the famed Pasadena Playhouse, and a close friend of Lietta Harvey. Guy was the station's program director. When he purchased the "Shock" package of movies, he suggested that they have someone host them; Sullivan suggested that Guy do it himself. He did the show for about seven months, and then left for a better program director's job elsewhere. His last two shows were the set-up for the new host: the penultimate one had him announcing that "the Ghoulita Doll" was coming, and in his last he "brought her to life." Thus, Ghoulita's first show was spent searching for Jeepers, who, in real life and the show's life, had disappeared. Sullivan was truly committed to the show; he continued writing and producing it when Harvey took over as host; did the same for Jeepers' Keeper; and when the Keeper left, he hosted it as the "Creeper."

California-born, Lietta Harvey loved making and playing with puppets as a child. She would put on puppet shows for her parents, younger brother, or whatever guests happened to be in the house at the time. She appeared in every grade school play that she could, and took dancing lessons. She decided on an acting career in high school; her drama teacher had her excused from other classes so that he could instruct her in the ways of stagecraft and directing. She never really considered any other career. She was accepted at the Playhouse, where her classmates included Gary Burghoff and Rue McClanahan. After college, she returned to San Francisco to be part of the first West Coast production of *West Side Story*. Another cast member, a young man named Martin Buchwald, later changed his name to Marty Balin and found fame and fortune with the rock band Jefferson Airplane (later Jefferson Starship).

Lietta moved to Hollywood in 1962, another struggling actress in dilapidated digs. And like other wanna-be actresses, she modeled, did local commercials and waitressed. Many of the Playhouse alumni kept in touch with her, including Jim Sullivan, who told Harvey about the auditions to replace Jeepers. The character was quite different from the ones she was used to playing, but a struggling actress needs to eat, so she auditioned. Never particularly a horror fan, Harvey threw herself into what she hoped would become her next role: binge-watching horror films and going to the library to bone up on the subject of horror. She ate and slept horror until she had a horrible thought of her own: She was auditioning for a female ghoul, and she didn't have a thing to wear. Desperately seeking ideas, she looked at the moth-eaten curtains hanging just a few feet away; she took them down and wrapped them around some black leotards. *Voila*, instant costume!

The following monologue (peppered through and through with demented chuckles) is from Lietta Harvey's April 1963 Ghoulita audition, the kinescope of which has been donated to the UCLA archives:

> Don't turn around! There's somebody behind you! If you turn around, they'll make maggot-meat out of you! Oh, there's nobody behind you, it's me, in front of you in your TV set... [Pulls a rubber salamander from her hair] Oh, it's Freddy! Hello, Freddy ... have you brought me a message from Jeepers? [Puts salamander up to her ear] What does he say? Good, good, you're going to hop on down to George Allen Rambler ... good ... what does he say about me? Oh, yes ... he still loves me, but he hasn't sent me my greasy gopher guts! Oh ... oh.... Freddy, Freddy, you'd better hop on down to George Allen Rambler ... that's it.... I wonder if, if there's movie stars at George Allen Rambler? Oh, you know, I was a movie star once, I, I was in the best pictures.... I used to get lots of fan mail ... oh, oh, those were the ghoul old days ... and Jeepers gets all the fan mail now, like this one: "Dear Jeepers, This letter is to notify you that the Grotesque Ghoul Society has just chosen you as 'Ghoul of the Year' ... also, I've chosen you as my number-one boyfriend..." [Disappointed] Oh ... oh, well, I want you to know that it wasn't my idea, it was my mummy's... See, she always says when she sees you, "Look! There's your boyfriend!" Naturally, this slightly angers me, so I immediately chop off her head! And this happens every week and she's beginning to look

a little silly now, because she only has two heads... Yes, I'm insanely in love with you, Jeepers, and every time I see you with your ghoul-friend Skull... [Looks directly into camera] Doris! I nearly die, my heart just splits in two... This can become a little messy, and I wouldn't want to get blood all over, because I just had my cell freshly padded, and that could be messy. Jeepers, if you read this on your program, I'll tell you a deep, dark secret.... I'll reveal who's been playing all those dirty tricks on you... Have you ever awakened finding yourself fully embalmed? And spikes drove through your chest? You have? Well, these are the works of people who don't like you... Well, I didn't know there were people like that ... well, I'm sure you do like Jeepers, and I'm sure Jeepers will be glad to know what you've told me ... until I see you next week, I remain Tammy Tamburlaine from Granada Hills ... thank you, Tammy, now we'd better get back to our picture.... Oh, wait a minute! [Reaches off-camera, and then pretends to cup something in her hands; then she wags her finger] I told you! One of you turned around ... maggot-meat!

The character got away with a lot of ad libs, as Harvey became more comfortable with the role. They attempted some pretty zany stunts, the outcome of which was not always successful, but the viewers at home didn't know if they were supposed to work out or not. Possibly this was the intention of the crew, who were always pulling pranks on her; on one such occasion, a cameraman climbed inside her coffin, crossed his arms and rolled his eyes up. This produced the desired effect of Harvey freaking out! One day after closing time, she and Sullivan took a prop skeleton to the office of the new program director and sat it in the chair behind his desk. They failed to take one other person into account: the lady who cleaned up the office at night. The cleaning lady quit the next day.

Having inherited the ghost-host spot from Jeepers, she also inherited his sponsor and most of his props and "family." The sponsor was George Allen Rambler, the car dealership repeatedly mentioned during the audition, which provided her with a car that had been used by Jeepers. The car, nicknamed "Palagar," had no engine and had to be pushed onto the set by the crew, to the accompaniment of engine sound effects and smoke. Her adopted family included Doris the skull (the "Doris" referred to the audition kinescope), Boris the stuffed werewolf and Pumpkin the stuffed rat.

Ghoulita had a fan club run by Mark Shepard, who was all of 12 years old! Here's the letter which accompanied the fan club kit, which included a photo of Ghoulita, a membership card and a Ghoulita pencil and badge:

> Dear Ghoulita Club Member,
> It is my pleasure to welcome you to the terroriffic cult. Mark Shepard informs me of all your ghoulish letters received. Oh, hot death, I'm so full of thanks! Every one of my horrid family is screamingly happy that you're with us. When I open the coffin lid, take pen in shaking hand, then you shall hear from me every two moons (two months). And when the full moon is frightening enough, we shall have a ghoulish randee-voo. I will send the bats winging to Mark with notice of when and where we shall gather. Keep up the horrific work... So until this Saturday, on Ghoulish 13. See you then? Ghoulita

In December 1963, Harvey left the show (which continued with new male host Jeepers' Keeper) seeking to broaden her show business horizons. She became the editor of the *Hollywood Talent News*, a trade paper for actors, and a partner in a night club, where she directed the shows and hired the talent. She wrote, directed and produced a show concerning child abuse, which played at many schools across the state; she also began teaching acting seminars, wrote the column "From the Director's Chair" for entertainment magazines and was a talent agent. Her financial talent for the stock market allows her to be semi-retired, although she still teaches the occasional seminar.

Grizelda MacCabre

REAL NAME: Karen Shnaubelt Turner Dick (1955–)

HOST: *Castle Blood Midnight Monster Hop* (2006–2008), HSTV, Channel 19, Uniontown, Pennsylvania; CSMTV, Channel 98, Maryland; RTN, Pittsburgh, Pennsylvania

BIOGRAPHY: Karen Dick is the daughter of Franz Shnaubelt, founding chairman of Costume-Con and creator of *The Whole Costumer's Catalogue*. Born in San Diego, she attended Helix High School and San Diego State University, where she got both a BA and MA in anthropology. But it was not only science that fired her imagination, it was also science fiction; at age nine, she started watching the anime series *Astro-Boy*; by 11, she was watching *Star Trek* with her dad. In the 1970s, Dick began to create her own costumes and wear them at sci-fi cons. In 1983, Dick, her father and Kelly Turner founded "Costume Con." Originally conceived as a one-off, the convention has been going for over thirty years. Dick has worked with her ex-husband Ricky Dick (Gravely Macabre) in his professional clown-costuming business and designed top-of-the-line corsetry and theatrical-quality Halloween costumes. In 1993,

Karen Dick as Grizelda MacCabre, 2006 (courtesy George "E-Gor" Chastain).

along with Dick, she co-founded Castle Blood, one of Pennsylvania's most famous spooky attractions, and the site at which the filming of the *Castle Blood Midnight Monster Hop* would be filmed. The two would eventually divorce, which also ended her association with the show. Her presence was sorely missed, as she was a low-key and knowledgeable hostess, but she let her beautiful costumes (and Gravely) do most of the talking. Grizelda's daughter Skully MacCabre has taken her mom's place on the show.

Halloween Jacqueline

REAL NAME: Jacquie Davis

HOST: *The Haunted Theatre* (2011–present), Cablevision of Monmouth Channel 77, Jackson, New Jersey

BIOGRAPHY: Halloween Jack is one of the most enduring of the new breed of horror hosts and a founding member of the Horror Host Underground. His wife Halloween Jaqueline is a (relatively) new addition to the show. Despite being tremendously busy with their projects and family, Jacquie found time to answer my questions in March 2016:

BC: *Do you like horror and science fiction movies?*

HJ: I'm a *huge* horror fan, and have been for as long as I can remember. It has truly become my passion and obsession. As for sci-fi; sorry, not so much. My love tends to sway more towards monsters, and less of aliens.

BC: *How did you come to be a horror host?*

HJ: I wasn't really looking for it, so much as it found me. I always loved Elvira, but she was really the only model of a horror host I had, until I first logged onto the Monster Channel and then became acquainted with Halloween Jack, who subsequently invited me to be his co-host.

BC: *Halloween Jack has been on for a lot of years. What made you decide to get in on the act?*

HJ: He asked, LOL. I was hesitant since my acting abilities were at zero, and the idea of speaking in front of a camera, or crowd, made my stomach turn, but thanks to Jack, I overcame it, and it even helped me overcome some pretty extreme phobias.

BC: *Was the character created by you?*

HJ: No, Halloween Jacqueline was Jack's creation.

BC: *When did the show start? When did you become co-host?*

HJ: The show started on Halloween 1999, but I didn't make my first appearance until 2011.

BC: *What's your day job?*

HJ: Photographer, and full-time mother and wife.

BC: *Do you help write the show?*

HJ: Jack is the creative one but he does encourage my input and ideas. Most of what we do is ad lib, so I guess you can say I help write when I come up with my own lines.

BC: *Do you do anything else in terms of production?*

HJ: No. To be honest, other than lighting issues, I have no practical understanding of *any* of the technical issues involved in the production, or editing.

BC: *Do you have any horror host role models?*

HJ: Yes, Elvira, Fritz the Nite Owl and my husband Jack. I was a fan of his show, long before I ever became a part of it.

BC: *What's the status of the Horror Host Underground?*

HJ: From the efforts of Jack and other horror hosts, it's still looming and hopefully making a comeback. To be honest, I'm not really involved in it. I don't really consider myself a real horror host yet, so I leave all of that to the heavy hitters.

BC: *What are some of your fondest memories of the show?*

HJ: The outtakes! Jack, "Little Jack" and I have the best time goofing around making the show. Even the screw-ups are a blast. When it stops being fun, it's time to quit. One of the funniest memories involves "Little Jack." Jack and L.J. did a skit that was a take-off on the Little Rascals where Jack was chasing him up and down the stairs. L.J. got so tired after running up and down, so many times, that he collapsed on the step. (No, he didn't pass out, just decided to lie down.) Even though it wasn't in the script, it turned out to be a hysterical scene.

BC: *What has been your most memorable personal appearance?*

HJ: *Horrorhound* Weekend, when Jack and I tied the knot, in front of all of our horror host friends, who are more like family.

BC: *Which do you prefer, TV or the Internet?*

HJ: I'm still a fan of TV … unless I could bring the computer to the couch, or bed.

BC: *Your husband's name was inspired by a line from the David Bowie song "Diamond Dogs." Any comment on Bowie's passing?*

HJ: It felt like a close family member died. I always liked his music, but Jack educated me on his life, and broadened my horizons on the full scope of his music career.

Hazel Witch

REAL NAME: Anna F. Inge

HOST: *Shock Theater* (1959–1960), WRVA Channel 12, Richmond, Virginia

BIOGRAPHY: Very little remains in regards to this show: a couple of still pictures and not much else except her memories, which she shared in *Virginia Creepers*:

> Well, the first show we mostly just did introductions to the movies, and then we embellished it and we kept bringing in people; you know, my mother was on one night; she took out her teeth and was boiling a potion, trying to get me to go back to the old broom because she wasn't very happy with me on a vacuum cleaner.… I was amazed because I had these real loyal fans that would call me and come to see me at the studio, and I was just amazed how well it was received, and we would schedule dates with Hazel and we went to the ball game … we had a 1913 Ford that we used, from a Ford dealership there in Richmond, and we would drive around in that, and Jeeves, who was my butler, we have fun or we would go out on these dates, whatever the contest was, and so we would have quite a bit of activity on the weekends and I would be very tired after we taped because I still worked as executive secretary and the producer and whatever, and I'd be very tired and I wouldn't take my makeup off … we were riding down the street and I just stopped at the stoplight and turned around, and there to the left or to the right to the driver and they would.… I'd just wink or whatever and they'd just go wild and go who in the world was that? But it was fun.

In the same documentary, Hazel fan Herb Tate reminisced, "I got to see them filming it one night.… It was really funny, everybody cracked up all the time, and then of course they'd stop the tape, and I guess they edited it, but it was fun." Inge shared this tidbit:

> She was just crazy and she was the last of the Virginia witches, you know the red-hot mamas, and she'd go, "Hi, Precious, *hahahahaha*," you know, that kind of thing. And they would see me, if I was out on a date or whatever; people would come up to me and go, "Hi, Precious," so that was the word… We always taped everything, filmed it actually, when we did go on these dates so we could use it for some of the people wanted to see themselves on television. People who watched television at that time really got involved with, like, Hazel the Witch, you know, oh, what does she do and they wanna know, 'cause I did some really crazy things too, but it was like, "What did you do last week?" and yet there were other television shows on, you know, national television shows and I was always involved with what was going on in the local scene, and people would always wanna look and see what we were doing.

Inge was married to actor Gordon Jump (*WKRP in Cincinnati*) from 1963 until 1992, when they divorced; they have three daughters, two of whom are actresses.

Ione

REAL NAME: Ione Rolnick (Citrin)

HOST: *Prize Movie with Ione* (1969–1975), WLS-TV, Channel 7, Chicago, Illinois

BIOGRAPHY: Very little is known about actress Ione Rolnick. Other than hosting

Prize Movie, her only other credit is *Suburban Roulette*, Herschell Gordon Lewis's low-budget tale of the wicked underbelly of suburban living. No footage of her as the host of *Prize Movie* exists. Based in Detroit, *Prize Movie* was originally an ABC production with a host named Rita Bell. Due to its success, ABC-affiliated stations in Chicago and New York tried their own versions; the New York version was hosted by former Hollywood star Gloria DeHaven, the Chicago version by Ione. The latter ran for seven years and was number one in its time slot. However, as Ione Citrin, award-winning abstract artist, she is very well-known. As she says on her website, "A native of Chicago, she is a former television star and commercial voiceover artist. Now she wins awards and sells her creativity through her hands instead of her larynx. Her art is as original as she is—bold, colorful, and highly decorative." And, as of this writing, it appears that she wants to be known for her art alone, as she didn't respond to emails or phone calls.

Isobel/My Dear

HOST: *Shock Theatre* (October 7, 1957–September 13, 1958), WCAU, Channel 10, Philadelphia, Pennsylvania; *Shock Theatre* (September 22, 1958–March 27, 1959); *Zacherley at Large* (April 3, 1959–June 20, 1959), WABC-TV, Channel 7, New York, New York; *The Zacherley Show* (October 9, 1959–December 9, 1960), WOR-TV, Channel 9, New York, New York; *Chiller Theater* (1964–1965), WPIX-TV, Channel 11, New York, New York; *The Return of Roland* (1985), WCAU-TV, Channel 10, Philadelphia, Pennsylvania; *Horrible Horror* (1986), Goodtimes Productions direct-to-video release; *Z-TV* (1988), unsold pilot

BIOGRAPHY: Is it possible to write about a character when that character never actually existed? Not usually, but when it's the wife of the Cool Ghoul, Zacherley, it is. She never made an appearance, and he only treated her to a stake a time or three, but she stayed with Zach throughout his career, be it as Roland or Zacherley. In John Skerchock's *The Zacherley Scrapbook* (Dark Dungeon Enterprises, 2001), Zach had this to say about her origin:

> The name was chosen because it was the first name of one of the producers. We never saw her [the producer], and no one ever saw My Dear, so it was an in-joke. Whether as Roland or Zacherley, the show never had any money for guests, so I had to invent a few friends—my son Gasport, who lived in a burlap sack, and my wife, My Dear or Isobel, who lived in a coffin. By the time I worked at my last TV station, the coffin was actually the canvas mail cart. We joked that My Dear may be an ape. She made ape noises, and I told the story of how we met in the jungle when she fell out of a tree. I was Mummy-Hunting at the time. She took my heart away, and I had a devil of a time getting it back.

Still, she was real enough to the viewers. Zach continued, "Not convinced at how popular Roland was, John announced one night that Isobel needed a new pillow for her coffin. So he asked each fan to send two hairs from his or her head to fill this new pillow. The station got flooded. We received over 23,000 pieces of mail. A bald man even sent an I.O.U."

This couplet comes from a Roland kinescope:

We've all seen the ghoul named Roland, but of My Dear, only her hand.
Could it be he has fear, because Igor is near, that he won't show the rest of My Dear?

In the *American Scary* documentary, Leonard Maltin recalled, "The setting was supposed to be some sort of dungeon, where we supposed he lived, and there was kind of an old laboratory table, and an old laundry bin, where his wife, either departed or undead, it was never quite clear, but he referred to her as 'My Dear,' and would always cast glances down at that laundry cart."

"My dear wife lived in a box, because we couldn't afford to have somebody else on the show!" said Zacherley. "We had a record of monkeys chattering, and we either sped it up or slowed it down, I forget which ... and she made a noise like [imitates a monkey], and I would answer her back the same way."

Ivonna Cadaver

REAL NAME: Natalie Popovich

HOST: *Macabre Theatre* (with Butch Patrick; 2002–2012), KHIZ-TV, Channel 64, Los Angeles, California

BIOGRAPHY: The following tidbit is from the now-defunct *Macabre Theatre* website:

> Butch Patrick, a.k.a. Eddie Munster, and Ivonna Cadaver, a timeless ghoul who has chosen to re-invent herself in the 21st century, haunt, tease, and tantalize viewers each week on the Los Angeles-based *Macabre Theatre*. The show *L.A. Weekly* declared, "It beats the living daylights of just about anything else being broadcast." Each week, Ivonna welcomes viewers into her own private dungeon where she engages in delectable debauchery and hosts campy—some say classic—horror movies such as *House on Haunted Hill*, *Lisa & the Devil*, and *The Brain That Wouldn't Die*. Butch Patrick of *The Munsters* delights in his signature segment "Haunted Hollyweird," as he visits haunted locations and tells true stories of the stars, movies, and scandals behind them. Join Ivonna as she delivers hip, irreverent, [and] cutting-edge humor "with a bite!" Some of her favorite segments include "Goth Trivia" (fun facts on the movie), "Ghoul Shopping Network" (her take on hot products in today's culture, with a macabre twist), and Ivonna's CD picks of the week, "Ivonna's Music Dungeon List)."

Other segments included "Ivonna's Eek Mail," her "Top 5" and a chance to win an autographed picture.

Her (also now-defunct) Horror Host Underground profile contained the following "biographical" details: "Born in Eastern Europe, a distant relative of the Romanovs, Ivonna began her career designing 'Burial Wear,' a thriving cottage industry during the Black Plague. After acquiring her mother's jewelry and dreaming of a 'life' at the Royal Court, she decided that she just couldn't wait around at the castle for her inheritance, declaring to anyone who would listen, 'If I can't have it all right now, then I'm out of here with Ivan!'"

She was interviewed by CNN one Halloween a few years back, with the blurb "Ivonna Cadaver replaces Elvira as the new Queen of Horror," which never quite came to pass. The vaguely annoying thing about the interview was that "Issues" segment host Jane Velez-Mitchell doesn't seem to care so much about why Ivonna was being called "The New Face of the Undead," and what she had done to earn that accolade; practically the whole interview was spent discussing her newfound sobriety. I wrote to Natalie in 2016 for an interview, and although she responded enthusiastically, she also added the caveat that she would have to check with her manager. Her manager must have said no, because I never heard back from her.

Jami Deadly

REAL NAME: Jami Edwards (1979–)

HOST: *Deadly Cinema* (2003–2005), NTTV, Channel 22, Denton, Texas

BIRTHPLACE: Texas

BIOGRAPHY: *Deadly Cinema* only ran for two years but it is still remembered fondly by fans all over the world, due to its drop-deadly beautiful host, the former Jami Edwards. Jami, an entertainer who was making a name for herself on the nightclub circuit, had an idea for a horror-hosted show, but found no takers until she got in touch with NTTV, a student station operating out of the University of North Texas. The show, which was like a much less obnoxious version of *Mystery Science Theater 3000*, came together with a cast and crew of Acting and Film students, which probably accounts for the short run. In that time, though, it won the Texas Intercollegiate Press Association Award for Best Television Production. In 2008, Matt Muhl and Scott Simmons respectively wrote and drew a comic book, *Deadly Cinema: The Movie,* to celebrate the show's fifth anniversary (even though it only ran for three years). As of this writing, it's being re-run on Roku and is available on DVD. In the documentary *Fade to Pink,* Jami said that when she created Jami Deadly,

> I wanted an original spin on the classic Vampira, Elvira horror hostess type of show.... I wanted to do things a little bit differently, and in my own way, putting a 1950s blonde bombshell twist to the whole thing. So I took my idea and shopped it around to all the studios in the area, and then I contacted NTTV, and I got in touch with a man named Mario. He thought it was a cool idea, and then I didn't hear from him again for another year ... and that's when he put me in touch with Matt [Muhl, the show's writer-director].

Jami Deadly in a classic publicity shot (courtesy George "E-Gor" Chastain).

Matt Muhl was just starting to get to know people, getting to know the staff, and he was in the NTTV staff room, and the program director at the time, Mario Pina, had a video on top of his desk, and it was *Werewolf in a Girl's Dormitory*. Muhl asked him about it, saying, "What is this for?" Pina just kept telling him about this show that Pina wanted to do, and Muhl said, "I want to be a part of this; I'll help out in any way." He said, "Sure, I'd love for you to help out." It turned out that Pina ended up graduating, so he wasn't able to do the show, and so he asked Muhl. He said, "You seem to be real gung-ho about this show that I was going to produce; how would you like to produce it?" In a heartbeat, Muhl said, "Yes, I would love to. I really owe it to Mario Pina, who passed the torch to me, and that torch was this show."

[Mario] said, "I know this guy that absolutely adores old horror movies, and he would love to help you write this and put it together; we have all the equipment here, the studio, the cameras," and I thought, "Great, this is finally what I've been looking for." Then I got in touch with Matt, and we talked off and on, and we finally did the first episode in October 2003. It was an original idea of mine to have a sidekick that was a severed head, just for the simple cheesy fact that you could stick a guy in a box ... that's something that they did in old movies, 'Look, we have an illusion of a floating severed head, but the rest of him is in a box,' and I always wanted to incorporate that in the show."

Alex Fuhrmann played Jenkins the severed head. He recalled, "Matt said to me something about *Deadly Cinema*, and I wasn't sure what it was, and he said Jami Deadly, and I was like, is that her real name? And they said no, of course not, that's a character she came up with." According to Jami,

Alex was great; he's this hilarious, hilarious guy, and we were very sad to see him go after episode two. The cast that we had starting out had a very good chemistry together, they had a good vibe, and we knew that after Alex had to go back to England, there was going to be a void there that we had to fill... [It was filled by Dante Martinez, who played the role of Raoul the Landlord.] [Martinez] wanted the stock, normal, human character, because in a cast of wacky characters, monsters and completely insane people, there's always the one normal character that is there to draw the audience in; you know, look, I'm just like you, having to be in this insanity, and this is what it's like to be in this wacky cast of characters. I think in the end, he wasn't so normal after all ... or maybe it was just the influence of us.

"Dante is a fool," Fuhrmann recalled affectionately. "He's hilarious ... a green light for me to do ... anything." Muhl had met Dante about a year prior at a Fourth of July party, and they became fast friends. Martinez appeared in Muhl's short film *Herman's Big Break*, which has no dialogue; Muhl thought Martinez was comedically gifted and asked him to join the show. Jami reminisced, "Dante's great; he has a natural acting ability, which is great, he seems like he just sort of stuffs down all this comedic ability inside of him and then periodically, it just kind of flies out and you think, 'Where did that come from?'"

Muhl had met a couple of other students named Zach Beseda and Brian Kelly, separately; it was serendipitous that the two came along when they did, because Muhl needed one of them to play a lawyer, but he accidentally cast both of them for a particular scene, and they both showed up. So Muhl came up with the idea of having *two* lawyers. "I got the camera on them and ... they just feed off of each other, and that is what they're great at doing.... I love these guys apart; together, they're even better." Jami Deadly laughed, "I really enjoyed their first appearance as very sleazy, horrible, horrendous lawyers, 'cause everyone hates lawyers..."

Drew Edwards played Chaney the neighborhood werewolf, Jami's "bad-boy" boyfriend. He drank too much, he was a womanizer, and he strutted around, threw popcorn at people and grumbled a lot. Edwards described him as a combination of Chewbacca, the Tasmanian Devil and Elvis Presley. Jami explained, "Chaney has been the love interest of Miss Deadly since episode one, when he showed his love by giving the best gift a woman could ever receive ... a customized bubble gum–pink coffin.... Every girl secretly wants a coffin; flowers, chocolate, put that out the window [*laughs*]..."

Jami stressed that the show was a group effort: "We've all got along great, I mean, there's no fighting or difficulty or attitudes flying around... It's long hours and a lot of work put into it, it really just comes down to you love being here and you're happy being here, you're putting together everyone's efforts into a project, and it's been great with everyone, seeing what they can bring to the table."

According to Brian Kelly, "It was just for school credit, none of us was getting paid ... and I think that anybody that comes down here is just pretty much putting themselves out for a good time ... and I'm doing this for a good time 'cause I'm a whore. If I can be on TV and wear makeup, I feel pretty." But comedy, as Steve Martin said, is not always pretty. Drew Edwards recalled that the atmosphere could be very tense. Muhl was always very stressed, and Edwards sometimes worried about him. They didn't usually have a lot of time to rehearse, only a couple hours a day over a period of three days, and they didn't have a lot of time to do much reshooting. Everybody joked around a lot, and that eased the tension, but sometimes it was like they were all going to jump at each other's throats. Muhl described the close quarters as a "kinetic experience." Beseda said that Muhl described it that way because Muhl put a lot of pressure on himself because of being on a schedule, but it always turned out really well, despite the occasional flare-ups. By the end of filming, they were all feeling tired and punchy, and very goofy, so sometimes that comes across on screen.

Jami concurred: "Yeah, we get tired and cranky, but at the end of the day, the next time you see people, there's no grudges held." Muhl related that the movie dub process is a very long and tedious one. "When the show first started, Matt, Alex and I would dub over the movie... With Alex, he would basically hit on me all the way through it, and I, in retaliation, would poke fun at the fact that he's a severed head, and he can't do much about it."

Alex Fuhrmann recalled that dubbing the movies "was so boring, because the movies were so bad; but then sometimes, it was good making fun of them, it's just that the jokes got a little bit tiresome." Zach Beseda agreed; "[The movies] are bad, not even fun to watch bad, just boring bad, and when you have to sit through even an hour-and-a-half movie where just, like, nothin's happenin', people are just in a room talkin' about stuff, you don't know what's goin' on, you don't even know what they're referring to; it gets a little rough..." Muhl declaimed that there was something "real charming" about the old movies that they used; that they wanted to be as entertaining as they can possibly be, but the movies just didn't have the budget to do it, adding that he thought that was reflected in the show itself. He said they did their best to make sure they had that bridge between the movies and the show and that he hopes that Jami and the rest of the cast forgive him for striving to be the best that the show could be.

Jami said, "I have always been a huge fan of bad movies; I just can't stop watching them.... I think it's that car accident type feel to it, you just can't stop looking at it ... and I've had to sit through so many of them that it's by choice ... and that's a little bit strange, but then, *I'm* a little bit strange, so it makes sense." She said of the dubbing, "It's a fun process... Then Matt ... the last few episodes, he made us sit there and do the movie dubbing twice in a row ... just to be sweet to us, because he knows we *love* doing it." Zach Beseda recalled, "It was fun to work with Jami because she actually has a good sense of humor, you know, and a lot of attractive girls don't." Dante Martinez put it more bluntly, saying that Jami caught him staring at her breasts a lot.

Fuhrmann said that the few episodes he was involved with were funny to start with; Jami would mess up a line, then he'd mess up a line, and they would just laugh because he thought what they were doing was so silly and stupid, but the nicest bit was off-camera where they'd just laugh and mess around all the time. Kelly called Jami a heck of a talent and a force of nature; he also says she has a very large following, and he can see why.

Jami also wanted to showcase her other talents: "During the series, because I also perform as a live performer, I kind of wanted to add that in one of the episodes, and I told Matt, 'I'd really like to work this song in,' and we thought this would be a really great end piece for our Christmas Spooktacular. 'Santa Baby,' which was originally sang by Eartha Kitt, and she sung it in a very breathy, Marilyn Monroe sort of way, in the '50s..."

Muhl gushed, "Jami is great, because she's not only everything you want in a star, but she's just the perfect woman, you know, smart, funny and gorgeous in every way possible. Working with Jami is a dream, because she's really easy to direct, she never complains, she has a real passion for this character and the show, and she's just incredible in every way possible. I adore her." Deadly returned the compliment: "Matt is great to work with ... he's been the backbone of the show. ...Matt is great, with all his pop culture references; you can tell he's very passionate about horror movies and campy, cheesy movies of all varieties from all different decades..."

The rest of the cast were equally effusive in their estimation of Muhl, calling him a good guy, a talented man, energetic, very persuasive, and would always show up every day they'd shoot ready to bring his and Jami's vision to fruition. "We both share the love of it, but sometimes, I think, you know, his love runs a little bit over," Jami sighed. "Matt wants things done a certain way, and it's usually his way, but he is giving if you suggest something and he thinks it will better the scene."

Kelly reckoned that Muhl knew they liked to play around, and so he wrote the characters pretty loose, which he said was a lot of fun, and it made the whole experience a lot of fun. Sometimes, though, Muhl paid the price for all his efforts; Kelly is pretty sure he got a concussion once or twice, because they were constantly hitting him over the head ... but there was also an occasion when Matt hit his head on the edge of a camera. Muhl thought the blood worked for the character, so he kept it in. Brian Kelly said that it showed Muhl's devotion to the show, and that if Muhl had died, he'd come back just to finish the show. From all indications, he was a "player-friendly coach," a good director who knew what he wanted, and got it; he allowed and encouraged the cast to have fun, just as long as they got the job done. Jami Deadly said,

> You know, the relationships we've made, just the basic aspect of filming a TV show, is a lot more complicated than I ever could have imagined. Me, I love pushing my own boundaries, I love exploring different aspects of what I can do, what I can accomplish, so to me it's completely rewarding, something you can look back on and say, see what I did. I'm proud of it. Even though it's extremely cheesy and campy, I'm proud of it, darn it.

Vampira: The Movie featured Jami and the rest of the *Deadly Cinema* crew. For the episode on which they showed *Plan 9 from Outer Space*, they went the whole nine yards; Jami appeared as Vampira and Muhl played Ed Wood in a series of skits. The skits were rather over-the-top, in the spirit of *Plan 9*, and Jami proved to be just as adept at doing Vampira as she was doing Marilyn. Jami also appeared in the documentary as herself, and she had this to say about Vampira: "This was during 1950s suburbia, and she was coming on the screen, a woman with long black hair and a long black dress, hosting her own show, which in itself was a feminist statement... She was hosting something on her own with this kind of cool, frosty sexuality, and I think viewers during that time were shocked and equally drawn to her because of it."

Maila Nurmi went from pinup model to horror host; Jami's career is the opposite. She moved on from *Deadly Cinema* to a much more lucrative career as a pinup model and burlesque performer (which served her well in her role of a burlesque performer in 2007's *Devil Girl*), rubbing elbows with modern luminaries of the profession such as Dita Von Teese. She has been featured in a diverse collection of publications, and is also an in-demand Marilyn Monroe tribute artist; she first appeared as Marilyn at the 2006 Texas State Fair. She has modeled for various clothing companies, including Poison Candy and Versatile Fashions. She was also did modeling for SuicideGirls, a website that features "neo-pinup" photography of "alternative models." At the site screamqueen.com, she was voted "Scream Queen of the Month" for September 2005. She now lives in Las Vegas.

Other Genre Credits—FILMS: *Fade to Pink—The Making of Deadly Cinema* (documentary), Cloudy Eden Productions, 2005 (Herself); *Texas Frightmare Weekend 2006* (documentary), Triple C Productions, 2006 (Herself); *Vampira: The Movie* (documentary), Vamp Productions, 2006 (Herself/Vampira); *Devil Girl*, Monkey Man Films, 2007 (Burlesque Performer)

Katarina

REAL NAME: Katarina Leigh Waters (1980–)

BIRTHPLACE: Luneburg, Germany

HOST: *Katarina's Nightmare Theater* (2011–2012); *The Hearse, Blood of Dracula's Castle, Incubus, Snapshot, Mortuary, The Survivor, Satan's Slave, Double Exposure, Whispers, The House on Sorority Row, Revenge, The Devil's Men and Terror, Mark of Cain, Satan's Blood, The Pyx, The Carpenter, Nothing But the Night, Final Exam, Devil Within Her* and *Humongous*

BIOGRAPHY: There are four types of women horror hosts in this book (five if you count the men that dressed up as females): The "Golden, Silver and Bronze Age" hostesses that had regular shows on local television; the "Modern Age" women who ply their craft on public access channels, YouTube and/or websites; two who played the host in theatrically released films, and two who have hosted a series of movies that accompanied said movies' DVD release. One is Morella and the other is Katarina. Out of all the women listed in this book, Katarina is the only one who came to the sisterhood after first finding fame as a professional wrestler.

Waters was born in Germany, then moved to England to go to college, where she received a Bachelor of Arts (with honors) in Film and Drama. But the squared circle beckoned; after arriving in England at 18, Waters thought that wresting was an American province until she saw an ad for a local show. She soon found out that there was a big difference between classical wrestling and American wrestling; the British version was devoid of the flash elements that have made American wrestling the joke it is today, and lost interest. Sometime later, though, she saw a couple of wrestlers on *The Jerry Springer Show*, which for some reason got her juices flowing again, and this time she saw it through. She wrestled professionally for the first time in 2002, and after going through several name changes and wrestling (er, "sports entertainment") federations, she is still taking it to the mat at the time of this writing.

Waters has made a side career for herself in films; she has directed, produced, written and acted. One of her favorite shows was *Smallville*, and Waters said in a wrestling mag that she was "totally obsessed with Lex Luthor." She wrote two episodes of *Nightmare Theater*, for the movies *Whispers* and *Humongous*.

Other Genre Credits—FILMS: *Sickness*, SaintSinner Entertainment, 2011 (Simone Foster); *Amanda and the Guardian*, Surreal Arts, 2011 (The Serpent Queen); *Bad Pixels*, Orgasmatron Films, 2012 (Valerie); *Zombies in the Basement*, Klubalturn Productions, 2014 (Dusty); *John Constantine—Hellblazer*, Drittyboro Studios, 2015 (Queenie); *Fantasy*, Loot Crate, 2015 (Knight); *Gospel*, Drittyboro Studios, 2015 (Vengeance); *Satanicus*, Creepersin Films, 2015 (Woman); *Killing Joan*, TODFILM, 2016 (Donna); *In the Woods—A Red Riding Tale*, Necrocity Entertainment, 2016 (Claudine)

Klara Kackel

REAL NAME: Unknown

HOST: *Klara Kackel's Kreepy Kauldron* (1974–1976), KHME-TV, Channel 46, South Bend, Indiana

BIOGRAPHY: The only information that the author has been able to dig up on Klara Kackel so far is contained in this letter from one Joseph Meeks in *Scary Monsters* magazine #10: "During 1974–1976 an independent station, Channel 46, from South Bend started up and began airing 'Klara Kackel' on Saturday Nights. Klara was a man dressed up as a witch, with a high-pitched gruff voice. She always welcomed her 'Little Dearies' to the show with her smoking, boiling cauldron which stood under a tripod, usually with a rubber chicken or two sticking out of it. She stirred it with her broomstick, and the occasional rubber bat flew by. She was known for her ... on-screen antics. Channel 46 went bankrupt, and was taken over by a religious station in 1976 or 1977."

Laraine Newman (1952–)

BIRTHPLACE: Los Angeles, California

HOST: *The Canned Film Festival* (1986), WWOR-TV, Channel 9, New York, New York

BIOGRAPHY: There are some horror hostesses whose careers didn't end with their horror shows (or end up *as* a horror show). Laraine Newman prospered both before and after her stint as a host. Born in L.A., she attended Beverly Hills High School, where she took her first Improv theatre classes. After graduation, she was rejected by four schools in England, so she went to Paris for a year to study mime with the legendary Marcel Marceau. She is best known as one of the original cast members of *Saturday Night Live*, which she was on for five years, and originated the role of Connie Conehead, teenage daughter of Beldar (the overrated Dan Aykroyd) and Prymaat (the underrated

Jane Curtin). In the 1993 feature film, the role was assumed by Michelle Burke; Newman played another Remulak resident.

After *SNL*, she signed on for 13 episodes of *Canned Film Festival.* They featured such golden oldies as the Mexican Wrestling Women classic *Doctor of Doom* (a.k.a. *Las Luchadoras contra El Medico Asesino*), *Robot Monster* and Ed Wood's *Bride of the Monster.* Unlike *Mystery Science Theater 3000*, the movies weren't interrupted with irreverent comments; *Canned Film Festival* kept the comedy to the commercial breaks—and even though the presentation was humorous, the show often offered valuable historical information about the featured film, as well as insightful comments about the often-overlooked assets of the films, such as the speculative scientific accuracy of movies like *Project Moon Base.* The movies were sometimes edited to the demands of the time slot, but the mutilations were nowhere near as extensive as *Reel Wild Cinema* (*see* Sandra Bernhard).

Newman, whose character was named Laraine, veered away from the ultra-sexy veneer that was the stock-in-trade of most other horror hostesses; instead, she was an usherette. In the context of the show, she was also the owner of the Ritz Theater, which had fallen on hard times, which forced her into such wacky measures as installing a Laundromat and enticing the few customers with a line of make-believe snacks, like the lip-smacking Butter Lumps (come to think of it, another instance of speculative accuracy), Chocolate-Covered Lug Nuts ("Robby the Robot's favorite snack") and Diet-Free Nutra-Cal Bars. The only real items on the menu were popcorn and Dr. Pepper, which was to be expected, since the show was sponsored by Dr. Pepper. Laraine the usherette was not the only inhabitant to be found within the walls of the Ritz; the show also featured her "mother," a shadowy figure who was never named, and communicated with sound effects. Other members of the supporting cast were Kathryn Rossetter as Doris, the middle-aged fan of romances, and her younger feminist counterpart Becky, played by Laura Galusha. Jack (F. Richards Ford) was a local newspaper writer and movie critic. Fitzy (Patrick Garner) was an all-purpose dirty old man and Chan (Philip Nee) was a childlike mute. Despite being aggressively marketed, the show only lasted one season.

The real Laraine became an accomplished voice actress in addition to her on-screen appearances, which include the classic adaptation of *Fear and Loathing in Las Vegas* starring Johnny Depp as Hunter S. Thompson. There are drug-fueled fantasy sequences a-plenty in the film but it cannot exactly be classified as a genre film, although plenty of her other roles are. She has done some memorable episodes of the animated *Justice League* and the various *Batman* series, like the delightful "This Little Piggy" episode of *Justice League*, where she does a hilarious turn as Medusa. In addition to her acting career, she is a contributing editor for the online magazine *One for the Table* and occasionally writes for *The Huffington Post*. She has also written articles for a variety of newspapers and magazines such as *The Los Angeles Times.* In a town (Los Angeles) not exactly known for marital solidity, she has been married to the same man for 25 years, and they have two daughters.

Other Genre Credits—FILMS: *Invaders from Mars*, Cannon Pictures, 1986 (Ellen Gardner); *Coneheads*, Paramount, 1993 (Laarta); *Witchboard 2* (*The Devil's Doorway*), Blue Rider Pictures, 1993 (Elaine); *Monsters, Inc.*, Walt Disney Pictures, 2001 (Voice);

Jimmy Neutron, Boy Genius, Paramount, 2001 (voice of Hostess); *Wall-E*, Walt Disney Pictures, 2008 (Voice); *The Haunted World of El Superbeasto*, Carbunkle Cartoons, 2009 (voices of Lefty/Kate/Courtney); *Tom and Jerry & the Wizard of Oz*, Turner Entertainment, 2011 (voices of Wicked Witch of the West/Miss Gulch); *Superman versus the Elite* (animated), Warner Premiere, 2012 (voice of Newscaster #3); *Monsters University*, Walt Disney Pictures, 2013 (additional voices); *Tom and Jerry—The Lost Dragon* (animated), Warner Brothers Animation, 2014 (voice of Elf Elder's Wife); TELEVISION: *The Coneheads* (animated): 1983, (voice of Connie); *Alfred Hitchcock Presents*: "The Jar," 1986 (Periwinkle); *Faerie Tale Theatre*: "The Little Mermaid," 1987 (Coral); *Amazing Stories*: "Miss Stardust," 1987 (Miss Schroedinger); *Monsters*: "Rouse Him Not," 1988 (Linda McGuire); *The Tweety & Sylvester Mysteries* (animated): "B2 or Not B2," 1995 (voice of Trudy); *3rd Rock from the Sun*: "World's Greatest Dick," 1996 (Candace); *The Tick* (animated): "The Tick vs. Education," 1996 (voice of The Flying Squirrel); *Perversions of Science*: "Panic," 1997 (Becky); *Superman—The Animated Series:* "Apokolips.... Now" (voice of Toby Raynes); *The New Batman Adventures* (animated): "Love Is a Croc," 1998 (Baby Doll/Mary Louise Dahl); *The Zeta Project* (animated): "Quality Time," 2002 (voice of Dr. Marion O'Keefe); *Justice League* (animated): "This Little Piggy," 2004 (voices of Medusa/Themis); *Wolverine & the X-Men* (animated): "Shades of Grey," 2009 (voice of Marjorie); *Batman: The Brave and the Bold* (animated): "The Power of Shazam," 2010 (voice of Ms. Minerva); *Beware the Batman* (animated): "Monsters," 2014 (voice of Diner Owner); *International Ghost Investigators*: "Laraine Newman," 2015 (Herself)

Lucretia

REAL NAME: not available

HOST: *Lucretia's Creature Features* (dates unknown), KOKH-TV, Oklahoma City, Oklahoma

BIOGRAPHY: Sigh ... move along, move along, folks, nothin' to see here. Just a few seconds of video footage survive, featuring a beautiful woman in lingerie and a spooky set.

Macabra

REAL NAME: not available

HOST: *Theatre of the Macabre* (1982–1985), WOWT-TV, Omaha, Nebraska

BIOGRAPHY: As the woman who played Macabra wishes to remain anonymous, it stands to reason that we can know little about her. There's no surviving video footage except for a "bloopers" reel available on YouTube, and so, once again, we can rely only on Elena Watson and memories; in this case, provided by Mr. "Disco" Stu Burns in an e-mail to E-Gor:

> I was doing a search for Omaha horror hostess Macabra and I ran across a reference to your web page [E-Gor's Chamber of TV Horror Hosts]. Macabra was a favorite of mine growing up, and I've always wondered what happened to her. The show aired on Fridays, 10:30 p.m. The company she worked for was Mutual of Omaha—the same folks that produced *Wild Kingdom*. Without hyperbole, she was one of the most attractive women I have ever seen, which may account for her beating out the other 150 applicants Watson mentions. Beyond the physical, however, her delivery was consistently intelligent and relevant without being so deep as to lose her younger viewers (myself included).

Watson portrays her as wearing "leopard-skin" tights. I don't remember anything like that. When I saw her, she would often wear something appropriate to the film she was hosting; e.g. Egyptian garb for *The Mummy*. Other shows would have her wearing a nightgown or an evening dress. Though her outfits were often form-fitting, they never approached the plunging décolletage of someone like Elvira; Macabra really didn't "show much skin." It was a tastefully done show.

My own experience with Macabra is somewhat limited. I grew up in rural Nebraska, and would only see Macabra when we visited my grandparents in Lincoln. My experience with the horror genre sprung from Kearney-based NTV's *Shock Theatre*, which featured voiceovers, but no visible host. Macabra was witty, but not outrageous like Elvira or [Macabra's] worthy predecessor, Omaha humanitarian Dr. Sanguinary. Macabra's narration perfectly suited the tone of the Universal classics that she introduced; serious, sensual, and with a *slight* bit of dark comedy. I have some friends of mine doing some checking for me. I'd like to tell Macabra what a great host she was. In my experience (which is substantial), she was the *perfect* horror film host.

Watson fills in a little biographical detail. The show's star was at the time a divorced local businesswoman who had a son, and the nature of the fan mail she received convinced her to remain anonymous. She worked for an insurance company, and was also going to university to receive her M.B.A. Watson says that the actress really enjoyed it, but obviously, she's had a change of heart. The station came up with the name and concept of the character. Macabra, like many other female hosts, did her duties from a couch and wrote her own scripts. When she started, there wasn't the usual snarky horror host's attitude towards the movie that she was showing, but finally, when faced with such dreck as *Dracula vs. Frankenstein*, she caved in and Told It Like It Was.

While writing this book, I called Stu to see if he had ever been able to find out anything more about Macabra. He was able to find out her real name, and what she does now (she's an assistant professor at a university, in the business school). But he warned me that people had tried to contact her, and they had, shall we say, not met with the best of receptions.

Macabra in a newspaper ad, 1983 (courtesy George "E-Gor" Chastain).

But, like it was with Moana, it was my duty to call and see for myself. I contacted her by phone on August 25, 2015; I told her who I was, who my publisher was, etc., and what my latest book was; I asked about Macabra. She said, "I'm going to have to end this conversation now." And then she hung up on me. I guess you could call that the last word on Macabra.

Madame Cadaver

REAL NAME: Patricia Ozmum

HOST: *Fright Night* (1989–1996), KHAS-TV, Channel 5, Hastings, Nebraska

BIOGRAPHY: A fan named Lee Peterson contributed the initial information for this entry to E-Gor's Chamber (used with permission):

> I grew up in Grand Island, Nebraska (birthplace of Henry Fonda). In the early-to-mid '70s, our local horror movie host was Madame Cadaver. As I recall, she showed movies on Fridays and Saturdays at 10:30 (a different movie each night), after the local news. It was definitely on Channel 5 from Kearney-Hastings. Her look was patterned on Vampira (I didn't know that at the time; I assumed she was an original)—black dress, pale makeup, [and] long black hair. I remember her show to be pretty straight, not a lot of clowning around or anarchy. She did answer viewer mail sometimes, though.

Peterson later added:

> I've finally some choice info about my local horror host, Madame Cadaver. After writing a letter to the editor of my hometown newspaper, the *Grand Island Nebraska Daily Independent* (I've been a New York City resident for nearly 20 years), I was contacted by a gentleman named Bob Booe, who was the creator of the program. Here's what he tells me:
>
> "I put the idea together to create a sales vehicle for an otherwise unsold segment of station air time—at the time, I was assistant general manager and program director of the station (KHAS-TV in Hastings, Nebraska). *Fright Night* first hit the air in the fall of 1969, in time for the Fall Sweeps. Madame Cadaver was played by a part-time employee of KHAS-TV named Patricia (Pat) Osmond [see correction below]. She would make her appearance by raising the lid on a coffin I had borrowed from a local mortuary. We attempted to create a scary set scene, complete with cobwebs, spiders, and scary lighting, etc., etc. Madame Cadaver would, after establishing each week's theme, intro old black & white scary movies. The station purchased a number of these old Lugosi and Karloff-type spine-tinglers. We would, on occasion, have locally prominent people appear as victims of The Madame by showing them chained in her private dungeon, or hanging from torture racks, etc., etc. PS—It was fun.

The correction came from Larry Cain of Columbia, Missouri:

> I came across [E-Gor's Chamber] and was delighted to find a reference to the Madame Cadaver show.... I do have one correction, on the spelling of the name of the show's host: it was Pat Ozmum, instead of Osmond. Other details are correct as nearly as I can recall. I was Sports Director of KHAS-TV from 1970–1976 and was well-acquainted with Pat. I was even a "celebrity" resident of her dungeon on one of the shows.

Madame Mortem

REAL NAME: Samantha Ramirez

HOST: *The Magnificent Madame Mortem's Midway of Madness* (2003), Horror Host Underground Network

BIOGRAPHY: This entry could well be called Madame Mortem's Post-Mortem, since she would appear to have vanished from public view. Her website is down, and there is no surviving video footage, not even on YouTube, which is surprising for a show of such recent vintage. She only did seven shows.

Madame Mortem made her debut in 2003 as a lead-in for the *Haunted Theatre* show starring Halloween Jack. The following information was collected from her now-defunct website:

You bring the chips, we'll supply the cheese! Born to a gypsy fortune teller and a carnival barker, the Magnificent Madame Mortem traveled the world with the Carn-Evil Circus. She never was really able to tell fortunes, but learned how to bilk folks for their hard-earned cash from her dad. Along the way, she hooked up with a smart-mouthed bird, Quoths the Raven, who was part of a traveling bird show that had joined the circus. The Madame won Quoths in a lucky hand of poker and the two became fast friends through their love of B-Movies, Monsters, and Horror Hosts, especially Madame Mortem's idols, Vampira and Elvira. Madame Mortem and Quoths were not well-liked by the rest of the carnie folk, and late one night, as the Madame and Quoths were "sleeping one off," the circus packed up and left them behind. Knowing they needed jobs, Quoths and the Madame put their love for all things Horror to work. Spending their last bit of money on video equipment, they began late-night broadcasts of *The Magnificent Madame Mortem's Midway of Madness* from her fortune teller's tent at the abandoned circus.

The show was a true family affair; Samantha Ramirez was Madame Mortem, Josh Ramirez played two ravens, Quoths and Uncle Nevermore, and Bob Ramirez played Cameraman Bob. And even though they only showed seven movies, there was a lot of diversity in the selections: the original *Night of the Living Dead, Carnival of Souls, King Kong vs. Godzilla, Suspiria, Dementia 13, Alice Sweet Alice* and *Diabolique*. I wrote to Paul Counelis, asking if he could get me in touch with Halloween Jack, to see if Jack knew anything about the current whereabouts of Madame Mortem, and he responded: "She is distancing herself from the horror host stuff, it seems; her [Facebook] profile is mostly Bible verses and information about her being born again. She isn't ashamed of it though, and may still be willing to be interviewed. Her name is now Sammie Lee Russell. I sent her a message, and will let you know what she says regarding an email interview." Halloween Jack sent her a message, but she never replied to any of us.

Malena Teves (1974–)

Host: *13 Nights of Fright* (2004), Fox Movie Channel; *American Scary*, POOB Productions, 2006 (Herself)

Biography: The beautiful and very talented Malena Teves is a part-time actress and model and full-time singer. She began her on-screen career as the co-host of *13 Nights of Fright* alongside Neil (*Sandman*) Gaiman. Gaiman said in *American Scary*:

> I had the meeting with the Fox people, and they said "Are you interested?" and I said yes.... Condition number one was that I got to come out of a coffin at some point, and Condition number two was that I had a glorious, silent, vampiric assistant of magnificent curvaceousness, because I thought that was part of the tradition. If you're gonna do it, you should do it all the way ... going out there and having the gorgeous Malena—she's not only gorgeous, but she's terribly funny, which means I actually get to do stuff and play off her, so I don't get stuck in front of the camera on my own. It's great.

To that, Malena replied with a laugh: "Well, I do talk. ...They'd say we want you to open the coffin, and I can't just walk up and open up a coffin, I'm very animated, so I would walk up to the coffin, and I'd stroke it, and pull it up slowly ... it was really fun." There was more fun behind the scenes in rehearsals, where Malena cracked everyone up with her *Chipmunks* impression: "Why don't you give it to me like you used to, Big Daddy?" "I don't think we're gonna use that in the show," he laughed. The show itself was lavishly produced, with a sumptuous set that looked like it cost more than all of the old hosts' sets put together, and Malena and Neil made a great team.

The musical side of Teves is in her blood—her father wrote, played, and sang, and her mother sang for the all-women group "The Chord Busters." Almost from birth, Teves' mom took her to stage performances of every kind, and by the age of five, Malena was acting, singing, dancing and participating in beauty pageants. By fourth grade, she was playing the violin. In high school, she was the leading performer in the dance company. In February of her junior year, she began taking college courses for high school credit, graduating early. Teves, who had already been modeling for two years, went to New York, where she continued her upwards trajectory by doing shoots for Tahari, Ann Taylor, Venus Swimwear, Ujena and Mary McFadden. Then it was off to Milan, where she modeled for Chanel, Max Mara, Gautier and Versace. Despite her record of success in the field, she was ultimately told that her face was made for acting, not modeling; she was "not editorial enough" and "too cute," which, translated, means that she wasn't built like a beanpole and her face didn't wear an expression of perpetual gloom.

Her modeling career cut short by the fashion fascists, Teves moved back to the City of Angels, where she began learning improv under the aegis of Dan Weisman at the L.A. Comedy Connection, and studying acting at Margie Haber Studios. From there, it was on to *13 Nights* and parts in movies, as well as returning to modeling and singing; she was the host of several jazz and blues spectaculars at the House of Blues in Los Angeles. Teves is a humanitarian as well; her "Fairy Godmother's Club" is devoted to making a difference in the lives of children that others don't care about. She certainly cares about them, having adopted a number in addition to her own. At the time of this writing (2016), Malena had just finished battling a serious illness for the last five years, and, when she could, continued to sing her songs and make public appearances. In 2015, she retired from Hollywood and now resides, along with her children and her husband Bruce, in an old colonial home somewhere in New England.

Margali Morwentari

REAL NAME: Neils Erickson

HOST: *Thriller Theatre Starring Margali* (1990–1993), WDBD-TV, Channel 40, Jackson, Mississippi; *Thriller Theatre Starring Margali* (1991), WXTX-TV, Channel 54, Columbus, Georgia

BIOGRAPHY: Margali Morwentari was a character created in the late 1970s by Neils Erickson, a Mississippi horror fan who sat on the board for CoastCon, the state's premier horror/science fiction convention. The character first appeared in the fantasy role-playing adventure game *Wizard's Realm*. Erickson was employed by Gamescience Corporation as an illustrator and editor in the 1980s and '90s. In 1990, Erickson turned the character into a horror host. Margali was the host of the Jackson, Mississippi, series *Thriller Theatre Starring Margali* from 1990 to 1993. It was amusing low-budget entertainment, produced on a shoestring, like many of the movies "she" showed. Drawing on memories of a famous New Orleans horror host, Morgus, Neils and his partner-in-slime Tim Hess, who was responsible for Hans, the hand servant, served up a late-night snack that really hit the spot for viewers. Hans, the hand servant, was, as you might have guessed, a detached hand, much like "Thing" of *Addams Family* fame. Erickson was also the voice of Wendel, the werewolf announcer. Hess sent an email to E-Gor with some much-appreciated additional information:

> I was co-creator-writer-director-producer of *Thriller Theatre Starring Margali* from 1990 to 1993. The program originated out of WDBD-TV in Jackson, Mississippi, and could be seen in parts of Louisiana and Arkansas. For a short time in early 1991, the program was syndicated on WXTX-TV in Columbus,

Georgia. The WXTX signal reached into Alabama, giving us coverage in five southern states. The program starred Neils Erickson as Margali Morwentari, along with a never-seen werewolf announcer, Wendel, and Hans, Margali's hand servant (digitally mastered by yours truly). The program won Silver Awards from the Mississippi association of broadcasters during each of the three years of production, and even though it was scheduled at midnight on Saturday, it was at one time the highest-rated movie on WDBD's schedule. Margali still makes regular appearances and is an annual highlight of the New Orleans Worst Film Festival. Hans is still attached to me, and helping to manage the promotion department at WZDX in Huntsville, Alabama. Neils now lives in New Orleans.

Marilyn the Witch

REAL NAME: Dolores Teachenor, a.k.a. Dodo Denney, a.k.a. Nora Denney (1927–2005)

BIRTHPLACE: Kansas City, Missouri

HOST: *The Witching Hour* (1958–1959), KCMO-TV, Kansas City, Missouri

BIOGRAPHY: Character actress Nora Denney appeared in films and TV and on the stage. She was known as Dodo for a time in her career; that name came from her real first name, Dorothy. Her career actually began with a horror host gig in her hometown when she hosted *The Witching Hour*. Her costume was the stereotypical witch's brew: long gray hair, jutting chin, warts, pointed hat and a black cape, a living version of EC's Old Witch. She did the show for about a year before moving up the ladder: She appeared on many TV series, including *Green Acres, Petticoat Junction, Hart to Hart, Get Smart, Room 222* and *That Girl*. She will be forever remembered for her role in 1971's *Willy Wonka and the Chocolate Factory*, where she played the mother of the bratty, obnoxious Mike Teevee.

Nora Denney as Marilyn—the Witch, that is, in 1958/59 (courtesy George "E-Gor" Chastain).

Other Genre Credits—FILMS: *Willy Wonka and the Chocolate Factory*, Wolper Pictures, 1971 (Mrs. Teevee); TELEVISION: *My Favorite Martian*: "My Nut Cup Runneth Over," 1966 (Woman); *Bewitched*: "A Gazebo Never Forgets," 1966 (Woman in Park), "Samantha Fights City Hall," 1968 (Mrs. Gurney); *The Ghost Busters*: "Who's Afraid of the Big, Bad Wolf?" 1975 (Sophia); *Tucker's Witch*: "Abra-Cadaver," 1982

Marlena Midnite

REAL NAME: Marlena Aude Metzger

HOST: *Midnite Mausoleum* (2009–), WQAD, My TV 8-3, Moline, Davenport, Quad Cities, Mediacom Cable Channel 716

BIOGRAPHY: Marlena Metzger was born in Dubuque, Iowa, and she was a deprived child—she had no local horror host to call her own. But it didn't take her too terribly long to remedy that, along with Blake Powell, a construction superintendent from Clinton, Iowa. Erika Hildebrandt, also from Clinton, responded when they advertised for a sidekick (Robyn Graves) online, through Myspace. By 2009, *Midnite Mausoleum* was running on ten public access channels in seven states, and by the time that the show had ended its run in 2013, it had expanded to 60 channels in 22 states. Whereas most hosts today do their thing via their own websites, YouTube, Roku or public access TV, Marlena and Robyn graduated from the Internet to actual broadcast television, and they continue to increase their considerable following. Marlena granted me this interview in late 2015:

BC: *How did you come to be a horror host?*
MM: I first discussed doing a horror host show with co-creator Blake Powell in the fall of 2008. We were both working on a comedy movie (that never actually got finished). He had grown up on the local ACRI *Creature Feature* and later, *Son of Svengoolie*; I had seen *Son of Svengoolie* on cable as well as *Zomboo's House of Horror Movies*, which was syndicated locally for a short time. Anyway, the discussion turned to creating a new show of that type, and within about a week or so I had the characters of Marlena Midnite, Wolfred and Franklin. I began making puppets for Wolfred and Franklin, as well as working on other character and set designs. We began test shoots in February 2009, and began putting our first 12 [web] episodes online in April 2009.

Marlena Midnite and friend, 2010 (courtesy Marlena Midnite).

BC: *Do you like horror and science fiction movies?*

MM: Usually of the older variety when it comes to horror; older horror-comedies more than anything ... some of the classic stuff like *The Raven, Comedy of Terrors, Pit and the Pendulum* and the classic Universal monsters, with *Creature from the Black Lagoon* as a particular favorite. Science fiction, I like a lot of older and newer stuff: *Monolith Monsters, It Came from Outer Space, It Conquered the World, Flash Gordon, Dune* and *Blade Runner*. I'm also a big fan of film noir.

BC: *Are you a full-time actress?*

MM: I am a full-time horror host, but *not* a full-time or even a part-time actress. Horror-hosting and acting are two entirely different things; I am simply myself on camera for the most part. It doesn't take any real acting ability to be a host.... I guess you might say that the limited amount of acting I do has to be written, at least in part, by me.... I could never just come in and perform something from a script someone else wrote.

BC: *Was any one host a particular inspiration for you?*

MM: Over the years, I have traded for and collected a ton of shows by different hosts on DVD or VHS, so by the time we did the show I was familiar with quite a few. Certainly Sven and Zomboo are an influence, and right about the time we started the show, I got a whole batch of *Commander USA* episodes from a collector.... I would say that Commander USA is probably the single biggest influence on me as a horror host. Other influential hosts would be Sammy Terry, Doctor Creep, Crematia Mortem, Count Gore De Vol, Doctor Madblood, the Bowman Body and Scarticia.

BC: *How is* Paynekiller *coming along?*

MM: *Paynekiller* finished principal photography in September 2014, and the "new" *Midnite Mausoleum* went into production that same month, so needless to say we crank out new episodes every week, and there is really no time whatsoever to cut *Paynekiller*. In January 2016 we will be taking some time to get a rough cut started, so maybe we can get it finished in the summer of 2016.

BC: *The IMDb lists* Midnite Mausoleum *as having only one season, in 2009. Has the show run continuously since then, or did you take a break of some sort?*

MM: The only reason there is an IMDb entry at all is because Carmela wanted to get her credits on there for the two episodes she was on, otherwise, we pay no attention to it. We ran on public access from 2009 to 2013, and we quit early in 2013. In summer 2014, commercial television came a-calling, and we have been there ever since.

BC: *What made you decide to come back?*

MM: When we quit the show in 2013, while we were literally tearing down the set, we made a list of sorts that said we will need this, this and this to return to doing the show.... Then in the summer of 2014, Tribune Broadcasting station WQAD TV8 in Moline, Illinois, said, "We'll give you this, this and this to re-launch your show on our channel," and the rest, as they say, is history. We currently run at 10:30 on Friday and Saturday nights.

BC: *Was the character created by you?*

MM: Yes, basically an extension of myself, so that part is simple. I worked for a while on the "look" before I settled on it.

BC: *Did you create the other characters?*
MM: Yes; Wolfred and Franklin at first, then Robyn, Cleo, and Creepy Charlie later.

BC: *Do you write and produce the show as well? Or Blake? Or is it collaboration?*
MM: We used to write it together in the early days, but more recently it is mostly me for the majority of the show, and Blake does the Wolfred and Creepy Charlie stuff most of the time.

BC: *Tell me about Blake and Robyn.*
MM: Blake is the show's co-creator and co-producer; he is the videographer and editor, as well as the voice of Wolfred. Robyn is my "human" friend on the show; she works for the Midnite Mailservice, and delivers my viewer mail. She is a lot of fun.

BC: *What are some of your fondest memories of the show?*
MM: Still making new ones every week! I really had fun shooting "The Maltese Bat," which was a set of film noir-style skits; also the "Tracking Moonbeast" segments we did last year. So there is always something new. I really like to get out and do location shoots when possible.

BC: *Are there any especially funny memories of the show*?
MM: On our Halloween episode back in 2009, I cut up a ghost-shaped piñata with a chainsaw, which came off really well, although a bit dangerous and messy. The Christmas episode that year was an absolute blast, with some great stuff with Robyn and Andrew Smith, the voice of our skeleton "Bones."

BC: *Which do you prefer, public access TV or the Internet?*
MM: Neither. The only reason we came back is because it was commercial broadcast television. The Internet is kind of a vast wasteland begging for viewers. I would hardly think doing a show there would even be worth the trouble because you are simply lost among a multitude of shows. Public access was very good to us in a way; it certainly got our show on in over 60 markets across the U.S. But there were very few that were actually keeping up with the new episodes as we put them out, and when they were supposed to run, and in what order. I am pretty sure there is a station in Louisiana that has been running the same episode for years. But I guess I would say it is a great training ground, so if I had to

Midnite Mausoleum with Marlena Midnite, 2010—send your little vampires to bed! (courtesy Marlena Midnite).

choose, I would choose public access. When we started on WQAD in October 2014, it didn't take long to figure out that broadcast television made everything we did previously look like a joke. Commercial sponsors, an occasional *good* movie, and a viewership that dwarfs public access were all things we learned about very quickly. We now do an annual event with the station called Boo at the Zoo every October at a local zoo; it is a benefit for the zoo, and people can bring their kids to trick-or-treat and visit the animals. The only place that the event is even advertised is by the station itself and our show especially, and we have over 10,000 people come to it each year—the numbers are just amazing.

BC: *How long do you see yourself doing Marlena?*

MM: Oh, I suppose for another year or two, but we will see. There is an always unforeseen thing that might end up changing everything, so who knows? But for now, I'm pretty content to keep doing what I'm doing for a little while.

Other Genre Credits—Films: *The Giant Rubber Monster Movie—Sascratch vs. Afrodesius* (short), 2011 (Marlena); *Dawn of Dracula*, Hammer Head Productions, 2013 (Victoria Van Helsing)

Medusa

Real Name: Jennifer Ashley Klein, a.k.a. Jennifer Richards (1947–)

Birthplace: Brooklyn, New York

Biography: This is the first of two entries that deal with actresses who played the part of horror hosts in a movie (the other being Lynn Redgrave; see below). The producers of both *TerrorVision* and *Midnight* failed to realize one important thing; they were obviously made to cash in on the Elvira phenomenon, but it seems that they didn't get that women like Vampira and Elvira were parodies, each in their own way, and it's very difficult to parody something that's meant as a parody in the first place. For instance, the James Bond films: the Flint films with James Coburn worked, the Matt Helm films with Dean Martin didn't.

The thing to remember about *TerrorVision* is that this movie is not about the horror host; she's just another purposefully obnoxious character in a cast full of them, although she does play an important part in the climax. It doesn't begin promisingly; the title tune is an absolutely terrible, generic New Wave theme song. There is a good choice of clips from B-movies, including *The Giant Claw, Earth vs. the Flying Saucers*, and *Robot Monster*. The cast is uneven. Richards' Medusa, like Lynn Redgrave's Midnight, is shown to be a real party girl, slutty, bitchy and cruel. The movie is ostensibly a satire, but a true satire would be more cohesive; *TerrorVision* just throws everything at the wall, hoping something will stick. Medusa certainly fulfills the stereotypical physical requirements and look of the horror hostess: cleavage, lingerie, stockings, all topped off with a wig of rubber snakes. But the character comes off as so unlikable; it's hard to believe anyone would watch her. Most importantly, the character crosses the line in terms of sleaziness, something nobody else in this book ever did. Many of them were certainly naughty; indeed, that was part of their appeal, but none of them ever extolled the audience to "call in and tell me about all your kinky ... nightmares"—the horror hostess as phone sex. This is one of the areas where the satire falls flattest. The "swinger" mom is played by the beautiful Mary Woronov, who manages to project both a frosty frigidity and hints of unspeakable decadence. And then there's the character she plays in the movie, which is performed with a perfect sense of irony that the other characters seem to be lacking. Veteran character actor Bert Remsen as the right-wing survivalist Grampa is mildly amusing, but the stereotype of the character is too easy a target, especially with some of the nutjobs that dominate the headlines nowadays, as if to prove fact is, indeed, stranger than fiction. On the other hand, Alejandro Rey, who, in a complete reversal of his image on the TV series *The Flying Nun*, plays a swinging Greek, and he swings in all directions. Curiously, he shows no interest in Mary Woronov, surprising her by telling her that he likes boys and that it is her husband he wants, not her, but then goes to their indoor heated pool for a quickie with the woman who accompanied him, only to find out the monster has consumed her, and he's next on the menu. If the monster hadn't eaten him, he probably would have tried to go Greek on *it*.

The plot, such as it is, concerns a dysfunctional suburban family. Mom and Dad are swingers, Grampa is busy reliving the last war and building up his arsenal for the next one, daughter is a Cyndi Lauper clone with a heavy metal boyfriend and, as usual, the little kid is the first one to spot the monster, only (wait for it) nobody believes him, least of all the local horror host, Medusa. The monster comes from an alien world on which it is a pet, albeit one with a taste for flesh and able to make the heads of his victims pop out and speak in their own voices. When its owner tried to exterminate it by turning it to pure energy, the energy bounced around the galaxy until it somehow wound up in the Putterman family's television set, where it proceeds to eat most of them and their attendant companions. Medusa is there for the big climax. I won't spoil the ending for those of you who insist on wasting 90 minutes of their lives.

Other Genre Credits—FILMS: *TerrorVision*, Empire Pictures, 1986 (Medusa); TELEVISION: *Star Trek—The Next Generation*: "Cost of Living," 1992 (Painted Dancer); *Superman—The Animated Series*: "The Way of All Flesh," 1996 (voice of Young Woman)

Midnight

REAL NAME: Lynn Rachel Redgrave, O.B.E. (1943–2010)
BIRTHPLACE: Marylebone, London, England
BIOGRAPHY: Some may quibble with the inclusion of Lynn Redgrave and Jennifer Richards (see above) in this book; after all, they only played the parts of horror hosts in movies. But the fact that an actress of Redgrave's lineage and stature would portray a horror host in a major motion picture does, I think, merit her inclusion. She was the daughter of Sir Michael (*Dead of Night*) Redgrave and Rachel (*Curse of the Fly*) Kempson, as well as the sister of Vanessa (*Blow Up*) Redgrave and Corin (*A Study in Terror*) Redgrave.

She trained at the Central School of Speech and Drama, and made her stage debut at 19. The following years were filled with National Theatre stage productions interspersed with the occasional film role; she garnered great acclaim for her performance in *Georgy Girl*, for which she won a Golden Globe and was nominated for an Academy Award. The film co-starred her mother, and spawned a worldwide hit with the title song by the Seekers. But the pressure of being the sister of Vanessa, who was getting more acclaim and more awards for her film and stage roles, made her emigrate to the U.S. in the '70s. She was based in California, but was a Broadway mainstay. She made many television appearances and continued her film career as well, and she admitted that many of her career choices for the next 20 years or so were, if not somewhat dodgy, then downright "terrible." The downright terrible choices included *The Love Boat* (which was announced by a real former horror host, Ernie Anderson, a.k.a. the legendary Ghoulardi), *Fantasy Island, Disco Beaver from Outer Space* and *The Happy Hooker.*

Midnight was not necessarily one of those bad career choices, but it ain't no *Georgy Girl*. What it was, was a weird movie. On the plus side, there's Wolfman Jack, Frank Gorshin and former *Playboy* centerfold Karen Whitter, who appeared under the name of Karen Lorre (she was married to producer Chuck Lorre). On the minus side is, as always, Tony Curtis. Okay, *Some Like It Hot, The Defiant Ones* and *The Boston Strangler* were great films, but not really because of him, and are more than offset by crap like the truly horrific *Boeing, Boeing!, Arrivederci, Baby* and *The Manitou.*

The film begins with Midnight pulling up to the studio where she'll do her show in a customized hearse, surrounded by screaming fans, to the tune of some of the most generic, synth-driven, vaguely New Wave music ever heard. Cut to her doing the show; it's live, and the audience is filled with teens dressed as though they just stepped off the set of *Rock and Roll High School*, chanting "Mid-night, Mid-night." Midnight does some dialogue straight from Vampira, including, "My nails are hemorrhage red" and "I don't give autographs, I give epitaphs." One of the movie's basic premises seems to be lifted from the Vampira story too; the station wants Midnight to sign over the copyright to her character, which she refuses to do. Redgrave plays Midnight as the mother of all bitch-divas; Elizabeth Taylor on a bad hair day, a "cougar" before the time the term was invented, whose choice of men in the film are as questionable as some of Redgrave's real-life career choices. For instance, early in the film, she finds she has a stalker. Does she call the cops? Of course not; she takes him home with her and sleeps with him. Curtis is a sleazy producer called "Mr. B," constantly surrounded by opulence and beautiful young girls in bikinis; you can almost see the coke oozing out of the character's eyes.

Cynicism is the order of the day; practically all the characters are turds, and once again, Hollywood is portrayed as the kind of place where no one in their right mind would want a career—which seems appropriate for these characters, since none of them are in their right mind. The rest of the film plays out like a twisted parody of *Sunset Blvd.*; Redgrave is clearly playing Norma Desmond with more than a touch of Katharine Hepburn. Her chauffeur is devoted to her, and she seemingly to him, but unlike the *Sunset Blvd.* chauffeur, he goes to much greater lengths to prove his devotion. Erich von Stroheim, as Max in *Sunset Blvd.*, seemed to know where the bodies were buried, so to speak, but Iggy (Gustav Vintas) is a little more proactive about it. When Midnight learns what he's done, she tells him it was … very naughty. Then she makes him drink poison. But, no matter; she's been letting her boy-toy drive her car anyway.

Redgrave's performance is so over-the-top that it's almost beyond parody. She, at 46, is still a very beautiful woman, and is more than able to pull off the physical aspects of her character, and at least make it believable that a much younger man could have been attracted to her. Midnight's look is certainly a take-off on Elvira's, but at the same time, it's different. Black wig, of course, but not as much cleavage or leg; no gowns for Midnight, she was strictly a tight leopard-skin print pants type of girl. But the mental aspects are quite another. It's never clear whether or not she believes the often supernatural threats that she levies against others ("I'll give you herpes on your pecker"), or just being overly dramatic, or just a nut; probably a little of all three.

Steven Parrish as the stalker, boy-toy, wannabe actor and just general all-around rat fink is terrible; he's like all those young, useless Hammer leading men of the '70s, only with that awful '70s blow-dried hair. Come to think of it, some of the hapless Hammer "heroes" had blow-dried hair, too. Beautiful Karen Whitter gives a good performance in a thankless role that should have "VICTIM" flashing in big red letters every time she's on screen. And riddle me this, Caped Crimefighter: When is Frank Gorshin in the dark? Why, when he agrees to appear in *Midnight*, of course. Like Whitter, Gorshin plays Midnight's agent in a role so obvious in "execution" that he should have worn one of the *Star Trek* red shirts. At least the film is cool enough to feature an extra who wears a black leather jacket adorned with Misfits and Samhain logos, and to include Shocking Blue's classic "Venus" on an otherwise horrid soundtrack.

Lynn Redgrave as Midnight from the movie of the same name, 1989 (courtesy George "E-Gor" Chastain).

Lynn Redgrave's career picked up again in the '90s with a number of good stage and film roles, including an Oscar-nominated performance in *Gods and Monsters*.

Other Genre Credits—FILMS: *Disco Beaver from Outer Space* (Television), 1978 (Van Helsing); *The Bad Seed*, Warner Brothers, 1985 (Monica Breedlove); *Midnight*, Kuys Entertainment Group, 1989 (Midnight); *Whatever Happened to Baby Jane* (Television), 1991 (Jane Hudson); *Gods and Monsters*, Lions Gate Films, 1998 (Hanna); *Lion of Oz* (animated), Lions Gate Films, 2000 (The Wicked Witch of the East); *Hansel & Gretel*, Broomstick Entertainment, 2002 (Woman/Witch); *Peter Pan*, Universal, 2003 (Aunt Millicent); TELEVISION: *The ABC Comedy Hour*: "Hellzapoppin'," 1972 (Herself); *Fantasy Island*: two episodes, 1982, 1984 (Kristen Robbins)

Millicent B. Ghastly

REAL NAME: Barbara Ends

HOST: *Monsterpiece Theatre* (1985–1986), WLEX-TV, Channel 18, Lexington, Kentucky

BIOGRAPHY: Millicent B. Ghastly was the host of Lexington, Kentucky's *Monster-*

piece Theatre in 1985 and '86; several websites speculate that the reason the show was short-lived was because "she looked like a bag lady," which is inaccurate. In all of the clips of the show that are available, her style can be more accurately described as "punk" or "New Wave": wild hair, sunglasses that resembled Fritz the Nite Owl's, an off-the-shoulder t-shirt (which read "ARRGH!") exposing part of her bra, and spandex pants. They also speculate that the reason may have been copyright troubles. Her sidekick was a store-bought Cookie Monster puppet that might have gone unnoticed, except that *Monsterpiece Theatre* was also the name of a recurring Cookie Monster routine on *Sesame Street*, they said. But enough with speculation, on to the facts, provided by Barbara's husband Steve.

As he said on his blog, "It was Channel 18's idea. We just happened to catch the pitch." In April 1985, Barbara got a call from a producer at the station. A rival station was running movies in the late time slot and WLEX, an NBC affiliate, planned on doing the same thing after *Saturday Night Live*, except that the station wanted a host, preferably an Elvira clone, for a "cult" TV show. After scouting talent at the local playhouses, the producer decided that Barbara combined the looks and comedic talent that would be ideally suited to the part. But nothing was written on paper, any descriptions or directions; the producer carried it all in his head. The offer was $50 a week (later raised to $75). She said she and Steve would think about it. They never did sign a contract, but the show went on. Their original commitment was for 13 weeks, including the October "sweeps," and if the show proved more successful than the un-hosted movies on the rival station, then the show would be renewed for 13 more weeks.

The look of the character was designed by Missy Holloway, who had recently come to Lexington via Seattle to be the costume designer for a local modern-dance company. She designed Barbara's whole look, from the wig on down, and Bob Andrews designed Millicent's makeup. Andrews, a cook at a local restaurant, stayed with the show throughout the entire run, becoming an on-screen regular. Originally it was intended that the show be entirely ad-libbed, but Steve decided that couldn't work and wrote the scripts to give the appearance of ad-libbing. They found their sea legs about the fourth or fifth show, when she became less of a Tallulah Bankhead or Elvira and more of a brat. So although she never had anything positive to say about anything, Barbara still gives the character a heart.

The Cookie Monster puppet was previously seen as a werewolf(!) during a showing of PRC's *The Mad Monster*, and stuck around to become a regular prop. They took to calling it "the Little Blue Guy." But, contrary to myth, nothing in the way of legal action ever happened. That was also the episode where they parodied Jack Pierce's Wolf Man makeup technique; they pretended to nail Bob Andrews' hand to a board, poured white glue over it, and then stuck globs of plastic Easter grass on his hand. On the show that featured *The Creeping Terror*, they came up with the Carpet Monster, which did resemble one of that film's terrors that creeped. On an episode where they were stuck for ideas right up until air-time, Millicent flung open the studio doors and did an impromptu live tour of the studio, which left the production room employees both flustered and amused.

The show ended because Barbara and Steve moved back east. That had always been their plan anyway; they never thought the show would last as long as it did. Interoffice politics had something to with that decision; one executive would tell them one thing, another would tell them to disregard what the first had said and only listen to him, and so on. It seems that the station wanted a more "conventional" horror-hosted show, and when they gave it to them, they were aghast. They also had a real penchant for skewering the station executives, who were *not* amused. This and other actions like the ones described above got them handed down the following edict:

> No more crew interaction.
> No more snarky dialogue.
> No more Bob's, Nathan's, studio visitors, pizza deliveries, or phone calls, fake or otherwise.
> No more puppets.
> No more references to anything outside of the movie.
> No more reading viewer letters on the air.
> No more run on graphics, crawls or animation.
> No more roaming around the studio on air.
> No more sound FX, visual FX, or any other FX.
> No more nothing that wasn't funny jokes or puns about the actual movie.
> The show would be Millicent B. Ghastly in a chair, talking about the movie, period. And if she doesn't care to offer that, somebody else is available and waiting for the opportunity.

If they'd added "No More Breathing," that pretty much would have covered everything. Needless to say, this decree from the station high sheriffs only strengthened their resolve to leave, which they did. Barbara and Steve are still married, and are both "touched and humbled" by the fact that people still remember Millicent after all these years.

Miss Misery

REAL NAME: Reyna Young (1983–)

BIRTHPLACE: San Francisco, California

HOST: *The Last Doorway* (2007–2009), Myspace; *Miss Misery's Movie Massacre* (2010–), KCTH Channel 27/AT&T U–Verse, Hayward, California

BIOGRAPHY: "The Queen of Horror in the Bay Area" started her acting career at age four; the next year, she began modeling children's clothes in malls. Since then, she has worn many other hats: producer, director, writer, film festival director and, of course, horror host. As a little girl, she saw the original *Halloween* and was instantly hooked on horror. Every year in San Francisco, she sponsors her own short horror film festival, "A Nightmare to Remember," with help from its co-sponsor and co-founder, her husband John Gillette. "Nightmare" features shorts no longer than 20 minutes, a raffle for the crowd and special guests. She also hosts a "Night of the Zombies," a "Zombie Prom" and the "Women in Horror" convention. She has self-published two books of poetry as well as a scrapbook relating the story of the making of her short horror films, and a how-to guide on getting started in independent filmmaking. She's the subject of her own comic book, *Miss Misery: A Haunting Desire* and hosts a separate anthology series called *Forgotten Tales*. She is in the process of creating an Internet comic series about a Gothic superhero called "Miss Massacre." She is not just an actress in the horror shorts she makes; she often directs, writes, does makeup, casting—everything, really. She's one busy woman, and she still took time to grant me an interview in 2015.

BC: *How did you come to be a horror host?*

MM: I wanted to reach out to indie filmmakers and give them another outlet to get their stuff out there. When I first started, I had a half-hour show called *The Last Doorway* where I went around to conventions and interviewed horror celebrities and indie filmmakers. I originally thought of the name Miss Misery because my favorite Elliot Smith song is "Miss Misery," that's where my name came from. After doing 70 episodes, I had the opportunity to host films. So I started *Miss Misery's Movie Massacre* where I host with my co-host, Mister Torture. We host horror films and do different segments in between like my favorite toys or a movie review. We are going on Season Five now. It's been great! We also now have a Roku channel through Timeless Television.

BC: *Can you tell us any more about* The Last Doorway?

MM: *The Last Doorway* first aired October 31, 2007. I put the show up on Myspace at the time because of my huge following there. I figured it would be better on there than on YouTube. It was a 30-minute show of interviewing celebrities and indie filmmakers, showing short films and talking about all things horror.

BC: *Do you like horror and science fiction?*

MM: Yes, I love to read anything that entertains me; I grew up with Edgar Allan Poe and Stephen King. Nowadays, I don't have too much time to sit back and enjoy a good book, but I do have my awesome collection!

BC: *When and where can the readers see your show?*

MM: It's about an hour and a half show that's on Chabot TV out of Hayward, California, on Channel KCTH 27 Saturday nights at 9 p.m. Also, again, we're on Roku. My first show, *The Last Doorway*, will be up on YouTube soon; I'll be putting up all my shows.

BC: *When did* Midnight Massacre *start?*

MM: We started the show, hmm, about four years ago and we're now on Season 5. It's been great; great feedback and awesome fans. I have a lot of fun filming the show. My cast and crew are amazing. I write the show and produce it with my husband John Gillette, who is also the other half of our film company, Last Doorway Productions.

BC: *What's your day job? Or are you a full-time actress?*

Reyna Young as Miss Misery (in a bath, not in misery), 2012.

MM: I do not have a regular job; I run my film company full-time. I do my show, and sell merchandise.

BC: *Was the character created by you?*

MM: Yes! I write the segments and choose the films. I like to have full control of my show. I'm weird like that!

BC: *Do you have any horror host role models?*

MM: I grew up watching Elvira, and then later on my father introduced me to *Creature Features*, which is what *he* grew up on. I then met Bob Wilkins and John Stanley at WonderCon in San Francisco. I have been good friends with John Stanley for years. I love him, he's amazing.

BC: *What are some of your fondest memories of the show?*

MM: Oh, I have so many amazing memories, but I think the best is when I brought on Ken Constantine as Mister Torture; he's my silent co-host. He's an awesome guy and has brought a lot to the show, and is so much fun to be around. I think bringing him into the show was a good move on our part. We have so much fun on this show. One time a bunch of us got together and shot a music video and I sang "Monster Mash." It took us three days to set up and one full day to film the video. So much fun!

BC: *Any particularly memorable personal* appearances?

MM: Every appearance is memorable. When I did the *Last Doorway* show, I had the opportunity of interviewing Weird Al Yankovich. It was exciting and nerve-wracking at the same time. I was actually nervous, and I got through it as cool as I could, but wow, it was an experience. He is so cool; it was definitely an amazing moment for me and my husband. I normally don't get nervous about doing interviews, I just do them—but it was truly an awesome moment for us.

BC: *Which do you prefer, TV or the Internet?*

MM: Well, I love both, but the Internet reaches a wider audience and goes out more, which allows me to have fans from Japan or Russia. I get fan mail from all over.

BC: *How long do you see yourself doing the show?*

MM: As long as my fans want me.... I love hosting and doing my thing, so I will continue to host as long as I can.

BC: *What's the state of horror hosting in the 21st century?*

MM: Well, I feel like the films that I show have been shown so many times from so many horror hosts, and I wonder if people get tired of watching them over and over, but no they don't, because they watch them to watch the host. They love and support us. I believe horror hosts will be around forever because we have amazing fans.

Other Genre Credits—FILMS: *Confession*, Last Doorway Productions, 2006 (director, etc.); *Sinner*, L.D.P. 2006 (director, etc.); *Confession 2*, L.D.P., 2007 (Victim, director, etc.); *Out of Print*, L.D.P., 2007 (Victim, director, etc.); *Confession 3*, L.D.P., 2007 (Victim, director, etc.); *Welcome to My Dark Side* (documentary), L.D.P., 2009 (director); *Miss Misery Christmas Special*, L.D.P., 2009 (Miss Misery, director, etc.); *Zombie Attack*, L.D.P., 2011 (director, etc.); *The End*, L.D.P., 2011 (director, etc.); *Little Miss Muffin*, L.D.P., 2012 (director, etc.); *Sally*, L.D.P., 2012 (Sally, director, etc.); *Under the Bed*, L.D.P., 2013 (director, etc.); *Monster of Golden Gate*, L.D.P., 2013 (Mary Anne, director, etc.); *Grindsploitation*, Body Bag Films, 2016 (director, two segments); *Forgotten Tales*, L.D.P., 2016 (Shannon Steels, director, etc.); *Doll Murder Spree*, L.D.P., 2016 (Mary Larson, director, etc.); *The 12 Slays of Christmas*, L.D.P., 2016 (director, etc.); *A Christmas to Dismember*, L.D.P., 2016 (director, etc.); *Interview*, L.D.P., 2016 (director, etc.).

Miss Shock

REAL NAME: Kathy Burns

HOST: *Shock Theater* (1959–1960) KENS-TV, Channel 5, San Antonio, Texas

BIOGRAPHY: It is said that behind every great gorilla is a woman. Well, that's not exactly what they say, but in this case, it happens to be very true. Director Joe (*The Howling*) Dante said in *Beast Wishes*—a first-rate documentary about Bob and Kathy Burns—that he doesn't know anyone who doesn't think the pair aren't wonderful, and I include myself in that number. Dante also said that when you think of one, you immediately think of the other, and indeed, Kathy has been instrumental in all facets of Bob's career. She has been married to Bob for 60 years; they got spliced in September, 1956. She met him when she was 14, and they tied the knot four years later. Kathy told the story of how they met in *Beast Wishes*: "I was one of those silly little girls who came home from school and put on their records and stood in front of the mirror and sang with them…. I wanted to be a musical comedy star. Bob took typing at summer school so he could graduate a half-year ahead of time; he sat behind me, and one day the teacher said, 'Throw the carriage,' and he threw the carriage—the carriage left the typewriter and went clear across the room!" Bob *says* that wasn't his intention, but he got the blame … and in the process, began the process of getting the girl. "I wrote him a little note; it said, 'Hey, you're funny.' He wrote and said, 'Turn around, leave me alone.' Then I wrote him back; I was persistent."

Bob had made his first amateur film effort, *The Alien*, and was showing it at a friend's house. As it turns out, Kathy knew a girl who knew the friend. After renewing acquaintances, they talked for a while, with the end result being Bob asked Kathy out on a date. "Our first date, we went to Bob's Big Boy and had a hamburger, and then went to what is now the El Capitan Theater—it was the Paramount Theater then—and Bob made a big fool of himself…" Bob had taken her to see her first 3-D film, *The Charge at Feather River*. "Towards the end of the movie, there's a big Indian raid, and they throw spears and arrows and all this, and the 3-D really comes at you, and you're ducking all the arrows… All of a sudden, he reared back in the seat with an arrow stuck in his chest, and the woman [behind them] just about had cardiac arrest! Everybody else was throwing off their glasses and screaming…" Bob, who had started a panic, discreetly hid the arrow in the shirt sleeve that it had originally been in; Kathy suggested it was time for them to leave. "So we left and got to the lobby, and the police were coming in…. Bob said, 'What happened?' And they said, 'Somebody got shot with an arrow, and everybody saw it happen, but we can't find him.' To which Bob replied, 'Gee, I really hope you find him…' I love people with imagination, I love spirit, and I love people taking risks and taking chances, trying something new, because that's the adventure of life. [Bob] had the adventure of life in his soul."

Chris Walas (makeup artist on *Gremlins* and *The Fly*) vouchsafed, "I think Kathy, even more than Bob, not only appreciates what the fans love; she appreciates the fans themselves. We go to conventions, and her eyes are on the people—the excitement in their eyes; you know, Bob and I will be there going 'Wow, that's the best Creature kit I ever saw in my life,' and Kathy will be over there going, 'Psst ... guys ... that little boy over there ... that's what you guys look like right now!' I mean, she really connects with that elemental, emotional fan experience." Tom Woodruff, Jr., and Alec Gillis (Amalgamated Dynamics Inc.) concur; Woodruff says that he "probably knew of Kathy before I knew of Bob; my favorite *Famous Monsters* magazine had a picture of William Castle and Miss Shock, and I remember as a kid looking at that creepy makeup, that big eye, and it turns out that's Kathy Burns! Kathy Burns is Miss Shock!" In *Monsterscene* magazine #5, Bob explained how it all came about:

> In 1959, I was in the Army in San Antonio, Texas. They had a local show up at KENS, the CBS affiliate up there, called *Shock Theater*. It was the time when they all had *Shock Theater*s. They had a host on it (simply called "The Host") named Joe Alston, a good guy. He looked a little like Orson Welles. He really did. He could sound like him, too. He was actually the announcer for the station. It was one of those things where everybody doubles for something else; in those days they just did that. I kept looking at the show, and it was just kind of boring ... nothing happened. And I thought, "God, we could do something for that." The Army was driving me nuts. I hated the Army.
>
> I called Joe [Alston] and said, "Hey, we'll be glad to do some monsters for your show if you'll just pay for the cost of what it takes to make them." They said, "Come on down and talk." So we went down and talked about it. They said, "Hey, okay, great, give it a shot." That's when we started doing it, started building monsters for the show so it would tie in with the movie a little bit. I did a werewolf thing for *The Mad Monster* and [made up] Kathy as the Bride of Frankenstein one time. It went over real well, and the ratings started climbing. So, Bill Castle was coming into [San Antonio] to promote *The Tingler*. The manager of the theater called *Shock Theater* to see if somehow we could go out and meet him at the airport for fun, and escort him back into town. So I was trying to come up with something, and I thought, "Jeez, I know ... he has to meet some dignitary. It has to *be* somebody." And then it just hit me. It has to be Miss Shock. That'll work. So I did this makeup for Kathy, and made this real nice banner saying *Miss Shock* and all this stuff. That's all we were supposed to do, meet him and split. And he said, "No, no, no, no ... you guys come back to the hotel with me, I want to get pictures." At least one of them appeared in *Famous Monsters* #66 of us presenting the (skeleton) key (to the city) to him. Bill Castle was a really neat guy.

Bob elaborated on Kathy's misadventure as the Bride in *Scary Monsters* #43:

> The week they showed *Bride of Frankenstein* was the week Kathy and I learned that the KENS art director was real jealous of us. A young, rather effeminate guy, *he* used to do all the work on *Shock Theater* until we came on the scene... He still designed the new sets and things like that, but he'd been eased out of his other responsibilities and was *not* happy about it. The week of *Bride of Frankenstein*, he got a bug up him for some reason, and he went to the station manager and said, "I want to do the wig for the Bride." Kathy had real long hair at the time, and our original plan was that she was going to tease it up and spray it real good so that it would stand up. But this art director *demanded* that he be allowed to make the wig; he made a big deal out of it, claiming that he knew a way of doing the wig that would be just perfect.
>
> Kathy made a great Bride outfit, and I did the makeup on her—it worked out so well, she actually looked a little like Elsa Lanchester. Kathy's a ham, and loves being in makeup as much as I do. And the art director, just as we were getting ready to tape the show, brought the wig in. He'd made the thing out of steel wool ... it looked awful. Here was Kathy—the makeup looked great, the costume looked great, and this hair was the crappiest thing you ever saw. There was nothing more we could do; it was time to tape the show, and so we had to use it. The skit went well, but the Bride wig was pitiful. And to make it worse, for the next day or two, Kathy was digging pieces of metal out of her back. The whole time she wore the wig, little bits of steel wool were flaking off and getting down her neck, and it really irritated her back. That art director was a real jerk. But at least we didn't have to worry about him again after that, because everybody including the director told him the wig was a pile of crap, he never again asked to do anything except the sets.

Bob and Kathy have one of the largest, if not the largest, collection of monster movie props in the world, artfully displayed and impeccably preserved. Whatever happened to the original costumes from, say, the Republic serials of *Captain America* and *Adventures of Captain Marvel*? They reside at Bob and Kathy's house. So does the Kong armature from the original (and still the greatest) *King Kong*, which led to Kathy and Bob getting cameo roles in Peter Jackson's badly cast (except for them) remake. What about the original model of the submarine *Nautilus* from *20,000 Leagues Under the Sea*? Yeah, they've got that, too. They've got the werewolf from *An American Werewolf in London*, and we'll let Kathy take it from there:

> When we got the *American Werewolf in London* wolf, which is quite large—it's about six feet long and stands about five feet tall—Bob put it at the end of the stairway coming down from our upstairs, and every time I came downstairs, it scared me. And I couldn't understand why it scared me so badly. But then I remembered that it was triggering a childhood memory I had; my mother played the classical music from "Peter and the Wolf," and every time the "Wolf" music came on, in my mind, that's the wolf I saw ... and when I first saw that werewolf, that was the wolf, and I finally had him move it to the back of the museum because I couldn't stand looking at that wolf all the time.

Of all the props in their museum, Kathy's favorite is the Time Machine from George Pal's 1960 film version of the H.G. Wells tale:

> It's Victorian, it's a jewel, and we had the hardest time getting that. MGM was auctioning off all their props. We had saved $1000, and that's all we had—boy, we thought we were rich—and we went to the auction with our $1000, and I said, "We've got to get that machine," and it went 1000, 2000, 3000, 5000, 12,000, it went up so fast, and we were so discouraged, we just left with our heads down. And that was it; we thought we'd never see it again. Well, the guy who bought it went broke, and so he sold it to a thrift shop in Orange County, and a friend of ours, Tom Sherman, just by happenstance went into that thrift shop and saw the 'Disc' in the back room, and he knew what it was. He called Bob and he said, "Get a truck—don't ask questions, just get a truck." So we got a truck and went down there; we didn't know what was going on, and we offered the guy the $1000. We had to completely refurbish it ... so a whole bunch of us restored the machine, and we had our Time Machine back.

Kathy and Bob don't do it simply to accumulate "stuff," nor do they sell the items. They have a very sincere and honest love of the genre and an intense interest not only in preserving its legacy, but sharing it. They used some props (and built some new ones) for the internationally famous Halloween shows which took place at their house. Every year had its own theme, determined, Kathy says, by asking one of their friends what their favorite horror movie was. The shows were incredibly popular and the sets and effects incredibly detailed, on par with (and surpassing a few) movie sets. It wasn't surprising, given the number of professional contributors like Rick Baker, John Landis, William Stout, Bill Malone, Joe Dante, Dana Gould, Greg Nicotero (FX, *The Walking Dead*), Dennis Muren (visual FX, *The Empire Strikes Back*; *Jurassic Park*), Pat McClung (visual FX, *Aliens* and *Die Hard*) and Steve Wang (creature FX, *Predator* and *Monster Squad*), who gave freely of their time and money to make the best show they were capable of for Bob and Kathy. The first really elaborate effort was covered on local TV; Bob, Kathy and others made it look as though a 1950s-style rocketship had crashed into the side of their house. Other shows have been based on *This Island Earth*, *The Thing from Another World*, *The Exorcist* (Kathy played the Linda Blair part), *Forbidden Planet*, *Creature from the Black Lagoon* and of course, *The Time Machine*.

Then there's the gorilla in the room ... literally. Bob has done a lot of work in

A rare candid photo taken by Paul Riggie at the 2006 Monster Bash, where, to the amazement and delight of the fans, Kathy Burns reprised the role of Miss Shock (courtesy Paul Riggie).

movies and television in a gorilla suit, most notably as Tracy in the original *Ghostbusters* television series. "[Don] Post made the hands and chest and feet and head," Kathy recalls, "and I made the suit." The ape was originally known and billed as "Kogar," but then Bob decided that he didn't want a menacing head, so Rick Baker built the head that became Tracy in 1974.

Dennis Muren opined, "If there had not been a Bob and Kathy, how many of us might have disappeared into the world of regular workdays and not stayed in the movie business? I could guess that Bob and Kathy Burns will be remembered for being themselves when there was nothing else like them. There was nobody else like Bob and Kathy, and there still isn't."

"I just wish the world was filled with Bob and Kathys; there'd be peace on Earth ... though you probably wouldn't be able to walk anywhere because there'd be so much stuff," laughs Rick Baker. Bill Malone, who found the original Robby the Robot from *Forbidden Planet* in front of a junk store holding cigars and restored him to his original glory, said, "I love Kathy because she's really into photography, and she always has these wonderful pictures, and I've gotten very envious of some of the stuff she's shot." But we are all admirers from afar; Bob has had a lifetime to love her: "It's hard to put into words what she means to me."

Bob and Kathy don't get out that much these days; both have suffered (and are still suffering) various health problems, but remain as active on the Internet as they can.

They know they have the love and respect of thousands throughout the world, and, as the Wizard said, "It's not how much you love; it's how much you are loved in return."

Other Genre Credits—FILMS: *Rocketship X-M*, Lippert Pictures, 1950 (production assistant and costume coordinator on the revised 1979 version); *King Kong*, Universal, 2005 (New Yorker); *The Lovely Bones*, Dream Works SKG, 2009 (Mall Shopper); DOCUMENTARIES: *Time Machine—The Journey Back*, 1993 (executive producer, Time Machine restoration crew); *Halloween—The Happy Haunting of America*, 1997 (still photographer); *Spine Tingler—The William Castle Story*, 2007 (Herself); *Bob Burns' Hollywood Halloween*, 2009 (Herself, writer); *Beast Wishes: The Fantastic World of Bob and Kathy Burns*, 2012 (Herself)

Misty Brew (1)

REAL NAME: Faye Fisher Ward (1961–)

HOST: *Creature Feature* (October 1982—September 1983), WRLE, Channel 26, Green Bay, Wisconsin

BIOGRAPHY: The information in this entry comes from a career-spanning interview with Misty conducted by the late, great Dick "Nitelinger" Golembiewski (R.I.P.) for the *Scary Monsters 2005 Monster Memories Yearbook* (reprinted with permission).

> After "Alexander" (of *Eerie Street with Alexander*) left the air in 1973, Green Bay was left without a horror host. That changed in 1977, when WLUK-TV began running *TJ and the Ant*. That show went off the air in early 1982. Later that year, a senior at the University of Wisconsin (Green Bay) answered a casting call put out by a new, independent UHF station, WRLE (Channel 26; now WGBA). Faye Fisher transformed herself into "Misty Brew," and "Titletown" had a new horror hostess Friday nights at Midnight! The first show ran on October 29th, 1982, and the last on September 9th, 1983. At first the show was run as a single feature, but later it ran as a double (and sometimes triple) feature. As such, it often started at 10:30 p.m. In June of 2004, Faye spoke with *Scary Monsters*:

SM: What was your background prior to hosting Creature Feature?

FF: I grew up in Eau Claire, Wisconsin, but went to school at the University of Wisconsin (Green Bay). I was a Visual Arts major in college. I had minimal acting experience, although I sang in the occasional high school or college musical production. I'm a singer-songwriter.

SM: So, how did you come to host horror films?

FF: My boyfriend David Ward, who is now my husband, was a theater major, so I hung out with all the theater people. At UW-GB, there was a place called the Alternative Theater Space, which was where students could do experimental productions. Just outside of it was a bulletin board, and WRLE had a notice for an audition posted on it. I had just come back after spending a year in Boston. Everyone kept telling me, "Oh, Faye, you'd be perfect for this," or "Faye, you have to do this!" When I asked them why, they'd say, "You've got the look!" So I said, "What the heck," and I went in and auditioned. The audition was on-camera, in the station manager's office, with a couple of crew people. I just ad libbed. They told me to tell a funny, spooky joke, so I made up a stupid "Two ghosts walk into a bar" joke on the spot. What I found was that they were really interested in how I looked on-camera. It was all about my facial expressions, poise, body language, and whether I could handle awkward moments. It lasted ten or fifteen minutes. A week later they called and wanted to hire me! The station manager had been out in Los Angeles, and had seen *Elvira's Movie Macabre*, back before her show was syndicated. That's where they got the idea of using a female to host the show.

SM: So, how did you come up with the character's name?

FF: The station manager was the one who came up with it. I wanted to be called "Natasha," or something exotic, but he said, "What do you think of this idea? You know how cauldrons are a brew, and how it's misty? What do you think about Misty Brew?" I rolled my eyes and said, "Well, you're the boss; OK!"

SM: How did you come up with the character?

FF: I never really set out to develop a character. I had to operate under some interesting conditions. The station manager was *very* religious, and as such, I wasn't allowed to wear anything too sexy. My arms had to be covered, and I had to wear long, high-necked gowns that covered my legs. Ironically, when they called to offer me the job, they had the publicist, a woman—who was my main liaison—ask if I would do something. She said, "Faye, I'm a little uncomfortable asking you this, but the station manager asked if you could 'stuff' and pad yourself up!" I said, "No; what you see is what you get here. I'm not going to do some stupid, cheesy Elvira thing." I didn't want it that badly. David told me that it looked kind of cool when I popped my eyeballs up really big; it became my trademark. I could do the scary "eyeball thing." I got my costumes from Glad Rags, which was a vintage shop. They had some beautiful stuff, like velvet gowns from the '20s and '30s. I'd go in every week and pick out what I was going to wear for each show. A trendy salon called Bananas did my hair. They did it up really big and put glitter in it. They also did my makeup. It was regular street makeup. They made my eyes dark. I had "cat eyes," and long, dark and defined eyebrows. I used red lipstick, and rouge on the cheekbones. They just highlighted what I already had. Once I saw myself, it helped me get into character. Here I was dressed exquisitely, with the makeup. There was a sexual edge to my character, but it wasn't overt. A lot of people said that it was classy, or...

SM: Sophisticated?

FF: I guess! I was just this classy, sophisticated and spooky person. There was no conscious attempt to develop a character. I had this dry sense of humor. I wasn't over the top like Elvira. A lot was tongue in cheek, and I put a fake spooky edge on it. Still they'd say to me, "Can you kind of put a little sex into it?" I'd tell them, "I'm wrapped up like a mummy, and you want me to be sexy?!" It was a challenge. The only way I could be sexy, spooky and alluring was through my facial expressions and body language. I was never lewd. I had young kids watching the show, so I never crossed that line.

SM: What did you use for a set?

FF: Initially, we didn't have a studio to tape the show in, so we did the first shows in the Riverside Ballroom. It's this really old ballroom in Green Bay. They had red velvet curtains on the stage. They also had this big old chair. It was freezing inside! We did the first four or so shows there, and I used to have a couple shots of whiskey to keep me warm. The crew was dressed in parkas. Just before we taped the first show, they asked me how I felt about using a coffin as a prop. I asked them what they meant, and they said, "Well, how do you feel about lying in the coffin and then coming out of it?" I said, "I see! You've already purchased it, and *now* you're asking me how I feel about lying in it!" I told them I was a little miffed, but I was 21 years old and pretty flexible, so I told them that I would do it.

SM: So, you started the show in a coffin?

FF: Yes, it started with me lying in it. I would open the top half of the lid, and sit up. Then I'd say, "Welcome to *Creature Feature*, our offerings tonight are..." That was it. The set was the coffin, a chair and, at the Riverside Ballroom, the red velvet curtain background. I'll never forget watching my first show. David and I made a reservation at a local motel for my parents, who were coming from Eau Claire for that night, so we could all watch it. Believe it or not, I didn't own a TV, so I never got to see my own show until December, when my dad bought me a 12-inch black-and-white set. Anyway, that morning, they called to tell me my sister Linda was in labor—she lived in Eau Claire, too—and being this was their first grandchild, they were going to stay 'til he was born. He finally came into the world at 6:30 p.m. Apparently they left to drive to Green Bay right after the birth. At that time, it was a three-and-a-half- to four-hour drive, and David and I didn't know when they were going to arrive, so we waited in the hotel lobby, where there was a TV—in case they got there after midnight. They walked into the lobby door, just as the show was starting. That had to be a very weird day for them, watching their first grandchild being born and then driving across the state in the middle of the night, arriving in a hotel lobby just in time to see their oldest daughter appear on TV as a spooky vamp in a coffin!

SM: Was the show scripted?

FF: Yes; the gal who served as the publicist also fancied herself as a writer, so she would write a script. She would have trivia tidbits about making the movie, the actor featured, or whatever. For the early shows, I would show up and be handed the script. I had to memorize it on the spot, because we didn't have a teleprompter until after we began taping in a studio. Later on, David and I wrote the scripts.

SM: Did you have a sidekick?

FF: We were two or three shows into our run, and they decided to use one of the cameramen. His name was Jim, and he played the organ at weddings and funerals. We would open the show with him playing spooky music and me in the coffin. We called him "Klystron." The reason was because at the transmitter site, the station had something called a klystron. [A klystron is a vacuum tube used to generate and amplify ultra-high frequencies.] It cost $600,000 to replace, and they blew one shortly after the show started. He didn't wear a costume, just a suit jacket. He never talked. He would just grunt! I would ask him, "Klystron, what was that number you just played?" He would grunt back, and I would say, "Oh, I just loved that!"

SM: Did you do any live appearances?

FF: I have a lot of favorite episodes. One of them involved my first live remote at a record store called Pipe Dreams. They were premiering an album by a group called The Bees. I don't know where they were from, but that night we were showing the film *The Bees*. Glad Rags altered a black velvet dress for me. It was gorgeous. They put huge raven feathers on it. I had this giant collar behind me made from them, and I wore rhinestone jewelry. They had a little stage set up for me in the store, with my coffin on it. There was a band in Green Bay at the time called John Doe and the Doo Dads. Two of their members owned the store. They were two brothers, and were goofy guys! They came dressed as bees. It was pretty tacky, but silly, fun. The store was filled with people who had come to see the live remote broadcast. I had no script, no teleprompter, nothing. It was the hardest thing I've ever done. I had to ad lib and come up with something to fill three-minute segments when we came back from the movie. I didn't know what was coming next, with a crowd of people standing in front of me, and we were *live*! So I invited kids to come up on stage. I had a lot of kids who were fans. I remember one little boy I invited on stage. His friends must have dared him to jump up and give me a kiss. It was so cute! A lot of people came in costume. At the end of the show, as I was saying goodbye, these two guys came in dressed up like Conan the Barbarian and his sidekick. It totally threw me off! I was standing on the floor with the camera six feet in front of me. The stage manager was giving me the signal to wrap things up because we were coming close to the end. Then he pointed to my right side, and I saw the two guys who were standing behind me and to the right. I was floored! David was kind of giving them the jealous eye [*laughs*]! In between segments, while the movie was playing, I would sit between my two bodyguards and sign autographs on 8 × 10s the station had made up for promotional purposes.

SM: It sounds like you had a lot of fans!
FF: I later found out that I had three fan clubs. One was at St. Norbert's College in Green Bay, the second was at Lawrence University in Appleton, and the third was at the penitentiary! I heard from a friend who knew someone who was a guard there that Friday nights the place would shut down, and about a thousand inmates sat in a room with a huge screen and watched the show!

SM: I guess it kept them in line!
FF: It was kind of creepy, because I would get letters from them. Some of the guys sent letters with sexual intent. One guy wrote to tell me about the perfect evening he would spend with me. This same guy wrote me every week. The station was afraid to show me most of the mail, because they thought that I'd get too flipped out. When I first moved back to town, I got an apartment, and was listed in the phone book. This was a month before I was offered the job of hosting the show. People would find out my real name, make crank calls and hang up. That's why I needed the bodyguards at the live appearances.

SM: Some people just can't differentiate between the character and the person portraying it.
FF: That's what I found out. People thought that I was like Misty, but I am so far from what she was. To me it was just an acting job that I did to pick up some money while I was in school.

SM: Were you asked by the station to do anything else?
FF: I remember that they wanted me to go to a University of Wisconsin (Green Bay) basketball game. They wanted to run a "Win a Date with Misty Brew" contest. They never asked me what I thought about those ideas ahead of time. They would just tell me what we were doing. Frankly, they didn't pay me enough for that! I got paid $50 a taping session. We would tape two shows and it took three, four hours to do that. After I graduated in May of 1983, I was working in Door County, north of Green Bay, and I would still drive back to tape four shows. I finally told them I wanted more money.

SM: What were some of your memorable episodes?

FF: Well, there was the time I got locked in the coffin. You know they don't make them to get out of! It was at the Riverside Ballroom. At the end of the show, I would be sitting in the coffin, talk about the following week's film, and then say, "Good night! Don't let the vampires bite!" I'd then close the lid. I'd have to prop it open with my finger so that it wouldn't click shut. I had a microphone on me, so I couldn't speak until after the director said "Cut!" This one time, I had an itch, so I scratched it—using the fingers that were propping open the lid. I heard it click. Klystron was still playing the organ, so I couldn't say a word. After the director called cut, I heard the crew laughing at me. I said, "This isn't funny, you guys; I have claustrophobia." They continued to tease me by saying things like, "Okay, let's pack up and go!" They left me inside for a few minutes. Another I remember was after we had moved into the studio and were playing around with the station's blue screen. We showed *The Man Who Reclaimed His Head*. Jim, who was Klystron, was just this head on a plate. I'd talk to him, and he would sing "I Ain't Got No Body." We used it again when we showed *Attack of the 50 Foot Woman*. I was gigantic, and Jim was about three inches tall. Jim had a crush on the 50 Foot Woman, and wanted to date her, so I told him to get about 50 roast chickens and a truckload of corn on the cob, and then call her back and ask her if she wanted to have dinner! We would do stuff where it looked like I was floating on the air. We did all kinds of silly stuff.

...Back when we were at the Riverside Ballroom, a friend of mine was taking a Film and Television class at the university. Dale Kuipers was the guest speaker, and my friend asked if I wanted to come along. Dale was one of the prosthetics people who did the wolf heads for *The Howling*. He was working in this little airless place in Hollywood and had inhaled so many chemicals that he came down with hepatitis. He was a Green Bay native, and because of his health he had moved back to town. Well, in class, Dale was wearing one of our *Misty Brew Creature Feature* t-shirts. He was a fan of the show. He had everyone come up and have a look at some of his prosthetics. So I went up with my girlfriend. I had no makeup on, and I had my hair back in a bandana. He was holding up a little monkey prosthetic. He was going to try it on someone. He went around the room, stopped at me and said, "You look awfully familiar." That's when my friend said, "She's Misty Brew!" My friends were awful! They were telling everyone who I was, but I didn't want anyone to know. He said, "I have been trying to do something for your show. I have been calling the station. I'll do it for free! I want to bring my prosthetics to make characters for guests on your show, if you're willing to do it." I was like, "Holy crap! This guy's a professional who works in Hollywood, and he wants to do *my* show—for free!" He was incredibly talented. We wound up becoming friends. I went to his studio, which was above one of the old theaters. He had a life-sized E.T., which was used by some orchestra out east when they did the music from the film, and all of these other incredible things. He wanted to work on *my show*—for free—because he dug the show! I had to talk the station into letting him come down and do an episode. He had a friend of his wear this monkey-like facial prosthetic, with long hair, and hairy hands with claws. It was *very* realistic. Misty sat down and had dinner with him during the midbreaks. David came on with mummified cadaver makeup, and served us dinner and drinks in this sort of classy setting. It was so cool! The station thought that he was going to try to worm his way in and eventually get paid, so they didn't want to let him.

I thought to myself that if this guy wanted to come and work with me, this could be a *really* classy horror show. Unfortunately, the station wasn't interested. It's a shame, as he was really talented; a true artist. He loved his craft. He already made his money by working for Hollywood studios, so he was doing this as a way to practice his art. I'm sorry to say I've lost track of him, and don't know if he's still with us. He was very sick back then. [The multi-talented Dale Kuipers—also spelled Kuippers—passed away on July 17, 1996, in Green Bay.]

SM: *I understand you were married in one of your costumes.*

FF: When we showed *Bride of Frankenstein*, I wore a beautiful, white satin vintage dress from the 1940s. I loved it *so* much! Glad Rags let me buy it for a reasonable price, and even included a hand-made French bridal cap that happened to match it. When David and I moved to Chicago, I had a bridal veil and blusher attached. David and I were married in 1984, and I wore that dress. David, an actor, had once played the Monster in the Peninsula Players production of *Frankenstein*—which later went to Broadway and bombed; I literally became "The Bride of Frankenstein"—a joke that was not lost on our friends. We were even married four days before Halloween!

SM: *Did you have a large audience?*

FF: I had a very large and broad audience. The station once told me that 100,000 people in northeastern Wisconsin watched the show every week! I had everyone from small children to adults. I remember one time I was riding the bus on my way to school. This one man sitting in front of me kept turning around and looking at me. Again, I didn't have any makeup on or anything. I said, "Oh, no, here we go again." He finally said to me, "I'm sorry I keep looking at you, but you look so much like that woman who does the show on Channel 26." I said, "You know, a lot of people tell me that." He then said, "I'm sorry. I'm actually on my way to the eye doctor to get new glasses, so I'm probably not seeing very well." I said to myself, "Oh no! I should have told him yes! You poor guy, you have good eyesight!" [*Laughs*]

SM: *Were you recognized a lot?*

FF: One night during the spring, I had gotten decked out for a night at a local tavern with some friends. I was walking there—it was about a mile away—when I was stopped by a teenage girl. She had just parked her car near an apartment building, and was going in to visit some friends. She walked past me, did a double-take, stopped, turned around and asked, "Are you Misty Brew?" I was a bit tired of unwanted recognition by that time, so I quipped, "Good guess," and kept on walking. She ran after me, stopping right in front, blocking my progress. She said that she couldn't believe it was me, and she asked if she could have my autograph. I told her I was in a hurry to meet some friends, and she offered to drive me. I accepted. In the car, she found a scrap of paper in the glove compartment, and again asked me for an autograph, which I gave her. On the way to the tavern, she kept saying, "Oh my God! Oh my God! Misty Brew is in my car! My friends are never going to believe this!" That's what happens when you're in a small town! You really begin to appreciate anonymity.

SM: *Why did you leave the show?*

FF: David and I were done working up in Door County—we worked up there through the fall of 1983—and we wanted to move to Chicago. The money wasn't enough. The station was talking about possible syndication, but nothing ever happened. It wasn't something I wanted to make a career out of. I still don't understand why that high school student was so excited over meeting someone who dressed in vintage clothing every couple of weeks to fill the gaps between commercials on a little UHF station. Why would anyone think that getting my autograph was a big deal? I was just some local college student who got a break, and hosted a cheesy horror show. It still amazes me.

SM: And that's the story of Misty Brew. A couple of other horror hostesses [the first in Missouri, the second in Alabama] used the same name some years later, but Faye Fisher was likely the first. She is still an artist, singer-songwriter and costume designer. Writer Paul McComas grew up in Milwaukee watching *Nightmare Theater* with Dr. Cadaverino on WITI and *Shock Theater* on WVTV. In the early '80s he was a student at Lawrence University in Appleton, Wisconsin, and watched *Creature Feature*. He was so inspired by Faye's characterization that he based the character of Kayla Drake's alter-ego, horror hostess Ivana Viktimm, on Misty Brew in his novel *Unplugged*."

Misty Brew (2)

REAL NAME: Anonymous

HOST: *Misty Brew's Creature Feature* (1985–1990), KBSI, Channel 23, Cape Girardeau, Missouri (2014–present), YouTube: KreepyKastle Channels

BIOGRAPHY: According to the info on E-Gor's website, the second Misty Brew hosted a shock show called *Friday Night Frights* "circa 1986–1989 or 1990." Initially I suspected that they were the same woman because they resembled each other, down to the almost exactly the same attire. But phone calls to the stations, etc., unearthed the results; they were indeed two different women; this version of Misty Brew is not only still going strong, via that ol' devil Internet, but was recently voted into the Horror Host Hall of Fame. But Misty's re-vamped website had that the show was called *Creature Features* and started in 1983. Wikipedia had the same info, although that was obviously taken mostly from Misty's website, and one has to take what one finds on Wikipedia with a grain of salt. So I simply wrote to the website (duh!) and received responses from Misty *and* her "Renfield," Timexx Seabaugh.

On E-Gor's website, David Windhorst provided this tidbit:

> I got in touch with Eric Dahl, sales manager at KBSI ... to find out more about Misty Brew. Though not willing to give me her real name—maybe she was stalked or something—he did offer this info: "It always aired late-night on the weekends so as not to offend any viewers. We had a lot of fun with it. We had to stay late to do the shoots, so all of the crew ended up getting in on the act. Our producer played a killer bee once, one of the production guys played Frankenstein, and I played a robber one night. The gal that hosted "Misty Brew" was really funny. Some of the outtakes were even funnier than some of the stuff we put on the air. We had a lot of fun poking fun at the movies and current events.... We didn't have a teleprompter, so we had to write out the scripts on cue cards and roll them underneath the cameras."

The following interviews were done for this book, this one with Timexx:

TS: I'm a singer, songwriter and stage performer; a time traveler and a wannabe cult leader or sideshow bally. I've done some acting and I'm a current producer for several Kreepy Kastle shows.

BC: *Did you watch* Creature Features *as a kid?*

TS: I was an avid watcher of *Creature Features* and a huge fan of Misty Brew. This was of course during the '80s when we only had three TV stations to watch. KBSI was a new local station that originally aired classic reruns, much like MeTV does today. On weekends, KBSI would show old movies, and on Friday nights it was *Misty Brew's Creature Feature.* This was really my first exposure to horror films. I had seen Baron Von Crypt in St. Louis and Svengoolie when I visited family in Chicago. They primarily showed old Hollywood monsters and B-movies from the '50s and '60s. It was Misty Brew that caught my heart. Her campy, funny style and her infectious laughter is what I liked. I had not yet learned of Elvira as her show was not aired in Missouri at the time. (She was considered too sexual for conservative Midwest viewers of the time.) On Friday nights you could count on me to be home in my room in front of an old bunny ear TV watching Misty Brew and *Creature Feature.* Later in the '80s, KBSI became a Fox affiliate station. And because of that, Misty was now showing current movies. My first time seeing classics like *Halloween 1, 2 & 3, Friday the 13th, My Bloody Valentine, Fright Night, Night Creatures* and *Ghoulies* were all aired uncut on Misty's show. I was also able to see Hitchcock films like *The Birds, Frenzy* and *Psycho* for the first time from my little bedroom TV. Like the scene in *American Graffiti,* I once made a late night walk across Cape to try and meet her at the KBSI studios. And just like in the movie, I was sad to find out her shows were pre-taped, and only the security guys were there at night.

BC: *You're pretty much responsible for Misty's second life on YouTube and Kreepy Kastle. Describe how that all came about.*

TS: It was a labor of love right from the start. One late night while listening to *Coast to Coast AM,* Mr. Lobo was the guest; they were discussing horror hosts and a book. I called in and asked why Misty Brew was not mentioned. He says that it was really from lack of information. He was aware of her and even owned a VHS of her show. However, outside of that, he was not able to get much information. He said he has even inquired with KBSI and was given very little information. At that point. I say that I am friends with several of the show's crew members, and that I would gather all that I can, and promised to post as much as I could online. Mr. Lobo encourages me to do so and ends by saying he would love to see it.

So the next morning I begin my search for Misty. After calling a few friends and making some inquiries, I found that I had known her for years. But I had been unaware that she was in fact Misty. Soon a meeting with her, and Bryan Uptain [one of the original *Creature Feature* writers and cameramen) was set up. It was in that meeting that a plan was hatched to bring Misty Brew back from the dead.

Websites were created, and new footage was filmed. We instantly started to receive love and support from the Horror Host Community. Who were all so happy to welcome Misty's return. Gar the Ghoul and Horror Daves were the first to acknowledge her awakening. Fendred's Domain of Horror made Misty a cool new logo. So after I came across KreepyKastle and its free 24–7 horror-hosted movies, I was shocked to learn how many other horror hosts there were around the country. Dale Kay and Halloween Jack were more than accommodating when approached about adding Misty Brew to their programming. Soon after, *Horrorhound* and the Horror Host Hall of Fame came calling. Misty Brew was inducted to the Hall of Fame in early 2015. After that, Mr. Maniacal stepped up and built a official MistyBrew.com website.

The fan support for Misty Brew was quite frankly overwhelming for us all. It was as if hundreds of people had been just waiting to find her. Old fans who, like me, remembered seeing her original TV shows, and even new fans who had just discovered her. People started sending her messages right away. They were watching the episodes on YouTube and Kreepy Kastle soon as we posted them. It was the fans and viewers that really brought her back to life. And they are the ones that keep her alive. As she always says, "Misty Brew Loves You."

BC: *What is your job with the actual show? Producer? Director?*

TS: Mostly I am a fan of *Misty Brew's Creature Feature* and horror hosts in general. For Misty, I'm an organizer and kind of personal agent. I'm basically her Renfield. I get things taken care of for her as needed.

And now, play Misty Brew for me:

BC: *How did you come to be a horror host?*

MB: I became a horror hostess ... hmmm, well ... [through] my love of TV and scary movies first off, then.... I was in and around the central U.S. in the mid–80s, flying around on my Varoom Stick, doin' a few aero-bat-tics, and I noticed a job opening at

Misty Brew, strong as ever in this shot from 2015.

Misty Brew (2)

the local Fox station for a horror hostess. So I decided to fly in and apply. They hired me on the spot! I made great fiends there,. I was happier than a vampire in a blood bank!

BC: *Do you like horror and science fiction movies?*
MB: Yes! Misty Brew loves Horror and Sci-Fi.... I don't like the really gory slasher ones, though. When I watch those, I feel like the monster that ate uranium—I get atomic ache! Some of my favorites are (old original ones) *Dracula, Frankenstein, Night of the Living Dead, The Fly,* the *Night Gallery* series, the *Twilight Zone* series ... really all the vampire movies, new and old. I really, really enjoy them all!

BC: *What other acting work have you done?*
MB: Well, I have done some television commercials, even one for Pabst Blue Ribbon ... after all; my name is Brew. Misty Brew's idea of a balanced diet is a PBR in each hand (or a Bloody Mary). I have done a few music videos as well. I have always wanted to do my own movie....

BC: *Was the character created by you?*
MB: Well, Misty Brew has always been, well, me, Misty Brew! I do my own makeup and hair, had some help with wardrobe and costumes, but if my producer would have had his way, I would have been in a black bikini—or less! ... Anyway ... some of my ghoul fiends stepped in and created a fun look.... I was really just being myself!!

BC: *What are some of your fondest memories of the studio show?*
MB: I have so many! I made a lot of new friends and met some really talented people: Paul, Chuck, Brian, Eric, Scott and Chris. Those guys are still working in the business. I also still keep in touch with them, and Brian is still contributing and supporting me with the projects presently such as the new Internet shows and appearances. I remember when someone brought in a real pig's head to the studio; it hung on my wall forever! And since they kept it cool in there, it just seemed to stay alive and fresh! After every show taping, I would throw a blanket on the floor next to him and have a pig-nic right in the studio. So after eating, we would sing some tunes ... "I Wanna Hold Your Ham" was one of his favorites! I really enjoyed the different themes we had for the shows; holidays (we'd do fun art and seasonal skits), guests like Frankie, Invisible Man, Freddy, local guests and Misty's Big Book with fan mail (I still have the letters and art sent to me). I remember how fun it was to walk out and introduce the shows from a standing coffin ... walked right out of it at the start and, at the end, I said, "Good night, human creatures, Misty Brew loves you," winked, blew a kiss, and back in the coffin I went, LOL! I loved my couch, too.... Frankie and I would dance ... fun! Also, disappearing in and out was fun! I also remember we used a large motorcycle in one skit, and carved pumpkins on others. We also showed clips from personal appearances such as monster truck fests, Halloween contests and several events.

The Fox station quit airing movies on Friday and Saturday nights, but didn't mind as it was the early '90s and I was getting tired of things, you know, like Bill and Hillary Clinton, Rodney King, Garth Brooks, capitalism and a sleeping government... Wait ... other than Rodney King, all the others are still here? So I decided I needed a break, and I was just really worn out, and you know, as a vampire, there is really nothing better than a rest in your personal coffin. So I got my nails done and went into a deep sleep. I did my nails so no one would nail my coffin shut!

BC: *What made you decide to come back?*

MB: Gotta thank my good friend Frankie for that, as well as Timexx, Brian and Bryan. You can watch the whole awakening of me, Misty Brew, on my YouTube channel. Look it up, human creature! There's also a comic book about it. Basically, Frankie was missing me and came up with some lame excuse to awaken me. But I am glad he did. You know, the Internet was really new when I fell into my sleep—only had car phones, really, no smart phones—now it has given me a new outlet and new look on hosting horror movies, which I really enjoy, and I have the power—I sound like He-Man—to do what I want when I want to, as well as have some horrific fun with the human breathers—I mean, human creatures, , on the worldwide web. You know, it wasn't too long ago that the web was done by someone named Charlotte!

BC: *You went from being a local host to the internet and going world-wide. What's the biggest difference for you?*

MB: I like the freedom the Internet has to offer, and I can make fiends worldwide, not just in Missouri—or Misery, as my fiends call it! I love talking to and seeing people comment from all over the world! YouTube, Facebook and my good fiends over at the Kreepy Kastle Internet show! Also, you are just a click away from chatting and sending film to other horror hosts as well! It is just so much fun! I am happier than a camel on Wednesday! Happier than a Slinky on an escalator! Happier than a witch in a broom factory! And I am happy that I had the chance to do this interview with you, human creature! Thank you soooo very much!

Here are a few more raw facts: *Misty Brew's Creature Feature* began in 1985 and originally aired every Friday night at 11 on KBSI and other markets spread over the Midwest and Southern states. She hosted the show until 1989, but reruns on some of those other stations kept her afloat until 1990. Twenty-three years passed before she revived the character (which must be a record of some kind, at least among horror hosts) on both a YouTube channel and the Kreepy Kastle website channel. She had a bigger than normal cast of characters and assorted guests; her "dearest friend" Frankie (the production guy), Zombie Mother, the Count, Freddy, Wolfie, Dead Thing, the Super Natural, JC & Ro Deo, Jason, Michael and even Santa Claus. Her personality developed from vampire seductress to weird woman, employing the jabs at the movies and current events described above. Along with *Creature Features*, she would occasionally host the station's prime-time movie at eight o'clock, as well as *Misty Brew Reviews*. Throughout the run of the show, Misty also hosted an annual televised showing of *Halloween*, on Halloween, naturally. Besides the usual diet of features, Misty would sometimes show local and independent films by up-and-coming filmmakers.

She had a fair-sized selection of movies to choose from. Along with the obligatory Universals (*Frankenstein*, *The Wolf Man*, *Dracula*, *The Invisible Man* and *Creature from the Black Lagoon*) and Hammers (*The Phantom of the Opera*, *The Curse of the Werewolf*, *The Kiss of the Vampire* and *The Brides of Dracula*), she also had an interesting mixture of old and new ... everything from William Castle's *Bug* to *Fright Night*, from *The Green Slime* to *Slaughterhouse-Five*, from *The Haunting* to *Re-Animator*. She hosted a yearly Halloween marathon as well. And then she was gone.

Then, she was back. In 2014, she launched a new YouTube channel. At first, they were simply "revamped" versions of her old shows, but before too long, Misty was back in the game for real, filming new footage, not having appeared to age a day in the intervening years. By the end of the year, she also hosting movies for the Kreepy Kastle website, where she has a regular slot in the schedule. She also makes convention appearances and has a comic book and an action figure based on Misty Brew. In 2014, she made an appearance as "Mini-Misty" in the animated short *The Adventures of Mini-Sven* by James Conway. Every year, during the holidays, she collects food and money for her "Feed the Human Creatures" charity. She has hand-delivered both food and cash to local non-profit food banks and animal shelters. And the cherry on top was being inducted into the Horror Host Hall of Fame on March 21, 2015; she was inducted by Janet Decay (*The Mummy and the Monkey*).

Misty Brew (3)

REAL NAME: Catherine Brewton

HOST: *Shock Theater* (1988–1989), WDBB, Channel 17, Bessemer, Alabama

BIOGRAPHY: The following biographical, career-spanning interview was done, again, by the late Dick Biewski and published in *Scary Monsters* # 56 (used with permission) as "More Misty Brew: Alabama's Sexy Shock Theater Hostess!"

Faye Fisher played the first version of Misty Brew... Shortly thereafter, Elvira went into national syndication, and several other stations picked up on the idea. Paul Bankston started his career at television stations in Tennessee and Louisiana before going to KBSI in Cape Girardeau, Missouri, and later WDBB (Channel 17) in Birmingham, Alabama. Catherine Brewton was hired by Bankston to play WDBB's version of Misty Brew in 1988. In early 2005, they both spoke with *Scary Monsters* about the show:

> SM: *Paul, how did the idea of a horror movie show on WDBB come about?*

Paul Bankston: When I was at KBSI, a bunch of us had the idea of running a horror movie show with a hostess. As I think about it, there was a guy who came from Wisconsin who worked with us, and it might have been his idea. In pretty much the same way that we decided to do it in Cape Girardeau, it was because at WDBB, we had a bunch of horror film titles in our library. In and of themselves, they aren't compelling reasons to watch the television station. We said, "Why don't we try [a hosted horror film show]? We might get the character on the cover of the entertainment supplement in the local newspaper, and if the character and the show get some attention, we might be able to attract men 18 to 34. With that audience, we may be able to attract some beer sponsors, etc." ... I started to develop the show, and went out and tried to find a gal to play the character.

> SM: *Catherine, what were you doing at that time?*

Catherine Brewton: I was working as a swimwear and lingerie model, and doing local and regional pageants for companies like Venus Swimwear, Ujena Swimwear and Hawaiian Tropic. I won the title of "Miss Hawaiian Tropic—Alabama" while I was Misty Brew. I was also doing promotional work for *Playboy*, Miller and Budweiser, and I was "Miss Dixie Speedway." I happened to be doing print and runway modeling for a boutique, Essence of Lace, which specialized in lingerie, swimwear and sportswear.

PB: We went to the boutique and suggested that they provide the clothing—or lack of, as we always found less was more! [*Laughs*] The boutique suggested that if we hadn't found someone to play the character, they might have someone who would be perfect for it.

CB: I wasn't aware of the station's auditions for Misty. The boutique suggested me to them, and I wound up meeting with Paul at WDBB. I had a second and third interview with him, and then I was hired!

SM: Where did the character's name come from?

PB: As I said, at KBSI, we had a guy who came from Green Bay, and we got the name from him. I just decided to use it down here, too.

CB: Brew and my last name, Brewton, were completely coincidental, but I believe it to have been a good omen.

SM: What was the character like?

PB: We were trying to make a poor man's Elvira!

CB: Originally, the character *was* a spin-off of Elvira. They wanted the dark wig and the black outfit. What we started out with was a gown or negligee, which was black and sexy, and was similar in appearance to Elvira's. I went with that for some time. At some point I went to Paul and asked if I could wear different outfits, as I thought it would be a better way of promoting the boutique. I wanted to wear a different outfit every week.

SM: I understand you wanted to change your hair.

CB: I'm really blond—and a bit of a rebel. I wanted Misty to go blond, but Paul wouldn't go for that! [*Laughs*] They did let me do the different outfits. That was a lot more fun! I tried to play her as fun and outgoing. I was quite young at the time, and more of a Dallas Cowboy cheerleader type, rather than an exotic seductress. The character developed over the time that I played her, and became more of one, but my Misty was still a playful sex kitten.

SM: What did you use for a set?

CB: We didn't really have much other than a couch. That was really about it. Believe it or not, mine was the same one used for the news. Most days we shot, we had to be off the set in time for the crew to re-do it for the five o'clock news. Later we started to use the blue or green screen and they would superimpose images behind me.

SM: Was the show scripted?

CB: Yes, it was. Most days, I never saw the script in advance. They would still be typing it into the teleprompter when I arrived on the set. I first saw it when it came on the teleprompter and improvised from there!

SM: When did the show run?

PB: It ran on Saturday nights at 10:30. I think it ran somewhere in 1988–1989. [Interviewer's s note: Scott Free helped me tremendously by researching the dates in the Tuscaloosa Public Library. As best as he could determine, the show started on September 24, 1988, and ran through December 17 of that year. It took a two-week hiatus for the holidays, and then returned on January 7, 1989, and ran in the 10:30 time slot through January 21. The show then shifted to 10:00 p.m. on January 28, and ran in that slot through March 11. It went off the air for two months, then returned for another 13-week run on Friday nights at 10:30: May 5 through July 28, 1989. A special Monday night double-feature was run on July 24, 1989. Thanks, Scott!]

SM: *Did you do any public appearances?*

CB: Yes, all the time. I even did some radio shows. I remember doing a *Star Trek* convention. That was quite a unique experience. I don't remember where it was, but I do remember that there were people who had seen the show. They would tell me, "You know, you look bigger on television than you do in person!" [*Laughs*] It was very interesting as all of these people came dressed up. That was my most memorable appearance. Then there was the time I appeared at a monster truck meet! They would send me out to various locations. I remember that we shot at a local haunted house. I couldn't see the teleprompter! There's one shoot I'll never forget. They had me standing in a coffin. I couldn't see a thing! Not only had I not seen the script beforehand, I couldn't see the teleprompter.

SM: *What were some of your favorite episodes?*

CB: They were the later shows, because I really saw some development in the character. I really did. Once I got tapes of the shows, I could view them and determine how to improve. I improved Misty's wig, and her wardrobe. I did a lot of things to improve her. We did an episode where I was talking to an off-camera cat, and our cameraman got creative and waved a cat's paw in front of the lens. That was kind of silly and fun! There was another one where I played a cowgirl. I was really into horses and cowgirls at the time, and got to dress like one. I was actually dating a thoroughbred horse-trainer at the time, so it was a lot of fun.

SM: *We Midwesterners loved the Southern accent!*

CB [*laughs*]: I didn't know the difference! I was living in Alabama. Everyone spoke the same! I thought that both the show and character had a lot of unrealized potential.

SM: *Why did the show end?*

PB: At the end of the day, it's all about money, and the revenue generated by the show. Trust me, if the ratings were low, but sponsors were buying it, we would have kept it on the air. I don't recall specifically, but it may also have been that we had used up our film titles and weren't prepared to go out and either renew those we had, or invest in any new ones. It had nothing to with Catherine, the character, or the films. It was more to do with our inability to sell the show to sponsors.

CB: I would have liked the show to go on, with more time to develop the character, but I had a great time. I was grateful to be able to do it.

SM: *It got you started!*

CB: It did! Up until that time, I had done modeling, but while doing *Shock Theater* I got bitten by the acting bug. I would always close the show with "Don't bite the bedbugs!" I like to say that I wasn't bitten by the bedbugs, but *was* bitten by the acting bug! ... I moved back to Atlanta after the show ended and studied acting at the Alliance Theater. I continued to work as a print, promotional and tradeshow model before relocating to Los Angeles. Although I had the opportunity to do film and video for *Playboy* and other companies in the adult entertainment industry, my goal was to work in the mainstream. Today, I'm actively pursuing my acting career, and have done independent films and shorts, as well as commercials. I still model on occasion.... Back when I did *Shock Theater* I was focused on modeling. Now that I'm focused on acting, it would be fun to bring my knowledge and training to Misty. We all start somewhere, and I was bitten by the acting bug because of it.

Theatrical: Zanuck, Passon & Pace, Inc. (818) 783-4890 x14
Commercial: Sylvia Ferguson & Associates (818) 380-3024

Catherine Brewton also played Misty Brew, in 1988–1989.

Here is an original sales proposal from WDBB and *Shock Theater*; it's a fascinating look at the inner workings of the station, and, as with anything connected with the genre, a valuable historical document. It goes under the title of "Misty Brew Promotions":

> The HOTTEST personality to happen on the Birmingham media scene is WDBB's "Misty Brew." She is (A) Promotion-Minded, (B) Exploitable, (C) Sexy, and (D) Only on WDBB. You can have "Misty Brew" exclusively, display signings on the set, and have personal appearances at your business. Here's the package: (A) Exclusive participation in *Shock Theater*. Over a thirteen-week commitment, you will be the exclusive advertiser by product category. This includes six (6) thirty-second announcements per show. (B) Signage on the set—actually on the set, when the show is shot, your sign or business logo displayed prominently. (C) During the thirteen weeks, "Misty Brew" will make one personal appearance at your place of business and sign autographs. (D) You will receive at a minimum, fifteen (15) promos per week for the show and/or a personal appearance. (E) Exclusivity. (F) Set signage. (G) Personal appearance. (H) Promos. (I) Thirteen weeks. Total $963.00 per week. THESE THIRTEEN WEEKS NEED NOT BE CONSECUTIVE!"

It took a few years, but in 1999 Catherine Brewton finally appeared in her first film, a genre effort called *Hot Wax Zombies on Wheels*. She has continued to appear intermittently in supporting roles, mostly in actioners and comedies, up to the present day.

Other Genre Credits—FILMS: *Hot Wax Zombies on Wheels*, Wax Rhapsodic LLC, 1999 (Nurse Lydia)

Moana

REAL NAME: Kim Norris
HOST: *Moana's Place* (1983–1985), WTTE-TV, Channel 28, Columbus, Ohio; WPTT-TV, Channel 22, Pittsburgh, Pennsylvania

BIOGRAPHY: This entry will contain only the barest of facts, mostly due to the fact that that's just how Kim Norris wants it. But it's not for lack of trying, I can assure you. After many days of research and phone calls to wrong numbers (sorry!), television stations and various Ohio state institutions, I finally learned where she is now employed. The television stations were no help at all. One of the stations that she appeared on did their best to try to convince me that her show was on a rival station. Ohio Horror Host Fan Supreme Vince Cornelius warned me that he'd tried to talk to her about four or five years ago, about appearing in a documentary, and been given the brush. Norris wouldn't appear in the documentary, wouldn't consent to an interview, and practically refused to acknowledge that part of her career at all. I thought that the intervening years might have made her feel differently, and besides, I had a book to write, so I was pretty much duty-bound to at least try. She was not in her office, so I left a message with all the pertinent details, but she did not return my call or email me. So all we really know about her is that she was the lovely host of *Moana's Place*, which lasted for a couple of years. After that, she did the Channel 28 News for a few years. She's married and has two children. She apparently is doing quite well, and is now doing government work, though I feel that Norris would not want me to divulge where she was doing it, nor where she's located; I respect her privacy and her opinion, and hope that this short piece does not violate it. Come back, Moana, we miss you.

Moona Lisa

REAL NAME: Jeanne Romer; a.k.a. Lisa Clark (1924–)

HOST: *Science Fiction Theater* (1963–1971), KOGO-TV, Channel 10, San Diego, California; *Fright Night* (1972–1973), KHJ-TV, Channel 9, Los Angeles, California; *Moona Lisa's Creature Features* (1973), KFMB, Channel 8, San Diego, California; *Moona's Midnight Madness* (1973–1974), KMOX, Channel 4, St. Louis, Missouri

BIRTHPLACE: San Francisco, California

BIOGRAPHY: "It's midnight, it's the moon, and it's me, Moona ... as in ... you know where.... Moona Lisa, girl-guide of the galaxies and heavenly hostess ... at home and entertaining..."

And so went Moona's opening intro to *Science Fiction Theater*, the only surviving video footage out of a career that spanned a decade! Curiously, too, she is introduced by the female announcer's as "San Diego's own Mistress of the Dark," when Elvira wasn't even an idea yet.

Moona's official KOGO-TV biography, from February 1966, reads thusly:

> Lisa Clark has made a great success of being two-faced! A KOGO-TV personality for nine years, she plays both her charming self and Moona Lisa, the only yet-revealed "Inhabitant of the Moon!" As hostess of Channel 10's Saturday *Science Fiction Theater*, she both performs and writes her own "far-out" antics that have made her one of San Diego's favorite personalities. Lisa is a top commercial spokeswoman, having represented a multitude of national and local television commercial accounts. Lisa, and her husband Jeff, co-host the award-winning public affairs show *KOGO's Corner*, broadcast each Sunday. This is the show, with guest stars, that announces San Diego's community activities. Miss Clark, a native of San Francisco, began her professional career in Hollywood. Later, she moved to New York and studied at the Neighborhood Playhouse while continuing her theatrical, motion picture, and television work. She has appeared on almost all the national dramatic shows. Lisa is an identical twin of Laura Mason (now working in Hollywood as an actress, and she also appears as Lynne Mason). At one time, the twins worked in pictures and in Ken Murray's *Blackouts* in New York for five years. She has appeared in local

San Diego theatre productions, perhaps the most outstanding being her appearance at Old Globe in *The Gazebo* opposite Victor Buono. Lisa and Jeff are the parents of David Lucien Clark, six years old.

Lisa Clark, born Jeanne Romer, was born in San Francisco and began her Hollywood career, with her twin sister Lynne, as part of a sister act, "The Romer Twins." This landed them five roles in seven years, the first in Alfred Hitchcock's *Saboteur* (1942), in which they had their biggest impact as the Siamese Twins. They also appeared in *Swing Out the Blues* (1943), *Hitchhike to Happiness* (1945), *Easter Parade* (1948) and *The Great Gatsby* (1949). The KOGO bio says that Lisa had "appeared on almost all the national dramatic shows," but I can find no mention of this in any other source, except the interview with Clark below. Her sister Lynne (sometimes spelled Lynn) appeared in many other movies, sometimes as "Laura Mason." Under this billing she appeared in *The Bowery Boys Meet the Monsters*, as a very Vampira-like vampire. In the camp classic *Queen of Outer Space*, she was one of Zsa Zsa Gabor's guard girls. And they did work for five years as part of the musical-comedy-dancing revue *Ken Murray's Blackouts*, appearing at Earl Carroll's Theater. When they were doing the show in 1947, Moona Lisa met Vampira! Or, rather, the Romer Twins worked with Maila Nurmi, who found employment that year with the *Blackouts* both as a chorus and hatcheck girl. This information comes from an interview in the great documentary *American Scary*:

An extremely rare candid shot of the Romer twins in New York City in the late 1940s (courtesy George "E-Gor" Chastain).

> When I was in *Ken Murray's Blackouts* as a chorus girl, there were two very beautiful twin girls who were also in the chorus line with me. [They were also a featured act.] There were only five of us all together. But these two were identical twins. They had pale skin and long, dark hair, very beautiful. And they were the Romer Twins, Lynn and her sister. And years later, when I got all done up as Vampira, I said, "This is the third Romer Twin; now they're triplets." Later on, when Vampira was not functioning on local television, Channel 9 decided to put on a lady like that. So they hired Lynn Romer and she was Moona Lisa. Very nice lady, but she was too soft and romantic to be compared to Vampira in any way, other than visually. But she naturally looked the way that I made myself up. Have you ever seen Moona Lisa?

Perhaps she was just confused by naming Lynne as Moona; the twins *were* hard to tell apart. But it sounds,

Moona Lisa

to these ears at least, like she was paying a rather backhanded compliment to Lisa when she said that she looked naturally the way Nurmi had to use makeup to achieve. And maybe just a whiff of envy that Moona was on the air five times as long as Vampira?

Anyway, back to Moona Lisa. We'll continue the story by letting Lisa Clark speak for herself. "An Interview with the Lovely Lady of the Luna—Lisa Clark" by Terence Sanford appeared in *Scary Monsters*; it is used here with permission, along with additional material. Terence asked me to preface the interview with: "This interview with Lisa Clark was conducted in 1991. Information from it was printed in *Scary Monsters Annual* #2 in 1994 and copied on websites and in print without permission or credit."

Terence Sanford: *Was getting into show business encouraged by your family?*

Lisa Clark: Our encouragement to go into films, stage,

Moona Lisa, 1970: "Happy Hallucinations, Honeys!" (courtesy Terence Sanford, © Lisa Clark).

and TV was precisely opposite—a heady dose of discouragement from older members of the family. All in the professions—"respectable." Show business? Never heard of it. Besides, what could two skinny twins have to offer, anyway? Well, a meaty part as Siamese Twins in the Hitchcock film *Saboteur*, for their introduction into show business. And, all this from a chance meeting in Del Mar at the races, with a major Hollywood agent, Lou Irwin, who was sure we were absolutely right for the part. Fortunately, Alfred Hitchcock agreed. By the way, Alfred Hitchcock was an absolutely charming, kind and, as is agreed by most who knew him and worked for him, a terrific director.

My twin sister, Laura Elliot, and I were always in drama school, acting, and dance class. After working in Hollywood, theater and films, we both went to New York City. My sister left after a while and I stayed and did many of the early television shows: *Kraft Theater*, *Robert Montgomery Playhouse*, *Rocky King* and *Martin Kane, P.I.*

My husband, Jeff, was a singer at the time. His agent was Mildred Fenton, who was the top agent in New York City. She left New York City to go to San Francisco, and married Bill Goetze. They had written to us, inviting us to come and visit them. We had written back, but didn't hear from them for a while. The reason was that they had moved from San Francisco to San Diego. Bill Goetze was the general manager of KOGO Channel 10, and Mildred was the head of public affairs.

My husband and I did talk shows. We did the first Mr. and Mrs. Show ever in San Diego, and did shows that had various names—*FOCUS*, *News and Previews*, and *KOGO's Corner*.

In 1963, the station bought a package of science fiction and horror movies. They asked me if I would be interested in hosting these movies. I said that appealed to me strongly since part of my background was as an actress. The show was called *Science Fiction Theater* [not related to the 1950s Ziv television series] and began in September 1963 on Saturday afternoons. The show continued weekly 'til June 1971. Frankly, I expected that I would be handed a script when I first

Moona with Mr. Monster, Forrest J Ackerman, 1972 (courtesy Terry Stead).

started, and I discovered there was none. It was up to me to provide the material. I discovered that, many times in a two-hour time slot, the movie would only be 70 minutes long. What did this mean to Lisa Clark? It meant that she had to write all the copy to fill in that amount of time. After the first few shows I found it to be quite challenging and rewarding because I didn't know if I could write this type of show.

TS: *How did you create the character of Moona Lisa?*

LC: I had always been interested in the moon. There was all the talk of going to the moon and that absolutely caught my imagination. I came up with the name Moona Lisa—obviously a steal from Mona Lisa. One of the lines I had written was "I'm Moona and she's Mona; she's that young upstart who hangs out at the Louvre." I really felt I lived there and built a life for myself on the moon. The show turned out to be the highest-rated program we ever had in San Diego, and that record holds true today. Channel 6 put football up to challenge me for ratings, but they didn't make a dent in Moona Lisa. The show was both a challenge and enormous effort because I had to screen the movie, had them put in the stop-downs where I felt they should go and looked at the commercials so I could find something to lead into after I did my shtick. So it was bits and pieces that I put together to go in and perform live. The show was black and white when we started. When we went to color, we also got some of the more advanced electronic goodies such as the ability to chroma-key.

TS: *The San Diego programs had great set, light and sound design. Who was responsible for this?*

LC: Channel 10 had the most creative departments. The floor men were graduates of San Diego State University, and this was their only creative outlet. Other than the fact that I wanted a mysterious setting, they designed everything. They were wonderful. Prior to the show, these graduates were floor men, messengers and tour guides. It was a wonderful time in television to do this kind of show because people came with ideas. I had several moon sets built during my years at Channel 10.

TS: *In January 1972, you started hosting movies at KHJ Channel 9 in Los Angeles. How did this come about?*

LC: I or someone presented me to Channel 9. Their current horror host, Seymour, was leaving to go to Channel 5. When I was hired and signed the contract, it was only supposed to be one movie every Saturday night. Instead, it turned out to be two or three movies every Friday night ... which meant I had to write copy for everything, which wasn't exactly what I had been hired to do. I found almost entirely throughout my career, I simply had to serve as agent, producer, writer and on-screen talent. I wanted to write my own show, because I saw myself as the only yet-revealed Moonling on the moon. We did a chroma-key effect of me when they came out of the Lunar Module, which was great fun because it really seemed like at last I did get them to the moon.

TS: *Why was Larry Vincent (Seymour) leaving Channel 9?*

LC: I don't really know. I don't think it was a happy departure. At least that was my feeling from him. Before I started at Channel 9, they asked me to come up to do a promo with Seymour. This promo would link his last show with my first show.

TS: *After about a year and a half in L.A., you were asked to host movies in St. Louis.*

LC: I was asked to host movies at CBS station KMOX Channel 4 by general manager Tom Baptista, who had worked at Channel 10 in San Diego and remembered Moona Lisa. His hope was to syndicate Moona Lisa on at least five other stations. But, general managers being very protective of their turf, this did not work out. I lived in San Diego but flew to St. Louis to tape the show, which ran for about a year. It was really tough, and not all that rewarding because I never got to see the show, or do many personal appearances, or meet many people. All in all, Moona Lisa lived for 15 years, and anyone who worked in television when you were your own everything can appreciate what the sense of accomplishment and stresses are.

TS: *Other than the one appearance on Channel 9, did you ever work with Larry Vincent again?*

LC: After I left Channel 9 and he left Channel 5, the people at Knott's Berry Farm called me and asked if I would be interested in doing a Halloween show with Seymour. I'd said I'd love to. So I went up to L.A. and we rehearsed a show. I think it was two weekends, but it was called a Halloween show. He came out of the hospital to do the show and we had a marvelous time. He was obviously a sick man at the time. I really don't know too much what he was like. We didn't get that close or friendly. I was willing to be his admirer, but I think he was very aware of the seriousness of his illness, and this undoubtedly colored his whole response to whatever was happening. I'm glad I worked with him; it was fun to do and it would be nice if he were still with us.

TS: *In some of your San Diego shows, you had a snake. Where did you get him from?*
LC: Whenever there was a show that had to do with snakes, reptiles or creatures that roamed the night, I would borrow Baby Clarence from the San Diego Zoo. I would go to the zoo early Saturday, then to Channel 10, and return him after the show. The late Chuck Shaw, curator of reptiles, was married to a girl who was a producer at Channel 10. He was very gracious about letting me borrow Baby Clarence. Later they gave him to me, because they were tired of getting him ready for me to take him. He lived with me for quite a few years. He was a hybrid gopher-bull snake (nine feet). I did return him to the zoo, and unfortunately he lived only a few months after that. They say he missed me terribly; I like to think that's true.

TS: *Did any funny events happen to you during your years as Moona Lisa?*
LC: Someone took a skeleton from one of the science departments at SDSU. In the control room, there were floorboards that could be lifted up to repair wires, and there was enough room to put a full-length skeleton. They knew someone would open the floorboards early in the morning to do some work, and there was the skeleton. I had nothing to do with it, but was blamed. I believe the skeleton found its way back to SDSU. Another time I borrowed an iguana from the San Diego Zoo to use for a show. When I was driving from Channel 10 to the zoo, the iguana got out of its bag and grabbed my right ankle. I had to get it back to the zoo quickly. I was pulled over by a policeman who asked why I was speeding. I told him to look down at my feet. He looked and saw not only these claws on my ankle, but this huge tail behind the driver's seat. He then said, "You're Moona Lisa, *go! Go! Go!*" He wanted out of that fast. Another time I borrowed the prop head of Macbeth from the Old Globe Theater. I used it in several different movies—*The Thing That Couldn't Die, The Brain That Wouldn't Die* and *Attack of the Mushroom People*. This head would talk to me, I did his voice. Moona Lisa would say, "Why don't we have a wonderful, interstellar, intellectual, egghead exchange? How does that sound?" Then he would say, "*Dumb!*" He was always putting me down whenever I would get overly grand. I was taking the head up to L.A., to use in a show, when I was pulled over at the San Onofre immigration stop. The officer was very polite, and asked me to open the car trunk. I said, "I'd be glad to." I opened the trunk with great flourish, and there was this head all by itself. The officer actually turned white. He recovered and said, "You're Moona Lisa." I asked him why I was pulled over. He said once in a while they pull a car over they wouldn't ordinarily pull over. My thought was since I regularly drove up to L.A. on Tuesdays to tape the show, it registered on a computer—this was the day she brings her creatures up.

TS: *Of the three cities where you hosted—San Diego, Los Angeles and St. Louis—which one did you like the best?*

LC: I have a great warmth and fondness for San Diego, because it was the most creative. It was a live show and I did it for eight years. The people at Channel 10 loved it because they warmed to it. It gave them an outlet for what they were doing which in turn enhanced what I was doing, and I had a terrific audience. The first thing I had to overcome at Channel 9 in L.A. was the fact that here was a lot of "what could little San Diego show us?" Well, as a matter of fact, the production values we had in San Diego so overwhelmed anything they had in L.A. When I first did the show in L.A., they had a curtain blocking the moon window. The people at Channel 9 were bored and disinterested until we got Jaime Shandera, who directed the show in San Diego, up to L.A. Then all of a sudden it was "Look what little San Diego can do!"

TS: *When did you leave Channel 10?*

LC: I left the station in 1985 and still occasionally work with a company every now and then in L.A., but then just as producer, writer and also voiceovers. But my career as Moonling, although it's in my heart and soul, ended there.

TS: *What do you think is the appeal of horror hosts?*

LC: I think people like to be scared. Not deadly scared with guns and killing. I think people like mystery. I loved Nancy Drew mysteries as a child. The mystery of walking into a haunted house. I think there's an element of loving to be scared by lightning or thunder. We respond to it. We know that it's an innocent horror; people are compelled to follow it. The host brings immediacy to it and takes us on our tour to something wonderful. It can be funny, it can be spooky. It's the child in all of us that still loves Halloween."

"Heavenly Tidbits," contributed by Terence Sanford: "When *Science Fiction Theater* aired, visitors to Channel 10 were given sugar cubes. No one complained. For the uninitiated, where you put some acid on a sugar cube and swallow it you get high. The station did not receive any complaints. San Diegans knew it was a joke and played along. In 1981, KHJ Channel 9 in Los Angeles asked Lisa to host movies again. She rightfully declined as they offered her a lower salary than when she hosted movies in the early 1970s. Maila Nurmi (Vampira) was also asked to host again and that offer fell through. Instead of a Moonling or Gothmother, viewers were stuck with a Valley Girl."

Jim Knusch contributed the following "Monster Memory" to *Scary Monsters #8*:

> [Moona Lisa] was the sort of personality that I wasn't readily used to; the sexy horror hostess. ...She was dressed in black, wearing a variation on the "femme fatale/vamp/black widow spider" type of slinky costume. The opening of her show depicted her riding in ... on what appeared to be an asteroid. Her theme song was a selection called "Lord of Lights" from an album titled *Zodiac*. Her on-camera activities included commenting on the evening's movie and doing some in-between bits during the commercial breaks. During a screening of *Invasion of the Body Snatchers*, she appeared as one of the duplicates emerging from a pod.... She was alluring, exotic and entertaining. Admittedly, [my friends and I] enjoyed her show more for her appearances than the horror films offered.
>
> One show carried the announcement that Moona Lisa was going to make a live appearance at a business establishment in El Monte. My roommate and I made a beeline on the day announced. She was out in front of the store on a platform, sitting on a throne-like chair. After distributing autographed postcards, she mixed a drink of "moon dust and moon juice" and disappeared into the building. As we looked around, we noticed that we were the only two adults in the crowd that had gathered. Unfortunately, both my roommate and I misplaced that autographed postcard.

In later years, I made several trips back to Los Angeles, and I have attempted to gather information on Moona Lisa. All I could get from reps at KHJ-TV is that she was brought in from a TV station in San Diego to replace Sinister Seymour when he moved over to KTLA-TV.

It has been reported by some, including Knusch, that Moona's theme song was "The Lord of Lights" from an album titled *Zodiac*. Her theme song was indeed "The Lord of Lights," but the Zodiac was the band, not the album. The LP, which came out in 1967, was called *Cosmic Sounds—Celestial Counterpoint with Words and Music*, and each sign of the zodiac was represented by a song. "The Lord of Lights" was the song for Leo.

Morella

REAL NAME: Glori-Anne Gilbert (1969–)

BIRTHPLACE: Hutchinson, Kansas

HOST: *Morella Presents Graveyard Theater: Morella's Blood Vision* (*I Eat Your Skin*, *The Blood Seekers* and *Blood Stalkers*); *Morella's All-Nite Spooktacular* (*Hobgoblins*, *House of Blood* and *The Cremators*); *Morella's Blood Flood* (*Grave of the Vampire*, *House of Evil* and *Guru, the Mad Monk*)

BIOGRAPHY: Beautiful Glori-Anne Gilbert portrayed the character in a series of direct-to–DVD compilations released and re-released by RetroMedia at various times in the 2000s. There is no mention of it on her IMDb page, nor is there any information about her or the character on Wikipedia, so the only information on the shows comes from the shows themselves.

Her stint as Morella was part of a long career as a B-movie actress; practically all the films she has appeared in are genre films. Either that or sexploitation, and often a combination of both. She has been one of the more durable "scream queens," appearing in movies (most of them direct-to–DVD), as opposed to the girls that just stick a pair of fangs in their mouth and take photos with horny nerds at conventions.

Each DVD features three movies; each movie has a new *Graveyard Theater* segment (*Blood Vision* had three movies, but only two *Graveyard Theater* segments). After a stock footage opening with a creepy castle and waves crashing against the shore underneath the titles, Morella would appear in a crystal ball: "Good evening, fright fans, and welcome to *Graveyard Theater*, a great place to dig up a date ... or bury your career. I'm your ghost-hostess with the mostest, Morella." Then she would do a skit that lasted a couple of minutes. That was the only segment featuring Morella; since there were no commercials, there were no bumpers, and no closing segment. There were no other actors; her only companion was a brain named Spud, floating in a tank that bubbled when Spud "spoke." The set was cramped but well-dressed, as was Morella (a form-fitting black gown with a plunging neckline that accentuated her more-than-ample bust). Like Elvira, many of her jokes were about that bust. Here's a typical example:

> You know, I just love reading about all my favorite stars in the weekly edition of *The Freakly World News*. Who's getting hitched, who's getting ditched ... but my favorite articles are the ones on plastic surgery... A little nip here, a little tuck there ... which reminds me of my own plastic surgeon, Dr. Lance Stitchem... Y'see, I wanted these really big ... hands. But he talked me out of it, so I got a tattoo instead. Boy, am I glad I got *that* off my chest ... not that I had a tattoo on my chest, I meant my hands ... well, not that I had my hands on my chest... Well, you know what I mean... Could somebody just please start the movie?

Other Genre Credits—FILMS: *Evil Ambitions*, B+ Productions, 1996 (Intern); *Vampire Call Girls*, 1998 (Heather); *Night Vamps*, EH Productions, 1998 (Hostess); *Killer Sex Queens from Cyberspace*, EH Productions, 1998 (Virtual Hooker); *Dream Witch*, Creative Productions, 2000 (Pamela); *Witchunter*, Evil Genius Entertainment, 2002 (The Blood Queen); *Blood Sisters—Vamps 2*, B+ Productions, 2002 (Heather); *The Thing Below*, Hellfire Productions, 2004 (Cindy Mayberry); *Curse of the Komodo*, Royal Oaks Entertainment, 2004 (Rebecca); *Countess Dracula's Orgy of Blood*, Frontline Entertainment, 2004 (Diana); *Komodo vs. Cobra*, Cinetel Films, 2005 (Darla); *The Witches of Breastwick*, 2005 (Rebecca); *The Breastford Wives*, 2007 (Laura); *Cry of the Winged Serpent*, Concorde—New Horizons, 2007 (Police Woman); *House on Hooter Hill*, 2007 (Sue)

Mrs. Lucifer

REAL NAME: Nancy Lee Dix

HOST: *Shock!* (1957–1959), KBAL-TV, Channel 11, Baltimore, Maryland

BIOGRAPHY: Dr. and Mrs. Lucifer were part of the "Golden Age," the first generation of horror hosts created at the time that the original *Shock Theatre* package was released to television. Dr. Lucifer, played by Richard Dix (no relation to the actor who appeared in such films as *Cimarron*), was a "quality" mad scientist, and the woman who took part in his "quality" experiments (which, naturally, were anything but), Mrs. Lucifer, was played by his real-life wife Nancy Lee Dix, whose character was a quixotic blend of the mildly kinky sexuality of Vampira, while at the same time projecting a June Cleaver brand of wholesomeness. Since she was Mrs. Lucifer, she and her husband have made their living by acting, mostly in stage productions, sometimes appearing together, as when they both appeared in the perennial *Arsenic and Old Lace*. She played one of Mortimer Brewster's aunts, while her husband played Jonathan. In a *Midnight Marquee* #46 article by Greg Mank, Richard and Nancy Lee discussed their horror host days:

> Richard: My inspiration for Dr. Lucifer was Charles Addams. Both Nancy and I are fans of Addams; we had all his cartoon books and liked his approach and sense of humor. Actually, in some instances, I'd take a cartoon that he'd already done and stage it; we'd visualize and animate the actual Addams cartoons.
>
> Nancy Lee: Mrs. Lucifer, too, came out of the Charles Addams books. She was a loving wife—a kooky lady, but nice and very much in love with her husband. The makeup, the wig and the costuming were the façade of the character, but in fact, she was a nice person and an everyday housewife—who just happened to cook bunny rabbits!

"TV's Nightmares," an article in the February 1959 issue of *TV Star Parade*, is an amusing, and surprisingly informative, piece on the show and its denizens:

> A macabre figure who comes off more mocking than menacing is Dr. Lucifer, a tremendously popular fellow in Baltimore, Maryland. In his laboratory at WBAL-TV (1 a.m., Saturday), his fiendish brain is constantly at work experimenting and creating—but his experiments usually backfire, and his creations are harmless, making him a bumbling sort of bogeyman. As a terror, he's all thumbs, and that's just the way Richard Dix, who plays the luckless Lucifer, plans it.... Though Lucifer works mostly solo, he is occasionally joined by the rest of his video family—his wife Grace, a daughter, Lucretia (played by the Dix's real-life daughter, Landra), and Baby Borgia.... At present, he's a (managing) director of the Children's Theater Association of Baltimore (where Nancy Lee was also heavily involved, as a secretary-treasurer-business manager) and president of the local AFTRA chapter.

Ms. Monster

REAL NAME: A.K. Smith

HOST: *Hel on Ice* (2004–), cable access Channel 29, San Francisco, California; Salem Access Television, Channel 3, Salem, Massachusetts

BIOGRAPHY: What do you get when you combine an orange and black "skeleton" track suit (think John Entwhistle or Glenn Danzig), ravishing red hair, blue body paint and copious cleavage? Why, you get Ms. Monster, of course! Ms. Monster, a.k.a. A.K. Smith, has been bringing horror and hilarity (much like the San Francisco 49ers) to the Bay Area for a dozen years. Aided by her "Monster Melons," Tit and Tat, as well as by her human companions Marc Nordstrom and Aaron Farmer (who are also the voices of Tit and Tat), she tries to make the world "a more craptastic place." Ms. Monster also has a few issues of her own comic book, which would make sense since the show is produced by B-Minus Comiks. Ms. Monster made it to the final rounds of the *Search for the Next Elvira* reality show, but despite being eminently qualified, she lost (while the woman who won never parlayed her victory into a hosting gig). Here is a blurb from her website: "Ms. Monster presents—*Hel on Ice*! [It's] not just a show, it's a way of life … er, death! Sit back and let your rigor mortis set in, while Ms. Monster and her Monster Melons, Tit and Tat, take you on a hilariously wild ride filled with B-Movies, shorts, cartoons, and, as always, puppets and gore! You'll bust out of your stitches, then hunger for your own entrails!" Yummy! The following is from her blog, from 2006:

> HEL-lo there my little beasties. I'm Ms. Monster from the late-night horror variety show, *Hel on Ice.* Come join us for our favorite B-Horror movie clips, our own animation, THE CEREALISTS, house bands, indie submissions, puppet gore, and a whole lot of murderous mayhem.... When we aren't trying to earn a crappy living bringing gore-filled nights to the cities of San Francisco, Davis, Berkeley, somewhere in Minnesota, Wisconsin, and Salem, Massachusetts, we are out drag-racing cars in our town called Hel and hanging out with the carnies. We tango with evil—the melons

2008 trading card featuring Ms. Monster and her Monster Melons (Courtesy Paul Riggie).

are the bringers of the apocalypse, after all—we love gore and we dance quite often with demons and other horror hosts.

I wrote to Ms. Monster in February 2016, and this is what she had to say: "Full disclosure—we have not filmed in a year, however, the latest six episodes are being launched with a new online television channel. The take-away is that while there are no Ms. Monster live appearances currently scheduled, new episodes are soon to hit the Internet airwaves. Sweet Screams!"

The Mummy (and the Monkey)
(See: Daughter of Ghoul)

Nina (1)
REAL NAME: Nina Catharina Hagen (1955–)
BIRTHPLACE: East Berlin, East Germany
HOST: *Sci-Fright* (1999), U.K. SCI-FI Channel, U.K., Ireland, and South Africa
BIOGRAPHY: Three women played the same character as a horror host, Nina. The first, and the only one actually named Nina (the show was named after her), was Nina Hagen, the Godmother of German Punk (not to be confused with Nena, the German New Wave songstress who had a worldwide hit with *99 Red Balloons*). She began to study ballet at the age of four, and was considered an "opera prodigy" at age nine. But alternative roads beckoned, and she left school at 16, moving to Poland to pursue her musical muse. A short time later, she returned to Germany and joined a cover band. In

Nina Hagen as the first Nina, 2000 (courtesy George "E-Gor" Chastain).

1973, she formed the band *Automobil*; in 1976, she left East Germany, along with her mother, after her stepfather was refused the right to re-enter the country. They went to Hamburg, where Hagen was signed to a CBS-affiliated label. The label encouraged her to broaden her horizons, and she wound up in London during the apex of English Punk. This had a great influence on her music, and she moved back to Hamburg, where she formed the Nina Hagen Band. Their tenure was short (she left the band in 1979), but they produced some memorable tunes; first and foremost of which (harkening back to her first band) was the cover of the Tubes' classic "White Punks on Dope," known in the native language as "TV-Glotzer." To be fair, the song was not a total cover; the tune remained the same, but the lyrics were completely different. Her operatic influences showed, and the band was praised for the combination of diverse sounds. Her singing style drew comparisons to Lene Lovich, whom she would later work with in the film *Cha-Cha* (1979). She continues to compose, sing, record music and tour.

Her small-screen career got off to a controversial start: In 1979, while appearing on an Australian TV show called *Club 2* (ostensibly to discuss youth culture), Nina began to graphically demonstrate (although remaining fully clothed) examples of female masturbation positions, after which she got into a rhubarb with a fellow panelist. The show's host was forced to step down. Her TV career had actually started five years earlier, but none of her appearances could hope to compete with *that*.

Sci-Fright was fairly elaborately produced, although, like most of the rest of any horror host's shows, seemed a bit cramped in terms of space. Nina Hagen, ever the iconoclast, was just plain zany, appearing in many different costumes and skits and just generally having fun. The two actresses who succeeded her were much more in the traditional mode (i.e. slinky, self-effacing sensuality). In a way, *Sci-Fright* was a bit edgier than the same type of show produced in the States. Most every horror host made fun of local or national politicians or current events, but *Sci-Fright* took it a step beyond—in a country that tries to live down THAT part of its past, *Sci-Fright* featured a comic Nazi named Klaus, wheelchair-bound but still fanatical in his devotion to Der Führer.

Other Genre Credits—FILMS: *Pankow '95*, Pandora Filmproduktion, 1983 (Jungfrau Maria); *Vasilisa*, Cosmopolita Filmproduktion, 2000 (Witch); *Seven Dwarfs*, Zipfelmutzen GmbH & Co. KG, 2004 (Bose Konigin); *7 Dwarves: The Forest Is Not Enough*, Zipfelmutzen GmbH & Co. KG, 2006 (Hexe); *Seventh Dwarf* (animated), Zipfelmutzen GmbH & Co. KG, 2014 (voice of Eisfree Dellamorta)

Nina (2)

REAL NAME: Indira Varma (1973–)
BIRTHPLACE: Bath, Somerset, England
HOST: *Sci-Fright* (2000), U.K. SCI-FI Channel, U.K., Ireland and South Africa

BIOGRAPHY: No Nina Hagen to play Nina on *Sci-Fright*? No problem! Just get a similar striking brunette—but one who looks nothing like her, put a wig on her, and *voila*! Instant Nina! Oh, well, it always worked on *Doctor Who*. Actually, it also worked here; Varma was a talented and beautiful actress. She was only there for a season, using it as a stepping stone to bigger and better things.

Other Genre Credits—FILMS: *Vintage Blood* (short), Hook Pictures, 2015; TELEVISION: *The Quatermass Experiment*, 2005 (Judith Caroon); *Torchwood*: "They Keep

Killing Suzie," "Everything Changes," 2006 (Suzie Costello); *Game of Thrones*: ten episodes, 2014–2016 (Ellaria Sand)

Nina (3)

REAL NAME: Rachel Louise Grant de Longueuil (Rachel Grant; 1977–)
BIRTHPLACE: Luzon, Philippines
HOST: *Sci-Fright* (2001–2002), U.K. SCI-FI Channel, U.K., Ireland, and South Africa
BIOGRAPHY: No Indira Varma to play Nina on *Sci-Fright*? No problem! Just get a similar striking brunette—but one who looks nothing like her, put a brunette wig on her, and *voila*! Instant Nina! Oh, well, it always worked on *Doctor Who*. Actually, it worked here, too; Rachel Grant was a talented and beautiful actress. She was only there for a season, using it as a stepping stone to bigger, but not necessarily better things. She became a member of the "Bond Girls Club" with her appearance in the dreadful *Die Another Day*, the merciful end of the Pierce Brosnan Era.

Other Genre Credits—FILMS: *Die Another Day*, Eon Productions, 2002 (Peaceful); *Brotherhood of Blood*, Brotherhood LLC, 2007 (Jill); TELEVISION: *Starhyke*: six episodes, 2009 (Lt. Comdr. Wu Oof)

Nocturna

REAL NAME: Anonymous
HOST: *The Bone Jangler* (2001–), Comcast Cable, Channel 6/10, Chicago, Illinois
BIOGRAPHY: "Enchantress Nocturna" is the wife of the Bone Jangler and co-host of his self-titled show. I wrote to Mr. Jangler several times requesting an interview with her, but received no response. When Paul Counelis interviewed him for *11:59 and Counting*, Bone Jangler offered no information about his co-host.

The Old Lady

REAL NAME: Ottola Nesmith (1889–1972)
BIRTHPLACE: Washington, D.C.
HOST: *Nightmare!* (1957–1958), KTLA-TV, Channel 5, Horrorwood, Karloffornia
BIOGRAPHY: Being a horror host was only the tip of the iceberg of her acting career, which spanned over 50 years; she made her first film in 1913. After appearing in such well-regarded 1930s films as *Becky Sharp* and *The Prince and the Pauper*, she made her first horror movie in 1941, Bela Lugosi's *Invisible Ghost*. She was also in *The Wolf Man*, *The Return of the Vampire* and two Val Lewton classics, *The Leopard Man* and *The Seventh Victim*. But it was in television that she really made her mark on the genre via three of *the* scariest episodes of Boris Karloff's *Thriller*, the standout episode being the adaptation of Robert E. Howard's "Pigeons from Hell."

As horror hostess of KTLA's *Nightmare!*, she never referred to herself as such, but the credits called her "The Old Lady." Greg Mank, in a *Movie Club* #12 article, describes her appearance thusly: "She wore an early 1900s dress, a black cape, a large, old-fashioned picture hat, and black lace fingerless gloves. She was carrying a fan, and a black ruffled silk parasol. It was macabre Hollywood showmanship, with a touch of *Sunset Blvd.* decay...." (It's rather surprising that so many of the actresses and historians cite Gloria Swanson's past-her-prime-but-refuses-to-admit-it, lonely, homicidal former movie queen character as inspiration for their own characters.) Former movie queen Mae Clarke, co-star of the 1931 *Frankenstein*, sued Ms. Nesmith for claiming, on the episode where she showed *Frankenstein*, to *be* Mae Clarke. Perhaps Clarke was not aware that it was a running joke on the show; Nesmith claimed that she played the

Ottola Nesmith caused quite a stir in 1957–1958 as the Old Lady, who claimed to be the female lead of whatever movie she was showing.

female lead in every movie that she showed! The case generated a ton of publicity, and Clarke pled her case to the court of public opinion. In the court of law, however, Clarke lost.

Other Genre Credits—FILMS: *Invisible Ghost*, Monogram, 1941 (Mrs. Mason); *The Wolf Man*, Universal, 1941 (Mrs. Bally); *The Leopard Man*, RKO, 1943 (Senora Contreras); *The Seventh Victim*, RKO, 1943 (Mrs. Lowood); *The Return of the Vampire*, Columbia, 1943 (Governess Elsa Walter); *The Son of Dr. Jekyll*, Columbia, 1951 (Nurse); TELEVISION: *Target*: "Edge of Terror," 1958 (Woman); *Thriller*: "Pigeons from Hell," 1961 (The Zuvembie); "Yours Truly, Jack the Ripper," 1961 (Rowena); "The Hungry Glass," 1961 (Laura Bellman); *Alfred Hitchcock Presents*: "Services Rendered," 1961 (The Woman); *Bewitched*: "The Trial and Error of Aunt Clara," 1967 (Aunt Enchantra)

Peaches Christ

REAL NAME: Joshua Grannell

HOST: *Canned Peaches* (1998–2001), CityVisions Cable Channel 29, San Francisco, California

BIOGRAPHY: Information adapted from Peaches' website:

> Peaches Christ was born in a small boating town just outside of "Charm City," Baltimore, Maryland. As a wee girl, Peaches would dream of becoming rich and famous. She aspired to bring celebrity and controversy back to her well-known family name. Surviving many years of Catholic schooling, where poor Peaches was often teased and ridiculed for being different from other girls, she vowed to turn her dreams into realities. Since the East Coast had nothing left to offer her, Peaches and her friend Martiny flew directly to San Francisco, where they've been ever since. Peaches soon found solace and friendship on the "underground" cabaret stage at Trannyshack, where she's been allowed to work through some of her painful memories and make a bit of a name for herself as a drag superstar. Martiny became known as the most flawed and tragic drag queen in all of San Francisco. She's also Peaches' official sidekick. Peaches is a huge film buff who has written magazine columns and reviews, though she is best known for her "Midnight Mass" film series at the Bridge Theatre. Playing hostess to a cavalcade of midnight movies, each with its own special pre-show entertainment, Peaches has won the hearts of sick and twisted San Franciscans far and wide. Peaches' award-winning cable access television show *Canned Peaches* is no longer on the air, but a compilation, *Too Hot for Cable TV: The Best of Canned Peaches* (available from the website), documents the misadventures of Peaches, Martiny and their dear friend, Squeaky Blonde. Peaches' alter-ego, Joshua Grannell, continues to make films in and around the San Francisco Bay area. His recent short films, *Season of the Troll* and *Nightmare on Castro Street*, have enjoyed international festival appearances. Ms. Christ and Mr. Grannell are featured in a short documentary, *Peaches Christ: Superstar*, that's also cruising the festival circuit. Look for her new film, *Grindhouse*, coming soon. Remember, Peaches loves you!

Peg Scott

HOST: *The Witching Hour-Shock Theatre* (1959–1961), WTVT, Channel 13, Tampa, Florida

BIOGRAPHY: Before there was Shock Armstrong, there was Ed and Peg Scott, a husband-and-wife team who hosted horror films on WTVT, Channel 13 in Tampa, Florida. There is some confusion over the show's name; different sources have remembered it differently, both as *The Witching Hour* and the standard *Shock Theatre*. The different sources are both quoted on "Big 13," a site devoted to the history of that station. The first, in an article devoted to the Scotts' successor Shock Armstrong, tells it thusly:

> A late-night horror package had been tried before on WTVT. *Shock Theatre* was originally seen in 1959. The program was hosted by Ed and Peg Scott as a creepy duo living in a spooky mansion. The show's

Peg Scott, 1960, with husband and co-host Ed Scott (courtesy George "E-Gor" Chastain).

title was based on a 1957 horror movie package sold by Screen Gems, a subsidiary of Columbia Pictures. The package was called "Shock," and offered a plethora of titles from the classic Universal Studios library.... The name *Shock Theatre* was already in use by several markets around the country by the time Channel 13 got into the game. WTVT's original *Shock Theatre* ended around 1961, leaving a vacuum in local horror programming.

A much more intimate portrait was offered by Jackie Walker, personal friend of both Peg and Ed, and the owner and operator of Option Dressing, a personal image consulting firm for both individuals and corporations. Jackie's father-in-law Ronny Walker had been an electrician in the 1930s and, on one of his nights off, had gone to see a traveling "tent show" produced by, and starring, the Rowley Family. Phil and Nina Rowley played the leads in Broadway-style revues, and were known professionally as "The Buddy Players." Their son Ed, a.k.a Buddy, sang and danced in the revues. Mightily impressed, Walker joined up with the show as an electrician and began life on the road. He and Ed became good friends, but eventually the time came when Walker and the Rowleys had to part company so that Walker could start a family of his own.

That he did, Walker and his wife Celia settling down in St. Petersburg, Florida. A quarter-century after he had left the Rowleys' road show, he and his missus thought that they heard a familiar voice announcing the station breaks on WTVT and called the station. He inquired as to the name of the announcer, and was told it was Ed Scott. Rowley, who had changed his surname to Scott, got on the phone, and Walker said, "Buddy, is that you?" Their friendship re-established, the Scotts soon paid a visit to the Walkers, and met their son Neil. They stayed in touch for as long as Ed and Peg lived.

In 1982, a now-adult Neil saw the Scotts at a local store. His parents were about to celebrate their 50th wedding anniversary, and he arranged for the Scotts to put in a surprise appearance. The surprise was well-received, and in the process, the Scotts met Neil's wife Jackie. She and Neil became close friends with Peg and Ed. The Scotts never had any children, just a couple of dogs that they adored, and so Jackie and Neil became "part of the family." They visited frequently, and were on hand for many holidays. They supported each other in good times and bad, especially when Neil's father and mother died.

Peg had been a USO showgirl; Ed had tried his hand at Hollywood as a bit player, and he was also a talented artist and musician. Jackie Walker wrote that

> years before the premiere of *Shock Theatre*, Scott and his wife Peg served as co-hosts of Channel 13's weekly horror movie package called *The Witching Hour*. They played an eccentric, spooky couple who lived in a haunted house. Like Shock Armstrong, they would introduce the scary movies and appear during the commercial breaks. Their haunted house was fairly elaborate for the time, and a chore for the crew to put up every week. Realistic cobwebs were created by diluting rubber cement and applying the webs out of a makeshift spray-painter powered by a vacuum cleaner. It was a technique similar to that used by *The Munsters* a few years later.

Obviously, this is where the confusion of the name of their show comes from, but since the same website offers competing versions, it becomes literally a case of "he said, she said," and in the absence of a definitive answer, both are offered up here as possibilities.

Before their joint venture of a show, Ed Scott was a booth announcer for the station. He then tackled the role of "3-D Danny" in a children's show that had originally been on WKY-TV in Oklahoma City; the role was played by station employee Danny Williams. The concept and format of the show were borrowed for a WTVT version produced by Ken Smith. *3-D Danny* was a series that showed cartoons, with science fiction bumpers; Scott was attired in a vintage 1950s spaceman outfit, with his robot companion named "Ruffnik," who was played by Lyle "Red" Koch. Their adventures took place on a flying saucer set. When the saucer was seen in flight, it was stock footage from *Forbidden Planet*. Scott played the role for three years.

According to Jackie Walker, Peg was always "a forward thinking woman who didn't see much in the future for live announcers, and started thinking of their life's work beyond the scope of television. Her epiphany came one night at home when Ed couldn't get his pipe to light and threw it at the wall in disgust, claiming that 'you couldn't find a good pipe nowadays.'" The light bulb went off over Peg's head: "That's it! We'll start a pipe and tobacco shop!" Edward's Pipe and Tobacco was located right around the corner from Channel 13. They were successful, and soon moved to a bigger building, which was still only a few hundred feet away from the station. Then they became more successful, with shops all over the country, and even their own pipe-manufacturing plant. According to Walker, "Ed loved the tobacco shop; that was his life. He loved being out front and talking to people, joking around. Peg was the brains.... Ed was the entertainer."

By the late 1980s, the Scotts decided that they would sell their business, and retired. But the years of smoking had not done Ed any favors: "Not long after they got to Deltona, he developed severe health problems with his circulation, probably aggravated by the smoking; he lost one of his legs. It was very hard for him and Peg because they wanted to travel. One of the most poignant pictures he drew for us at the time was a field of flamingoes with their legs tucked up, and Ed is there too with his leg tucked up." His health continued its downward spiral, and Peg put him in a health care center, where he died. After his death, Peg Scott left Florida, and soon passed away as well.

Penny Dreadful (1)

REAL NAME: Rose Marie Earp (1933–)
BIRTHPLACE: Kansas City, Missouri
HOST: *Son of Chiller* (1960s), KMBC-TV, Channel 9, Kansas City, Missouri
BIOGRAPHY: Rose Marie Earp played the first Penny Dreadful, but, like some of the other early hostesses, no photos, video or audio survives to give any indication of what the show was like. Living in Kearney, Missouri, she is 83 as of this writing. I attempted to contact her for an interview, but her number is unlisted, and, not knowing what her situation is, I was hesitant to dig deeper.

Penny Dreadful (2) (A.k.a. Penny Dreadful the 13th)

REAL NAME: Danielle Gelehrter
HOST: *Penny Dreadful's Shilling Shockers* (2006–2015), over 100 cable TV stations throughout the Northeast
BIOGRAPHY: You know the old saying about how you don't miss your water 'til your well runs dry? Well, that hoary old cliché still holds true in a lot of cases, and it certainly applies to the fans of Penny Dreadful. Danielle and her delightful crew were staples of the convention circuit—until all of a sudden, they weren't. This was due to the most tragic of circumstances, the untimely death of her husband. All of monster fandom grieved, and word had it that she had retired the character. Checking her website while researching this book, I saw that she was doing a couple of conventions and/or personal appearances as Penny. I wrote and told her how much we miss her at Monster Bash and asked if she would consider doing an interview for this book. She not only agreed to do the interview, but the foreword as well.

PD: I've been involved in theatre performance and improvisational comedy for over 20 years. I studied theater at San Francisco State University, and am a graduate of both San Francisco Comedy College and Improv Asylum in Boston. Some of my favorite theater roles include Medea from the eponymous Greek tragedy by Euripides, the Wicked Witch of the West in *The Wizard of Oz* and Frau Blucher in *Young Frankenstein, the Musical*. I also teach college and have BA degrees in creative writing and literature, and an MA in English. My favorite color is purple; I love ice cream, and have a tattoo of a bat on my right arm.

BC: *Do your students know you're Penny?*

PD: I never tell my students that I'm Penny, but some of them have recognized me or Googled me and found out about it. Usually, on the rare occasion when they recognize me, they'll quietly approach me after class and ask. I'll put a finger to my lips and say "Yes. Shhh!"; however, one time a student flagrantly asked me at the start of class and bellowed, "*So how's Penny Dreadful?*' I quickly replied, "I don't know, we're not speaking to each other," and commenced class as usual. A couple of faculty members have recognized as well. One professor approached me and asked, "Excuse me, are you Penny Dreadful?" I laughed and said, "Yep." He replied, "I *thought* it was you, but I wondered why Penny Dreadful would be walking around on campus! Wait'll I tell my wife about this!" It turns out he and his wife were fans of the show. After that, he invited me and a colleague to come speak to his radio production class, which was really fun. While I normally wear a lot of black clothing, I look quite different outside the Penny getup—no pointy hat, less makeup, and definitely less cleavage—so I'm always pretty surprised on the occasions when somebody actually recognizes me.

BC: *Have you always been into horror films?*

PD: I've been a fan of classic horror films since childhood. My Uncle Valdemar used to give me his *Famous Monsters of Filmland* magazines, and he'd show me Universal and Hammer films as well as episodes of *Dark Shadows*. He also gave me a book of Poe stories, and used to scare me with his Pickwick horror records. I credit him for warping my young mind. I toyed with the idea of getting a hosted horror show off the ground in 1998. My good high school friend Ivan Bernier, who plays Dr. Manfred Von Bulow the monster hunter on *Shilling Shockers*, and I discussed it back then, but we had no clue how to go about doing it and didn't know how many public domain movies there were. Growing up, we were both fans of Commander USA on the USA Network, and we also loved local programming like *Creature Double Feature* (no host at the time), Willie Whistle, Captain Bob (who were both kids' show hosts) and stuff like *The Movie Loft* and *Dialing for Dollars*. We really missed the feel of local programs as we noticed that cable TV started erasing all those shows from the airwaves. We both possessed a desire to bring that type of show back. Later, in late 2004, I discovered a show called *Ghoul-a-Go-Go* which inspired me quite a bit. Through that great show, I discovered there were horror hosts all over the country making amazing programs using public domain films. At that moment a light bulb, or perhaps a candle, went off above my head and I realized we could actually get a show like this going. We started taping in September of 2005, and the first episode aired in January of 2006.

BC: *Was the character created by you?*

PD: Penny came to me when the time was right. I was in rehearsals for *Medea*. One day I was backstage and started joking around with the two boys in the show, making morbid puns. The idea of this vengeful sorceress from Greek tragedy making bad jokes seemed very horror host-like. In fact, I always do Penny's eye makeup like Medea's as a

Penny Dreadful, 2005 (courtesy Penny Dreadful/photo by Rebecca Paiva).

little homage. It also struck me that I'm from Massachusetts, and there has never been a witch-themed horror host from my home state. It just seemed like a no-brainer to me that New England should have a witch horror movie host, and I decided to go ahead and do it. I called myself Penny Dreadful in reference to the serialized tales of terror and crime from the 19th century. I used that name on the radio for a time and also used it when I was a singer in a rock band. It fit very well for the horror host persona. Incidentally, the name of the show, *Shilling Shockers*, also comes from serialized tales of the supernatural which appeared earlier in the 19th century. I called Ivan up and asked him if he wanted to revive the idea of the horror host show we discussed years earlier, and asked him if he'd be the cranky, semi-retired monster hunter next door—a Van Helsing type, and my foil in a sense. He heartily agreed. I also asked my husband Magoo Gelehrter if he'd like to play the werewolf husband and sidekick of Penny Dreadful. I described it to him as a non-speaking role. The Wolfman would snarl and growl, but wouldn't "talk." He smiled and said he'd do it, and then he named the character Garou after the French term for werewolf, *loup-garou*. Magoo was always *very* funny, and was a master of slapstick comedy. We both loved the classic comedians so much, and we'd often watch the Marx Brothers, W.C. Fields, Burns and Allen and so many more. He really turned Garou into something special. We shot a couple of episodes, and then my good friend from college, Rebecca Paiva, came on board to help out. She soon took on the directorial and editorial duties and really helped establish the look of *Shilling Shockers*. She also played the recurring role of Penny's friend Luna, an escaped mental patient with a genius intellect.

BC: *Is Rebecca Paiva related to Nestor Paiva, the great character actor from* Creature from the Black Lagoon?

PD: Alas, she is not related to Nestor as far as she knows. She gets that question all the time.

BC: *And you were a singer in a band? I was, too! Can you tell us a little bit about the band, you know … the name, how long you were together, or any releases?*

PD: We were called Sh!tty K!tty. We were a punk band. Our "hits" included "Surf Zombie," "Yeast Infection" and a punk version of "Purple People Eater." Our drummer Meredith MacKnight is amazingly talented. Our guitarist April Reed was a phenom and our first guitarist Trey Harrison was quite good, too. April is a rock star. She and Meredith added some legitimacy to our band since they were actual musicians, and very good ones at that. Magoo (Garou) was the bass player and we called him the Sid Vicious of the band since he couldn't actually play bass at first. April taught him a few licks and he picked it up as he went along. He actually got quite good at it by the end of the band's short-lived series of gigs, but he could only really play the songs April taught him for our sets. I was the singer, and sounded like a cross between a donkey and a car accident. In other words, I was awful! If you look up Sh!tty K!tty on YouTube, the above-mentioned songs are up there. We played a few gigs over the course of maybe two or three years. It was lots of fun and I miss it a ton.

BC: *What's your favorite Marx Brothers movie?*

PD: Do I have to pick just one? I love *Duck Soup* and *A Day at the Races*; classic Marx Brothers genius and craziness. And then I also have a fondness for *At the Circus*. Who doesn't love Groucho singing "Lydia the Tattooed Lady"?

BC: *Were you inspired by the original Penny Dreadful? What do you know about her?*
PD: While I was not directly inspired by Rose Marie Earp, the original Penny Dreadful horror hostess, I do consider her a spiritual ancestor in a sense, and sometimes refer to her as my great, great, great grandmother Penny Dreadful the First (I am Penny the 13th). As I understand it, she was a wonderful horror hostess with an otherworldly

Penny, who is anything but Dreadful (courtesy Penny Dreadful/photo by Rebecca Paiva).

quality about her delivery. I've seen pictures of her and she was beautiful. I also really like the balaclava that she wore. I certainly wish I could've met her.

BC: *What are some of your fondest memories of the show?*

PD: There are so many fond memories. There was a very arduous day on a Rhode Island beach where we were taping our *Seventh Seal* episode. We were there for many hours. After we finally finished, we realized there was a group of people sitting on a blanket watching us. It turned out they were a very friendly bunch who happened to be of Swedish descent. They thought it was great we were showing the Bergman film and offered us food and beer. We joined them and they proceeded to teach us Swedish drinking songs. It was the perfect ending to that very, very long day. I also remember how much fun and how exciting it was to tape the very first show. The premise was very flimsy and we sort of made it up as we went along. It was a blast!

BC: *Are there any especially funny memories of the show?*

PD: Yes! So many! Here's one: We almost got arrested during the taping of the *Dementia 13* episode! We shot at the old Danvers State Insane Asylum in Danvers, Massachusetts. New England is filled with weirdness, and every season we'd do at least one or two shows where we'd go to a strange place. In this instance, we decided to shoot at Danvers. Well, at the time, they were in the process of tearing down the asylum to put up condos. We snuck onto the property and shot a few scenes, but I wanted to get really close to the Kirkbride Building, which was the most magnificent building on the premises. We went down a dirt path which led to the Kirkbride Building, but the place was surrounded by a fence. However, we found a space underneath the fence that a person could fit through. Rebecca (Luna) was in a straightjacket, and as she began to crawl under it, we saw a police cruiser tearing across the grounds, coming right for us. Ivan (Von Bulow), who was filming, and Rebecca both turned tail and ran back down the path as I—in the witch outfit—shouted, "We can still get the shot before he gets here! Come back!" I looked back, realized the cop was getting much closer, and then ran down the path with Rebecca and Ivan. I can only imagine what the police officer must have thought. Luckily, we had most of the footage we needed including a great shot outside the tuberculosis ward. I still wish we could've gotten that shot near the Kirkbride Building, though. It would have looked amazing, but it's better than being arrested, I guess.

BC: *On one hand, you're keeping the tradition of the local horror host alive by appearing on television; on the other, you have access to technology that the original horror hosts never dreamed of. How does it feel to be local, yet international?*

PD: At first, I focused very much on New England as our "zone" and didn't make much of an effort to expand outside of the northeast region because I wanted to bring back the idea of a local show. We wanted to echo the tradition of the classic horror hosts. I also didn't want to step on the toes of hosts in other regions. During the early period of the show, I just never really considered the Internet as a viable option for broadcast because I was focused so much on the idea of local TV. I used the Internet mainly for advertising. I also tried very hard to maintain the Penny persona as a living entity. Like a clown, the horror host isn't supposed to "take off the makeup" in public. I tried to keep my real name separate and always stayed in character for interviews and public appearances. Garou was also very much behind this idea and never broke character in public when he was dressed as Garou. Wrestlers use the old carnival term "kayfabe" to describe this type of thing, and that is very much what we tried to maintain. If you listen to interviews with Morgus the Magnificent, you never hear Sid Noel. He is 100 percent Morgus. However, the Internet made the kayfabe route absolutely impossible! A little Googling easily yielded our real identities as well as out-of-character photos of us, so I came up with the idea of making Danielle Penny's doppelganger. She is a creature conjured up by Penny who looks exactly like her. The two have a hostile relationship with one another. And so, as the show went on, I adapted and decided to embrace the Internet a bit. I lightened up a little. We also sent shows to places that streamed the show online, which added to our viewership. It's great hearing from people all over the world who watch the show via streaming video online. It's a really fun feeling to know you are reaching people from all over the place.

BC: *As a classically trained actress, do you prefer comedy or drama? I heard that you made a wonderful Frau Blucher in Young Frankenstein, the Musical.*

PD: That's very kind of you to say. Frau was so much fun to play, and the cast and crew on that show were the best. I adore them very much. I love both comedy and drama, but I prefer comedy. There's no feeling in the world like the feeling you get from making people laugh. It's a rush like no other.

BC: *Word had it that you had retired the persona of Penny. What made you decide to bring her back?*

PD: I never really retired Penny. Penny is part of me, so she'll always be lurking … waiting to cast a spell. I announced that I was ending *Shilling Shockers*, which I have. Without Garou, there is no more *Shilling Shockers*. It didn't feel right continuing the show without him. Yes, I've hosted a number of solo episodes in just about every season, but that isn't the point. Garou was the heart of the show. I simply didn't feel it was appropriate to continue it without him as part of it, and my cast and crewmates agreed. Penny Dreadful will still be around, though. She won't let me off the broomstick that easily. Penny wants to live and I dare not deny her! We'll do Halloween specials and live events from time to time, and who knows; maybe I'll launch an entirely different show someday.

BC: *You just released Season 9 of* Shilling Shockers.

PD: These are the last episodes with Garou—we shot all of his scenes early on, per his request—and they also feature a continuing storyline in which I lost my powers and try to get them back. We released these seven new shows to all of our TV stations for Halloween. Season 9 is now out on DVD via our website (plug, plug). As I said, even though Season 9 is the final season of *Shilling Shockers*, Penny Dreadful will still appear in annual Halloween specials. I may even reboot the show under a different name at some point—*Penny Dreadful's Cobweb Cinema* or *Penny Dreadful's Witching Hour* or something. We shall see. Or maybe I'll just unleash a brand new horror host persona and start again from the ground up. I have an idea for a horror hostess that has never been attempted before, as far as I'm aware. I think it'd be really fun to try that out and see what happens.

BC: *You're the reigning queen of the active horror hosts.*

PD: Do you really think so? I appreciate the sentiment, but I still feel we never really got as far with the shows as I wanted to take it. I think we could have done much more with it and taken it to a bigger platform. We never really tried to do that. That said, I sincerely appreciate the fact that people found us anyway and that some of them enjoyed our antics. I refuse to play stupid. Penny is smart, knows the genre, and wields a vast array of supernatural powers. I tried to channel some of the gravitas of the classic horror actors into her, while also trying to channel the silliness of the comedians and cartoon characters that I love. Whether I succeeded is not for me to say. That's for the viewer to decide. Because she's a witch, I think there's an archetypal appeal about Penny. There's that sense of forbidden power mixed with a sense of humor and maybe a little bit of crazy. We also went deep into the mythology of the show and explored a variety of ideas, themes, styles and tones. Most importantly, I think, is the fact that despite her sometimes sinister delivery, Penny is actually quite friendly. I have always felt that the horror host should be a friend to children, and this is part of the appeal. For all the trappings of gloom and cobwebs, Penny loves her "Dreary Ones"—both the young and the young at heart. Rebecca added a *lot* to the show by making it look so professional. *Shilling Shockers* was funded by our DVD and merchandise sales for years, and the final season was funded by an Indiegogo campaign. We were working on a very low budget and it's a testament to Rebecca that she made it all look stunning. That's because she's a prodigiously talented individual who wore many hats during the run of the show. She directed the episodes, played a variety of roles, did the lighting and camerawork, edited the shows, and designed and maintained the website. Garou and Von Bulow were the true comic relief on *Shilling Shockers* and added so many ideas and gags. Ivan wrote some of the funniest scripts. We both grew up with local TV here in the Boston area and shared a love for those shows. And as I said earlier, Garou was really the heart of the show. His humor, sweetness, and sense of jubilant fun created an atmosphere of levity and joy. Eric Parks, the assistant to the director, came on during Season 7 and helped us immensely in a variety of ways, from playing characters like Dr. Jekyll to holding the broom mic [*sic*]. Eric has been an amazing and necessary presence during the latter portion of the show's run. *Shilling Shockers* was *very* much a group effort.

I think it's safe to say that I speak for all the fans and pros who attend the Monster Bash that we all hope to see Penny again, preferably much sooner than later.

Ravena, Goddess of Stonehenge

REAL NAME(S): Julianna McPherson, Brandi Lynn Coppock

HOST: *Friday Fright/Stone Circle Cinema* (1997), KTCI, Channel 3, Tri-Cities, Washington

BIOGRAPHY: *Friday Fright*, which premiered in October 1997 in Washington, featured Ravena and her trusty sidekick, a one-eyed, mute dwarf named Anok; the show ran for 26 weeks. The first Ravena was Julianna McPherson, about whom little is known. The surviving footage shows her to be going for the blonde bombshell look a few years before Jami Deadly; her costume was a black leather bra, a faux leopard-skin loincloth, black thigh-high boots and a luxurious white faux-fur coat. She also conformed to the stereotype of the dumb blonde when she looked at the camera and proclaimed, "Now we'll get back to *White Zombie*, starring the great Bela Lugosi as Dracula." Now, it's not like nobody has made a mistake before, and one hopes that it was done intentionally, but still…!

Then the actress switch was made to Brandi Lynn Coppock and a title switch was made to *Stone Circle Cinema*. Coppock was a former model for *Playboy* and also modeled for the *Fighting Force* video game, for the character of Alana McKendrick. Her career after *Stone Circle Cinema* was slight; she had roles in a few movies and television shows, plus a cameo in the Pamela Anderson series *V.I.P.* She also danced with Ricky Martin in a video and appeared on stage in *The Salem Witches*. Her last film role to date was in a horror-comedy (actually, it was more a horrible comedy) called *Trees 2: The Root of All Evil* (2004). As Ravena, she affected a slight costume change: a different black leather bra, now accompanied by a matching loincloth. She kept the thigh-high boots as part of the ensemble, but lost the white fur coat and gained a broadsword. She also changed her hair color. Anok also wore a slightly different costume.

Other Genre Credits (Brandi Lynn Coppock)—Films: *Trees 2—The Root of All Evil*, Pioneer Motion Pictures, 2004 (Agent Bentley)

Robyn Graves
Real Name: Erika Hildebrandt
Biography: See entry for Marlena Midnite
Host: *Midnite Mausoleum* (2009–) WQAD, My TV 8-3, Moline, Davenport, Quad Cities, Mediacom Cable Channel 716

Roxsy Tyler
Real Name: Carmela Hayslett
Host: *Roxsy Tyler's Carnival of Horrors* (2010–2014) Facebook
Biography: Roxsy Tyler is another one of the new breed of female horror hosts who thrived on the Internet. She continued the tradition of great Philadelphia horror hosts (probably the only great thing about Philly, with the possible exception of their cheesesteaks) but typified the D.I.Y. ethic essential to the modern host. Roxsy was not your stereotypical horror hostess. Eschewing the regulation "uniform" (form-fitting black gowns, cleavage, lots of leg), she wore a form-covering long black leather coat, jeans, t-shirt and, the best touch of all, a top hat. And whereas most horror hosts continue the grand tradition of sneering at the feature they were showing, Roxsy acted almost as if she were being made to do the show against her will (she actually said this in one of her promos), as if she could care less about what the movie was, or if a movie was even being shown. But that only served to underscore the difference between a character and the person playing her, because one couldn't find a nicer or more caring person. And that's not to say the character was off-putting; on the contrary, she was endearing and hilarious. In one of Roxsy's funniest skits, she and her co-host, Chuck, challenged each other to find a blind date on the Internet, and wound up with each other. Of particular interest is the short film she used to end the show, *Roxsy and Me*, discussed at the end of the interview below. She provides a short description of the film, but neglects to mention the appearance of Karen Scioli and Bob Billbrough, both as their real selves, and a real treat, reprising their iconic roles as Stella and Hives; it's definitely a moment where one might find one's eyes misting up a bit. She was also kind enough to put me in touch with Marlena Midnite and Sally, the Zombie Cheerleader.

BC: *I know the "Tyler" part of your character name comes from Steven Tyler. Where does the "Roxsy" come from?*

RT: "The Rock," now more commonly known as Dwayne Johnson. He was my favorite wrestler at the time. People used to chant "Rocky! Rocky! Rocky!" when he was talking or when he was in the ring. So the Roxsy is something that I tried to make comparable to that. Did you know that when I was a teenager, I was on a talk show because I was such a fan of his? I actually didn't want to be on the show, but people convinced me that I might meet him if I followed through with it. I never did meet him or even get so much as him favorite-ing a tweet. It's been 16 years and I'm still waiting, unfortunately.

BC: *Is Aerosmith your favorite band?*

RT: Aerosmith is my favorite band. My musical tastes are all over the board. I love the music my parents grew up with in the '60s and '70s like Hendrix and Zeppelin, but I'm also into heavier stuff like Rob Zombie, Dethklok and Finntroll. Most of the time, however, I'm very stuck in the '90s grunge period. I listen to a lot of Soundgarden and Stone Temple Pilots.

Carmella Hayslett rocks a top hat as Roxsy Tyler in 2012 (courtesy Carmela Hayslett, photo by Christian J. Grillo).

BC: *Is your makeup influenced by Alice Cooper?*

RT: It was not, actually. I'm not too keen on doing my makeup so one day I just smudged my eyeliner down my cheeks, and declared it an "I don't care" move. It stuck. People have called me Alice Cooper at conventions. To which I reply, "It is pronounced Rox-si."

BC: *Do you like horror and science fiction movies?*

RT: I love them! My mother was a big classic horror fan, so I grew up with a lot of the films which I, and the other hosts, show on our shows. I was also a Freddy Krueger kid. If you grew up in my generation, or close to it, you're either a Freddy kid, a Jason kid or a Michael Myers kid. Though I love watching all three, my first choice was always Freddy. I grew up with a love, fear and respect for all things dark and fearful.

BC: *How did you come to be a horror host?*

RT: I had never intended to be a horror host. I had written these stories about the Roxsy Tyler character. These stories were also read by Blake Powell, co-producer of *Midnite Mausoleum*. We had been friends for years, and he had just started *Midnite Mausoleum* with Marlena. I was really excited for him. I was getting everyone I know to watch the show and friend them on Myspace—Myspace was the thing at the time—and I asked Blake how funny it would be to have Roxsy on the show, off the paper and in the flesh. Next thing I knew, I was on my way to Clinton, Iowa, not only to meet Blake in person for the first time, but to be on the show. I intended for it to be just something silly I could do with Blake and a wonderful opportunity to meet his friends on the show. Before I knew it, I kept being asked by the horror community and the horror-hosting community if I will go back on *Midnite Mausoleum* or possibly have my own show. Well, my husband and I run a production company—we've put out four feature-length films—so we figured that we'd try doing a show since we had the resources. We started airing in spring 2010.

BC: *What's your day job?*

RT: I have many day jobs. I guess the most dominant one would be that I am a video editor. I've edited films, music videos, programs and trailers, but mostly I provide a fast and affordable demo reel service for actors. I also make and sell my own soap and candles. My husband and I also locally sell vintage furniture.

BC: *I understand you and your husband are also involved in some other very special work.*

RT: We rescue animals—lots of them! We currently have four cats that are all rescues. We have tons of fish. We had a crayfish named Zombie that we rescued from the marketplace. He was going to get cooked and eaten. I wanted to save at least one, and he turned out to be one of the most awesome pets I ever had. Then we have our 12 turtles. Most of them were rescued from Chinese gift shops where they were being abused and mistreated. Two of the turtles were dying right there on the shelves, but we got them, nursed them, had PETA get the shops to stop selling them, and then those two turtles made full recoveries. Most of my turtles are named after Hindu gods, Shiva, Ganesh, Vishnu, Buddha, Brahma and Varuna; the others are named after television characters. We have a greenhouse with a big turtle pond.

BC: *Are you members of PETA?*

RT: We are not members of PETA, but we worked together with them when we rescued our first four turtles. They were very helpful.

BC: *Was the character created by you?*

RT: Yes, completely. She started out as a character in stories I've written, and now she's so much more.

BC: *Do you have any horror host role models?*

RT: I grew up watching Elvira, but I never dreamed that I would one day do what she does. I did a lot of research on other hosts when I started my show. There are very few horror hosts I don't respect. It takes a lot of love to do what a horror host does. There's never a promise of making any money. There's never stability. There's just that love of horror that usually sustains them. I like Elvira a lot. I also really look up to Stella, the

Maneater from Manayunk, not just as a host, but as a person outside of hosting. I've had the pleasure of being friends with Stella, and it's safe to say she's become my idol.

BC: *Do you really think zombies are stupid? I kind of agree with you. Personally, I think they're way overdone.*

RT: They are overdone. They are stupid. Technically, they really are stupid, no matter how many brains they eat. I find them to be really cool-looking but so very non-threatening.

BC: *Your character has a real attitude, a real persona. How did that develop? Is she you?*

RT: That's a hard question to answer. I'm a very shy person in general. I don't talk very much. I'm never in the middle of a crowd. You take me out of that hat and makeup and I become very hard to find. I think Roxsy Tyler is part of me that gets hidden away when I'm not on camera. It's very liberating to be her. She's who I would be if I were a more confident and carefree person.

BC: *The character doesn't play up your physical attributes like some hosts did or do. It's refreshing. Is that because you want to be judged for your talents rather than your beauty, or was that just a conscious decision to be different?*

Another shot of Roxsy Tyler with her signature look (courtesy Carmela Hayslett, photo by Christian J. Grillo).

RT: There's enough horror hosts out there that play the sex card. The world didn't need one more. I didn't think about it too much when I started. Roxsy is just Roxsy. Roxsy Tyler always had a male dominance about her. Some can even say she's gender-confused. Roxsy Tyler is sexy because she's not trying to be. I realized that over time. Personally, I think it's hard to hold people's attention if you bank too much on your looks. That will get people to look at you, but what's going to keep their attention, or prevent them from moving on to the next pretty girl? I don't think it was intentional that I didn't "sex up" the character. I don't sex myself up in general, and that may have well spilled over into Roxsy's character too.

BC: *Do you write the show?*

RT: Yes. Sometimes I got stuck and asked my co-hosts or supporting actors to help me. Everyone on the show was talented at writing. I was just the one who had the most time to dedicate to writing the scripts. The scripts were always loose anyway, because we'd end up improvising a lot, but the scripts were good for nailing down storylines because we liked relating our "problem" in the show to whatever the problem was in the film we were showing.

BC: *What stage of development do you think the Internet horror host is at?*

RT: Everything is becoming an app and being designed to be more convenient. Horror hosting is becoming more available. You no longer have to wait for a certain time on a certain day for your favorite horror host to come on. I don't know if it's good or bad but it's happening. I think the good side of it is that it increases the chances of more people finding horror-hosting shows because even in horror hosting's rich history there's so many people who still don't know what it is or where to find it. There's an entire subgenre of horror that is under the radar, and it's full of great entertainment with wonderful, insane characters. Most of which couldn't be found before because most people were in bed by the time they came on TV. If horror hosting was ever going to become a bigger thing, I think it would be right now.

BC: *Do you have a favorite episode?*

RT: Oh boy. It's hard to narrow down which episode would be my ultimate favorite. We did one episode where we were hosting a short horror film from Australia, and it was about these two people breaking into a house and murdering the people in it. So my partner Chuck and I played it up like there was an intruder at our *Carnival of Horrors*. We loaded up on weapons and Chuck's character is the "kill-happy" guy, so he was looking for trouble. At the end of the episode, it turned out that it was just my former co-host coming back to get his stuff. That was probably one of our funniest episodes. The charisma between Roxsy and her co-hosts was that they absolutely did not get along. It was a group of people, running a carnival, and always trying to kill each other.

BC: *Are there any dysfunctional memories of the show*?

RT: We did an entire episode drunk before. I mean, we could. If we had been working for a studio or an outside producer, we would have never done that, but we were doing the show for ourselves, so one night we did a drunken episode. The kicker is … you couldn't even tell we were drunk!

BC: *What's the future look like for Roxsy?*

RT: I'm not entirely sure. Roxsy isn't hosting horror films any more, but wants to remain in the public eye. I think she'd make a good host for something else, like a game show or a reality show. Could you imagine Roxsy tearing up some pretty blondes on a reality show? Now *that's* entertainment! I've been dabbling with ideas on what to do with her. I think her brand needs to expand into new territories. People used to try and cast her in their films, but I was a serious actress trying to keep her persona away from the persona of being another character. I regret that now. I think Roxsy Tyler would have easily become a name in horror films. Maybe it's not too late, right?

BC: *When was your last show*?

RT: My last show was about two years ago…. I think. We ended it by making the short film *Roxsy & Me* as the conclusion to the web series. Me, my husband, and my friend Chuck all played exaggerated versions of our true selves. The plot was that I quit to pursue a serious acting career—totally not true—and when I quit, the fans turned against Roxsy, until Roxsy, who's sitting somewhere in my psyche, decides to repossess my body. It was pretty funny, but unless someone is a fan of the show or knew us personally, they probably wouldn't get it. The real reason I quit ... it was a lot of reasons. I would have went on forever if we had a bigger audience, but then Facebook started putting a cap on how many people see your posts. Facebook was where most of our fanbase came from, and now we can't reach them without spending money. I think if I had the resources to better market the show and the character, then Roxsy Taylor might have been almost famous. Not quite famous, but almost famous—and that's good enough for me. Another reason was that it was getting fuzzy about what was public domain and what was not. Something that is public domain one year is suddenly not public domain the next year. So for a season we tried showcasing independent filmmakers who had short horror films, but we didn't get enough films to air an entire season. A lot of them we couldn't show because a lot of them had nudity or too much cursing. We tried to keep the show PG because kids were watching too. Also, there were a lot of films where people were using licensed music without permission, and we didn't want to be liable for stuff like that. I would love to continue the Roxsy Tyler legacy. I have qualms about suiting up again, but as for producing my own show—that's all in the past for me. I've been there. I've done that. It's time to do other things now.

Other Genre Credits—FILMS: *Booley*, Potent Pictures LLC, 2010 (Rose Booley); *Deer Crossing*, Potent Pictures LLC, 2012 (Olivia Brice); *Apocalypse Kiss*, Potent Media, 2014 (Katia); *The Sugar Skull Girls*, Potent Pictures LLC, 2016 (The Pale Witch)

Sally, the Zombie Cheerleader

REAL NAME: Nichole Brooks
HOST: *Zombie Cheerleader's School of Horror* (2005–2006), *Monster Madhouse* (2006–2008), *Zombie Cheerleader Presents...* (2008–)
BIRTHPLACE: Jefferson, Maryland
BIOGRAPHY: I first became aware of Nicole Brooks when I watched *American Scary* for the first time. Who was this person? This is what she had to say in the documentary: "I'm sure if you're an adult, a B-movie is not particularly scary, but if you're six or seven or eight, it's terrifying, and Count Gore helped pull that out a little bit for me by just watching him and letting off a little steam. He was a part of what was called the Horror Host Underground, which is a conglomerate of horror host fans throughout the country."

I found out that shortly thereafter, Nichole Brooks had morphed into Sally, the Zombie Cheerleader; Carmela Hayslett (Roxsy Tyler) put me in touch with her, and even though bogged down by sickness and overwork, she was kind enough to grant me this interview:

BC: *Do you like horror and science movies?*
ZC: I'm partial to both sci-fi and horror. I enjoy horror movies with atmosphere, depth, mystery and suspense. Needless to say, I enjoy older, vintage horror movies. Yes, yes, blood and splatter are fun but give me a creepy flick with twists and turns in the plot. Well, I guess that makes me an Alfred Hitchcock fan, but I digress. As for sci-fi, I'm a complete zombie Whovian and Trekkie. I show mostly horror films on my show, but I will sneak in an old *Tales of Tomorrow* episode.

Sally the Zombie Cheerleader: "Beware, Fleshies!" (courtesy Nicole Brooks).

BC: *How did you come to be a horror host? Was the character created by you?*

ZC: It all started as a gag present around 2003, and the character has been growing ever since. At the time, I was chatting on an old Yahoo message board called the Horror Host Underground. I posted queries to other horror hosts and fans about doing my own horror-hosted show, but I needed to develop a character. Sally was born from a gag gift from a fan. The gift consisted of a stock cheerleader's costume. The fan found the cheerleader's costume in a thrift store and sent it to me. I liked the costume so much that I wore it at my first Cinema Wasteland convention in 2003 and then at the 2004 Scary Camp in Dayton, Ohio. Everyone seemed to like the look. I developed a name for the character, Sally. The name Sally is in honor of the heroine from Tim Burton's *The Nightmare Before Christmas*. Sally's original goal was to teach all monsters, mainly zombies, how to survive the "fleshie" onslaught. (Fleshies is a term I use to describe humans. It's fleshie or hufu. I think someone took hufu.) It was us zombies against the fleshies. I used old horror movies as teaching aids in my class. The show ran from around 2005 to 2007. I felt I succeeded in educating the monster masses, so I moved on to more of an insightful show with old horror—visiting strange locations, horror conventions, and trying to figure out what all those fleshie holidays mean. I'm a zombie, my brain is dead; I have a lot of questions.

My inspiration for becoming a zombie horror host can be traced all the way back to my childhood. Ah, the halcyon days of a young zombie. My love of all things horror began when I was a small child. I grew up watching Count Gore De Vol, a late-Saturday-night horror host on DC's Channel 20. Count Gore was incredible. The Count was chock full of horror information about the movies he hosted, interviewed numerous famous guests, and he hosted classic horror films. Thanks to Count Gore, I was able to watch the unedited version of *Night of the Living Dead* at the tender age of eight. I was scarred, and hooked for life. Oh, how I loved those long Saturday nights! Since I was so very young when his shows aired, I had to quietly turn on his show without anyone—parents—noticing. After I became a zombie, I met Count Gore many times and we joined forces on the Horror Host Underground. I now consider Count Gore to be a good friend. Count Gore is the best vampire in the world, bar none.

BC: *Do you write the show?*

ZC: I generally write, shoot, edit, produce and present my own show. My main co-host is Slo-Frank from *Monster Madhouse*. I have mostly branched off and concentrated my own show, but I do try to make special appearances on the *Monster Madhouse* show from time to time. Sally is a multi-faceted zombie.

BC: *When did the show start?*

ZC: I do believe my first show aired around 2005. It started off as the *Zombie Cheerleader's School of Horror*; the *School of Horror* lasted a couple of years until I decided to just go with *Zombie Cheerleader Presents....* I like investigating fleshie lore, holidays and traditions right now. My show is still very active.

BC: *Tell us about the* School of Horror.

ZC: The *School of Horror* was a place where all monsters could go and learn how to defeat, or understand, fleshies. During my *School of Horror*, I examined countless classic horror movies and tried to learn what fleshies were doing. I only seemed to learn that not all horror movies are very classy, and not many fleshies make sense.

BC: *What made you decide to go solo?*

ZC: I was, for the most part, solo. I did join the *Monster Madhouse* gang for a couple of years around 2006, but this zombie moved to a new lair. I have to fend for myself, eventually. I don't mind working as a solo, but I love having Slo-Frank around as a co-host. We monsters work well together.

BC: *What's your day job?*

ZC: Day job—zombies have day jobs? Right now, I think I'm too busy not dying, but if I had a day job, it might have something to do with medicine.

BC: *Have you done any other acting?*

ZC: Well, not as such, but I do a mean zombie.

BC: *Are you also a wrestler? I've seen videos to that effect...*

ZC: I consider myself a professional fleshie wrangler.

BC: *Do you have any horror host role models?*

ZC: Count Gore De Vol—that vampire was the making, and death, of this poor zombie.

BC: *How did you come to appear in* American Scary?

ZC: I was approached by Sandy Clark. Around 2005, he and John Hudgens traveled the states looking for interviews with horror hosts and fans of horror hosts. I participated in the interview for *American Scary* as a fan. At that time, I was a budding horror host. I was just shaping Sally at the time. *American Scary* is a good documentary. It does capture the essence of horror-hosting based on the horror hosts they were able to interview.

BC: *What are some of your fondest memories of the show?*

ZC: I loved working my children into the skits. We created commercials, played with dolls, and blew things up. It is fun to sit back and watch my kids grow and change as the seasons and years go by on the show. Not only did my show change, but my kids changed too. We all had fun filming the shows, and it was good family fun. Well, good zombie family fun. Some of the funnier moments of the show were during the taping of the Uni-doll bomber episode. At one point, the Uni-doll bomber blew up all of my daughter's—she was known as Zombette on the show—dolls. We could not stop laughing. It's amazing how much fun you can have with a few firecrackers and a big box of old dolls.

BC: *Has your show been on television, or is it strictly the Internet?*

ZC: The show was broadcast in the Midwest and as far as California on public access for a few years. Currently, I can be seen in Fairfax, Virginia on Channel 10, the Vortexx, my YouTube channel (Sally Zom Bie), and Kreepy Kastle.

BC: *How long do you see yourself doing the show?*

ZC: Sally may creep around in front of the cameras for a few years. Heck, she just might morph into something entirely new. I guess we shall just find out soon enough. For the moment, it is safe to say that Sally will be around, lurking in the shadows, and playing with the other horror hosts. We are one big, creepy fangmily.

BC: *Why do the Baltimore Ravens suck?*

ZC: I don't know if they suck, but since they're Ravens, I bet they peck a whole heck of a lot.

BC: *Have you any advice for their cheerleaders*?

ZC: Yeah, if a zombie runs after you, don't just cheer at it, run for the hills. If you don't run, that zombie just might bite you on the arse, and you'll wind up just like me!

Scarticia

Real First Name: Annette

HOST: *Horrible Movie* (circa early– to mid–1970s), WAPT-TV, Channel 16, Jackson, Mississippi

BIOGRAPHY: All that we have on Scarticia comes from three emails to the "Chamber" website (used with permission). First up is a note from "Marvin Gardens," who worked on the show and provided a photo of Scarticia (not reproduced here):

> I worked production on *Horrible Movie*—much like Morgus, only we had a female, Scarticia. Her real name was Annette, and she was the personal secretary to the station manager during her day job. *Horrible Movie* was around 1971–1972. I did Scarticia's makeup, and painted the background set for her. If you remember "Momma's" portrait hanging beside Scarticia's rocking chair—holding a dead rat by the tail—I painted that. Otherwise, I was usually on studio-cam, except for a few times I made an appearance as Dr. Choke Throttle. Our director at WAPT chose the absolute *worst* films ever made to feature. One of our biggest sponsors was a hippie boutique called the ZZAP Boutique. We had a really good time doing that gig.

The other two are from Richard Dube, which have been combined for editorial purposes (overlapping info, typos, etc.):

> Shortly after WAPT Channel 16 debuted in Jackson, Mississippi, in October 1970, they debuted a Saturday night movie special called *Horrible Movie*. For the first time ever in Jackson, I believe, we had a horror host-hostess. Her name was Scarticia. She was more like Morticia Addams than Vampira. She wore a lot of makeup and wore an outfit like Morticia's. She was entertaining; not gorgeous like Vampira or the later horror hostesses, but she was worth watching. She spoke in a deep voice, and wore white makeup with lines painted on her face. She had a gravedigger assistant, "Scoop Gravely," played by legendary, beloved local D.J. Ed Hobgood, and a nemesis called "Black Genie," played by a black girl. The set was kind of plain, as I recall. They ran a Universal package including the older classics, as well as Hammer's *Brides of Dracula*, *Curse of the Werewolf*, *Kiss of Evil*, etc. Scarticia always welcomed viewers at the start of the show with "Good evening, animals," and ended it with "Unpleasant nightmares." She was very entertaining, and I have a lot of fond memories from the show. In one skit they announced Scarticia would "streak" on TV; what it amounted to was a naked doll pulled across the front of the camera. Ah, the memories. Scarticia's *Horrible Movie* lasted about three years. In April 1977, WAPT brought the show back with a new AIP movie package, but without Scarticia. The [hosts] dressed in fright masks and carried axes, chainsaws, etc. The movie package [also] featured a few European films. It didn't last too long. I never met Scarticia, but I swear I saw her several times at the wrestling matches at the Mississippi Coliseum. A woman came regularly wearing a Jackson WAPT jacket, and sat across from us. Based on her build and face, she looked like Scarticia without the makeup. I tried getting info from WAPT, but I got no response. They changed management a few times, and the new ones probably have no idea what or who Scarticia was. [Author's note: They don't.]

Rhonda Honey Shear (1954–)

BIRTHPLACE: New Orleans, Louisiana

HOST: *USA Up All Night* (1991–1998), USA Network (cable)

BIOGRAPHY: To answer your first question: yes, that is her real middle name. How cool is that? A name befitting a true Southern belle, who graduated from John F. Kennedy High in 1972, and Loyola University in 1977 with a B.A. in Communications. She tore up the beauty pageant circuit, winning over 40 titles, including Miss Louisiana in 1975. While in college, she appeared in an AIP flick called *J.D.'s Revenge* which served to whet her appetite for the screen. Also while still in school, she whetted men's appetites by appearing (fully clothed) in the *Playboy* pictorial "Girls of the New South." It was the first of six appearances in the magazine, including the full pictorial spread in October 1993.

After graduation, Rhonda became the youngest woman ever to run for public office in New Orleans, losing by a mere 135 votes; but New Orleans' governmental loss soon became Hollywood's (and the world's) gain. Sometime soon after graduating from Loyola, she moved to Los Angeles, where she took classes at the Academy of Dramatic Arts and auditioned for the Bob Hope special *Starmakers*. She passed the audition, and it seemed like she was on her way, doing bit parts, mostly in television. The biggest movie she appeared in before she became a horror host was Mel Brooks' silly *Star Wars* parody *Spaceballs*.

Shear wasn't the stereotypical horror host; unlike most of the women discussed in this book, she appeared as herself. No spooky name or makeup, no wigs, no long black gowns, no macabre sets, not a hint of Morticia Addams in sight. Rhonda was devastatingly sexy enough on her own terms, and soon enough, people began watching the show, not for the movies she was showing, but for Rhonda. In a *Draculina* #24 interview, she said about that audience, "My fans are extremely expressive, [and] because I talk directly to the camera, people feel like they really know me, as opposed to acting a particular role. So it's like they really know the character of Rhonda, so they really express themselves to me."

USA Up All Night originally began in 1989, with Gilbert Gottfried hosting the show on Saturday from New York. Halfway through the first season, it proved so popular that a Friday edition was added, with Caroline Schlitt hosting from Los Angeles. When Schlitt quit in December 1990, she was replaced by Shear less than a month later; Rhonda's first show aired on January 4, 1991. In 1995, the Shear show was moved to New York. The program eventually changed its title to *USA Up All Night with Rhonda Shear*; Gottfried continued to alternate hosting duties with Shear up until the end of the show's run.

"Many breasts have popped out," when she was asked about the funniest thing that happened while filming *Up All Night*. "At my second show, I was at the UCLA Mardi

Rhonda Shear kept fans *Up All Night* for years. Autographed photo from 1998 (courtesy Paul Riggie).

Gras, and I was doing a pie-in-the-face thing. I was actually throwing pies at my producer, and a breast flew out; the students were surrounding me and no one told me because they were in such awe—or in shock." (I'd bet heavily on the former.) "I didn't even know, I was having such a good time, and my crew was too new to me to tell me anything, too. Another UCLA frat house has a room they can flood; they can make it into a swimming pool inside. They've been doing it for years. I was there during rush week, and we were taping from there. They have these little boats, and I was in a boat, and ... one of the kids pushed me overboard... You could see straight through my dress. I've had a lot of strange things happen with UCLA..."

Rhonda's control of the content of the show ebbed and flowed. She had a large say in it until it moved to New York. The pace was faster in New York so they had to prep faster because they started taping four or five shows at once, cranking them out in two or three days, instead of just one a week. The producers came up with ideas, but they always asked if she wanted to do them or not. One of her favorite things was on-the-street, on-the-spot interviews; the show moved away from that for a while, but around the middle of the run, they let her start doing it with frequency again. On the show, she ran the gamut, doing everything from portraying different characters to interviewing fellow celebs to covering amazing events to hanging from the ceiling. She was nothing if not versatile, even when the blood was rushing to her head.

During the show's heyday, she was a part of Purrfect Productions' "Sex Symbol Dynasty"; other members included fellow genre stars Monique Gabrielle, Julie Strain, Linnea Quigley and Dian Parkinson. Their specialty was fetish videos, and Rhonda, praise J.R. "Bob" Dobbs, participated in a few. *Las Vegas Bust* was a "behind-the-scenes look at busty Rhonda Shear and Monique Gabrielle in action at a photo shoot and their night in a Las Vegas casino, gambling and dancing." But that video paled in comparison to *A Shear Delight*, which featured Rhonda, in sheer lingerie, very up-close-and-personal, and included food-smashing with her feet.

Rhonda says she's "somewhat" of a B-movie fan, but readily admits that she couldn't run off the names of them and their stars and such, like she thought she should after all those years of hosting them (and, uh, being in them). But then again, she never considered herself strictly a horror host, not in the Elvira vein. Though the show started with sexploitation and horror fare, it soon broadened its horizons and featured ... well, just about anything, including a heapin' helpin' of the network's own made-for-TV movies. Shear said she thinks she is associated more with movies that have bikinis in them than with the horror genre.

The *Draculina* interview was done in 1995, before the end of the show, and before she embarked on a completely different career course. She said that she had just signed a new three-year contract. But she also noted that the USA Network had just gotten a new president (Barry Diller), and that he might suddenly get the notion that the new prez could very well decide that he had better ideas for night-time programming ... and that's exactly what he did. Desiring a more upscale audience, the network did away with the B-movies, the hosts and, soon, the whole show. At the end of that new three-year contract, Rhonda was informed that it would not be renewed. She ended the interview by saying that she had no plans to get married; that it was "scary," and she wasn't ready to give up that "total freedom" yet.

In January 2001, Rhonda was taken off the market when she was reunited with Van Fagen, her high school sweetheart, and created a whole new market for herself, and a whole new career in lingerie. She launched the companies Shear Enterprises and Rhonda Shear Intimates, which she designed, and started selling them on the Home Shopping Network; she was soon to be seen on shopping channels worldwide. In 2010, Rhonda designed the Ahh Bra, now the #1-selling bra in the world. And yes, she makes millions of dollars, but she gives a lot, too. In 2011, for example, she was the event chairperson and a sponsor of the American Cancer Society's "Making Strides—Put on Your Pink Bra" event. This gave her many chances to meet with women who were struggling with the treatment, or following surgery, and needed bras that were affordable, comfortable and feminine. She was touched by their strength, and began donating products monthly to women's shelters, as well as continuing her nationwide work with charitable organizations that fund research and are designed to empower women. Obviously, there's a lot more to Rhonda than meets the eye.

Other Genre Credits—FILMS: *J.D.'s Revenge*, American International, 1976 (1942 Girl); *Galaxina*, Marimark Productions, 1980 (Mime/Robot); *Spaceballs*, Brooksfilms, 1987 (Woman in Diner); *Frogtown II* (a.k.a. *Return to Frogtown*), York Pictures, 1992 (Fuzzy); *Earth Minus Zero*, Lethal Intent Productions, 1996 (Penny Cooper); *Prison a-Go-Go*, Worldwide International Picture Studios, 2003 (Jackpot); *You Are All Going to Die* (short), 2013 (Herself)

Sister Susie

REAL NAME: Joyce Sterling

HOST: *Chiller Theater* (with Chilly Billy Cardille; 1976–1984), WIIC-TV, Channel 11, Pittsburgh, Pennsylvania

BIOGRAPHY: Joyce Sterling, a.k.a. Sister Susie, was a member of the Chiller Theatre Family, which included Norman the Castle Keeper (Norman Elder; died in 2000), Stefan the Castle Prankster (Steve Lunchinski; died in 2009), Terminal Stare (Donna Rae) and Georgette, the Fudge-Maker (Bonnie Sue Barney). Chilly Billy, in a 2001 interview with the author and Paul Riggie, had this to say:

> They let me add a family after eight or ten years. I used to write the skits, but we never memorized them, we just ad libbed, and in that way it was spontaneous. They were a lot of fun to work with.

Also worth a mention is a distaff member of the Chiller Family, "Common-Eltha." Featured in the 1965 commercial breaks as a spokes-ghoul for Commonwealth Heating & Plumbing, she was made up as Vampira and seated in a tub. She was played by Marilyn Eastman, who starred in the original *Night of the Living Dead*. Another *Night of the Living Dead* player, Karl Hardman, head of Karl Hardman Studios, produced the commercials and did Marilyn's makeup.

Skully Macabre (See: Grizelda Macabre)

Stella

REAL NAME: Karen Scioli

HOST: *Saturday Night Dead* (1984–1990), KYW-TV, Philadelphia, Pennsylvania

BIRTHPLACE: Philadelphia, Pennsylvania

Stella

BIOGRAPHY: Stella, known in real life as Karen Scioli, hosted *Saturday Night Dead* on KYW for seven years, following the station's broadcast of *Saturday Night Live*. They were a clever lot, those chaps at KYW. But people forgot all about the title as soon as they laid eyes on the buxom Stella.

Karen hailed from Philly, which explains the "Man-Eater of Manayunk" appellation (it's a working-class neighborhood near the Schuylkill River); she was also known as the Daughter of Desire. As opposed to Misty Brew, who was told to be sexy, but not too sexy, Stella was under no such constraints, probably due to the later hour. Stella took much pleasure from half-clad hunks; she often had one or two hanging in her dungeon to fulfill her unspeakable desires. For instance, in one 1987 show, Stella smeared whipped cream on the chest of one of those young men, and then began to eat the whipped cream with a spoon. "There's a little slut locked up in all of us," she told the *Philadelphia Inquirer* in 1986. But it was all done with a nod and a wink; Stella's personality and skits could be described in the same way as one critic described the James Bond movie *Thunderball*: "It stands on tiptoe at the outermost edge of the suggestive, and gazes yearningly down into the obscene."

Stella's official biography included the following information: "Stella was born in North Libido, New Jersey ... a small village outside of Atlantic City. She is the only child of traveling hecklers. Her parents dropped her in a plastic bucket at Fifth and Shunk, in front of Guido's Hair Weaving and Plumbing Supplies, but for all intents and purposes, she was raised by a flock of pigeons. Reincarnated 37 times, Stella remains the typical ghoul next door." The real woman behind Stella's delightfully deviant behavior and cantilevered cleavage was actually a Philly-born actress and homemaker who weekly costumed herself in a push-up bra, slinky black gown, a feather boa, false eyelashes and a mole on her right cheek to become Philly's sexiest horror host. As she said in *American Scary*: "You put on cleavage late at night when people are drunk, word gets around, and they're gonna watch. It was the cleavage; you know, you show up with the cleavage of death in a black evening gown, everybody wants to see this... It was a big thing, I'm sure Elvira went through that, too." This was confirmed by Walter Betson, an original *Saturday Night Dead* fan: "You couldn't turn it off. No matter how bad the B-movie was, I had to keep it on to find out what

Stella, the legendary Man-eater from Manayunk, strikes a glamour pose in the mid–1980s.

Stella and Hives were gonna do next, because you never knew what was gonna happen. There were, uh, obvious reasons why I wanted to see Stella on Saturday night..."

According to Scioli, "Stella was not a vampire, she was not dead, she was not undead; she was a vamp. She was a loser, she was a big loser; she was greedy, selfish and mean-spirited ... and everybody loved her!" She had help; other regulars on the show included Stella's canopied bed, which she called "Beda Lugosi," (it talked and vibrated), Skeeves the Butler (Bill Brown), who was replaced by Hives the Butler (Bob Billbrough), Cousin Mel (Glenn Davish), who was constantly being told to shut up, and Iggy, a faceless, towering dungeon monster who ate anybody that Stella didn't like. But all the viewers ever saw was Iggy's arm; the arm and Iggy's voice were provided by the multi-talented Davish. He also played mad scientist Dr. Schuylkill. Psycho psychic "Madame Tofutti" (Donna Ryan) and (actress) Kathy Robinson rounded out the cast. She also had guests, such as Rip Taylor and Zacherley, of whom she professed to be a big fan. During Zach's TV horror host days, said Scioli, "he came on about 11 o'clock at night, which was very, very late, and he terrified me, but I was so intrigued and fascinated by him, that we would beg, 'Oh, please let us stay up,' and Mom was like, 'You're going to have nightmares,' and we said, 'Oh please, let us stay...'" In turn, she inspired the same devotion: "Most of the people who come up to me today, and they watched it, hit puberty with me ... so they would sneak downstairs and watch *Saturday Night Dead* at one o'clock in the morning, and it would scare the living daylights out of them..." Stella became a Philly legend: "My show was a ratings winner. These were the days when only a small part of the population had VCRs, so people actually stayed up at one o'clock in the morning to watch the show."

Set in Stella's haunted condo, the show featured such supernatural delights as séances, furniture that moved on its own, and a victim reduced in size and trapped inside a bottle of Mrs. Butterworth's pancake syrup. The show didn't just rely on the standard public domain movies or the usual Universal and Hammer offerings; it utilized such "gems" such as *Night Fright, Shivers, Zombies of Sugar Hill, Zombie Lake*, Al Adamson's shameful *Dracula vs. Frankenstein* and *The Legend of Boggy Creek* ("starring no one"). The show's opening consisted of a Duke Ellington number underneath the announcement, "This is *Saturday Night **Dead***, starring Stella, the man-eater from Manayunk!" According to Bob Billbrough, "Even though we had a bigger budget than, I think, a lot of horror show hosts, it was still a low-budget show." Scioli was more succinct: "Our show was so cheap, I would buy inflatable dolls at the porno shop, and it was like an extra actor that we didn't have to pay!"

Scioli was old-school, a local host: "Even today, I think the only local programming you see is the local news, or a couple of magazine shows that you'll see on Sunday mornings." Billbrough concurred: "It's something that we've lost ... we've lost the possibility of making a mistake, and the possibility of not being perfect on camera, and that's a shame. I think I'm very lucky to have grown up in a time when there was home-grown television.... There's a creativity that's been lost.... That's why somebody can talk about an Ernie Kovacs, and get a smile on their face. Even though they might've seen only one thing Ernie Kovacs had ever did, it was new, it was fresh, it was original, and it was theirs."

Like more than a few of the hostesses in this book, Karen wrote her own show: "I

Karen Scioli gives us a big smile as Stella in 1984.

didn't realize that I was going to have to write the show; when I was hired, I just thought somebody would hand me a script or whatever every week. I had all of these great ideas, and I used them all in the first two shows! I'm, like, 'Now what am I gonna do?' But then when I said, you know, 'I can't do this, I can't write every week,' and the producer would go off and write a script, and then I would hate it, and I'd say, 'I'm not saying that, it's horrible,' and then I'd rewrite it... It's a discipline, you fall into a pattern."

Scioli wears the badge of horror host with pride: "I've been off the air since 1990, and I'm constantly getting new batches of photographs printed up because I still get asked for photographs. I am so honored to be part of this bizarre, weird subculture.... Hey, look at me, I'm a Jersey housewife, you know? I'm shocked that it's still out there and still exists and is still talked about; I was always surprised when it was actually going on... It's really thrilling to be part of that whole culture.... I like it." Billbrough does, too: "My time with *Saturday Night Dead* was like play... We called ourselves the KYW Brat-pack, because we got away with murder! We got away with double entendres, triple and quadruple entendres. We'd entendre on top of entendre. Nobody stopped us; we were the kids in the candy store."

In 1997, Scioli and Robert Dunbar co-wrote Scioli's one-woman show *Bats*, which ran at the Society Hill Playhouse. It received an Honorable Mention in the ALR "New Play Search" and was a semi-finalist at the Pennsylvania State Theater's "New Plays Festival." She was featured in the documentary *American Scary* in 2006 and in the film *Apocalypse Kiss* in 2014. The still-striking Scioli now stars on WOGL's *Breakfast Club* (as "Rere Dinucci"), along with Ross Brittain and Valerie Knight. On April 15, 2015, she was a featured guest at Philadelphia's "Creature Features: As Seen on TV" live event. She's a member of the Horror Host Hall of Fame.

Other Genre Credits—FILMS: *Apocalypse Kiss*, Potent Media, 2014 (Adrian's Mother); DOCUMENTARY: *American Scary*, POOB Productions, 2006 (Herself/Stella)

Stella Lugosi

REAL NAME: Jo Rowan

BIOGRAPHY: "So ... there are ... two ... Stellas! *Two* ... Stellas!" This paraphrase of the great Bela Lugosi's line from *The Thirteenth Chair* is appropriate. After all, everybody's heard of *the* Stella, the Maneater from Manayunk, but while researching this book, I stumbled across buried treasure: Stella Lugosi. This is the tale of the Great Lost Horror Hostess.

It all started with only the faintest memories from fellow author and Bela Lugosi expert Gary D. Rhodes: "My first *Famous Monsters* was bought in 1981, I think. Though I was watching horror films on TV starting around 1976, there was no host at that point, in Oklahoma or Texas, who I saw. Oklahoma City's Count Gregor had, I think, gone on hiatus, and the town's Stella Lugosi (whom I later met) was also long gone from the tube by then. By that time, the woman who played her was teaching Dance at Oklahoma City University, where my eldest sister studied under her; ballet, etc. I never really knew much more than that, though I have to say, it is a great name, Stella Lugosi."

The woman who had played Stella Lugosi was in reality Jo Rowan, who still teaches at OCU. Rowan is a dancer, master ballet teacher and choreographer. She founded, and is director of, the American Spirit Dance Company (which has toured worldwide) at Oklahoma City University; there, she is also Professor of Dance. She was trained at both the School of American Ballet and the Bolshoi Ballet in Moscow. She has performed in ballets and operas across the U.S., including the Cincinnati, Dallas, Garden State and Metropolitan Ballets and the Cincinnati, Dallas, Philadelphia and Tulsa Opera. Rowan has been an instructor for all the major dance companies, such as Dance America and the Boston Ballet. She has created dance instruction in all types of media, and was the principal researcher on Michael Allen's *How to Make It in Musicals*. Rowan has performed nationwide in Actors' Equity musicals, as well as in TV commercials and the short-lived PBS series *The Consumer Survival Kit*. She has received numerous awards and honors; in 2009, she was chosen for a National Association of Dance and Affiliated Artists Lifetime Achievement Award. She just wasn't a horror host.

So how does she still rate inclusion in this book? Read on. The following conversation took place on January 4, 2016:

JR: I can tell you about the background of what this was, but I don't think it's something you're trying to do. You're trying to get people who actually had a show that was running, and people watching it, and I really didn't get that far. [My show] had some splashy moments; I showed it could be funny.... I have VHS [copies], although I don't know if they still work, because they've been out in a very cold garage since 1980. I think it was 1980 that I pitched it. It *was* produced; we did a number of segments, but whether it actually ran or not, I'm not really sure. But it was not picked up. But I enjoyed it, and I thought it was very funny. We used to lip-sync to Donna Summer's [*starts singing*] "Dim All the Lights." There were a whole lot of different things, mist, and smoke, and fog, and a red chaise…. I costumed it with a blood-red, full-neck, drapey gown, and black chiffon things hanging off the back of the gown, all the way down, long sleeves at the arms, and a crazy-looking wig. It wasn't so much like the classic, dark-eyed, Addams Family Morticia look, you know that? This was a different take on things. But the powers-that-be on Channel 9 here in Oklahoma City did not pick it up. So it was a gig and I gave it a shot. I like doing lots of different things in life, so I've not only been a ballerina, but I've also worked as a comedian, lots of musicals, I worked at Actor's Theater in Louisville, so I've done a lot of … stuff. So, I mean, I can answer some of these questions, but it didn't actually run.

BC: *I'm just happy that you got in touch with me, because some people, particularly ones that have accomplished as much as you, simply refuse to acknowledge that part of their career…*

JR: Why would that be?

BC: *I don't know.*

JR: I don't either, because if they put time into it, and if they thought it was funny, and if they enjoyed doing it, I would think that there wouldn't be a problem with that, I mean … what is it? Some kind of advanced hubris, like they don't want to have been a horror host? I think it's a funny idea.

BC: *I guess they've moved on from it or something and they just think they've gone beyond that, or maybe they're embarrassed, I don't know. So, what was going to be the name of your show?*

JR: Well, I was Stella Lugosi; I'm the one who thought that up, because I'm a Martian Irish person who likes to make puns on words. …I have boxes of VHS tapes, because, as a dancer, there's a lot of stuff that I've got. I'd have to see if I could find it, because when it comes to the VHS stuff, I've got the pitch and the production and all of that, but I don't have any promotional pictures because it didn't get around to having anybody put that kind of money into promoting it within the community. There was never any kind of advertisement for it in the papers, because they didn't pick it up but I do have all the shows; that's probably where this guy, who unfortunately I don't really know or remember—and I don't want him to be insulted by that, because I guess we knew each other back in the '80s, but, see, I teach about 200 kids a year, and they all graduate and go on, then I get a new group, so it's hard for me to remember everybody, I must've taught thousands of people since I've been here in Oklahoma City.

BC: *Well, he didn't say that you taught him, you taught his sister.*

JR: So maybe he saw it when I was showing it, because I have a warped sense of humor, I thought it was funny, and I used to show the kids, like, you don't just have to be a dancer, you can do lots of things! Be a triple threat; sing, act, you know, don't get so hung up on yourself that you think something is beneath you. I just wanted them to see what their professor, who was the chair of the department, what kind of stuff I would do to have fun… So I don't know whether you're doing anything on people whose things did not run [*laughs*], but that's the situation!

BC: *Well, as Jimmy Stewart would say, that's a very interesting situation! Why didn't they pick it up?*

JR: I'm not really sure. TV is a very precarious [business], you really don't know what's gonna go and what won't go. There's so many things that are pitched during that week, what do they say, the swaps or whatever…

BC: *Sweeps?*

JR: Yes, the sweeps. And then they go and do three episodes and they're not picked up … or somebody's a newscaster and all of a sudden they're gone because they need somebody younger. I think television is very precarious. They can't go into it thinking "I've got a job," you've got to go into it thinking, "Okay, I'm not gonna worry about this, I'm just gonna pitch it. You know, they might pick it up, they might not, but it's not life or death! It's not like 'Oh my goodness, I put my soul into this'; no, I just think up goofy things." Like for the kids, I had a chicken costume, and I was the Barnyard Weather Chicken [*laughs*], and I used to say, "Okay, kids, be sure and tell your parents that tornado is coming near your barnyard!"

BC: *Well, how did you come up with the idea of doing it in the first place?*

JR: God only knows [*laughs*]! I don't know, I think there was a guy on television that had a lot of black around his eyes and a big top hat, kind of looking like Jack the Ripper rather than a vampire, and I thought, "Holy cow, that is so stupid, what they need is a woman doing something, but to not be ugly or scary, but sort of like seductive in a certain way..." because I lounged on a sofa with a whole bunch of steam coming at me, you know, mist and fog, and I'm going, "Cough, cough, 'Dim all the lights'" and I'd fall off the sofa, that's the kind of stuff it was. That's what it was, and I thought it was really funny, but the guy in charge of Channel 9 did not, so that's where it went.... But they produced it, you know, he gave me a shot. I pitched it to him in his office and he said, okay, go and try it, and then I got a producer, one of those gung-ho kids. And they went into their props, and got the darn couch out and I read the script, and ... that's the way it went. Who can say? Who knows what goes on in someone's brain? When something is tremendously wonderful, why don't they think so? [*Laughs*] Why didn't you think that was good? I was sexy, not ugly ... it was funny and good, and coughing with all the smoke coming in there ... one time, I came out of a crypt.... They had a coffin and a whole bunch of dirt...

BC: *How many episodes did you do?*

JR: I think three or four, there weren't very many.

BC: *Did you have any sidekicks or anything?*

JR: No, no.... I wrote it, I costumed it, and I performed it, but they produced it. There was a circular staircase that went up to nothing; they green-screened it in the back, and I would take off from the circular staircase, with a big fan blowing my black chiffon out the back. I still don't know why they didn't pick it up, it was so good!

BC: *Well, I suppose there's no accounting for taste. But it's a great name!*

JR: Yeah, that was such a great show, and it died [*laughs*]. And then, see, Seinfeld came, and he did his show about nothing, and his worked. How do you know, you know? Mine was sort of about nothing, but it was fun. I don't care; as you can see, I went on to many, many other things.

BC: *Oh, an incredible number of things. You've performed on stages all over the world.*

JR: Yeah, for PBS I was the main goofy person for *Consumer Survival Kit* when that was on in the '80. I played a laxative! There were three of us; one was Bulk, that was this big, fat, tubby guy, and the other one was.... I don't know, there were three different kinds of laxatives, I don't even know which one I was, but I wasn't Bulk! And that one went! That one was picked up! My sexy red dress with the high décolletage, the big wig, "Dim All the Lights," that was not picked up; too bad. You know what could be? Oklahoma's very conservative ... I might have been a little bit over-the-top. I'll tell you, Bobb, I'm still a little bit over the top for some of the people here in this city.

BC: *I know the feeling...*

Suspira Sheridan

REAL NAME: Kathy Brown

HOST: *The Ghastlee Movie Show* (2008–2013), T-W Cable Channel 20, Dayton, Ohio

BIOGRAPHY: A. Ghastlee Ghoul was a mainstay of the neo-host movement for over 20 years. One of the co-founders of the Horror Host Underground, he married Suspira at the October 2003 Cinema Wasteland convention: the world's first horror host wedding. He and Suspira have, er, given up the ghost, choosing instead to work on other projects, including their house. Ghastlee has done a lot of interviews but very few, if any, have been done with his wife, Suspira. She granted me this interview in February 2016:

SS: I'm originally from Massachusetts. I've been watching horror movies since I was five. The scarier they were, the more I enjoyed them. I still remember my mother would walk in and say, "How can you watch that stuff?" Then I began to collect horror props to terrify the neighbors and work in various haunted house attractions.

BC: *How did you come to be a horror host?*

SS: I was introduced to Ghastlee (Bob) by my very special friend Dr. Creep from *Shock Theater*. He brought me to Bob's show wearing a Santa hat and told Bob that I was his Christmas present. I started appearing on *The Ghastlee Movie Show* as a regular, and I thought, "Great, I'm having fun hosting movies that I enjoy."

BC: *Was the character Suspira created by you?*

SS: I created Suspira as a vampire because they are my favorite characters. I shortened the name of one of my favorite Euro-Horror movies, *Suspiria*. Bob uses his middle name Hinton in a lot of his work, so I kept my family name of Sheridan with my character.

BC: *When did the show start?*

Kathy Brown as Suspira Sheridan, with her husband, A. Ghastlee Ghoul, in a 2011 photo.

SS: Bob had been doing his show for 20 years; I came on during the last five seasons. We did a few specials for the Monster Channel, and I hosted a short spin-off called *Suspira's Twisted Toy Shop*.

BC: *You said you were no longer doing new shows. When and why did you stop?*

SS: We stopped doing shows because Bob got tired of doing them and said he ran out of ideas. The rest of the cast tried to help, but Bob was producer, director and cameraman. The rest of us didn't have much choice.

BC: *Some of the other, newer hostesses in this book have already called it quits as well. Do you think the movement is dying out?*

SS: I only see some of the horror hostesses at conventions occasionally, so I really don't know why they stopped doing shows. I know Penny Dreadful, Janet Decay and [Sally] the Zombie Cheerleader still do shows.

BC: *You carried on the tradition of great horror hosts from Cleveland that started with Ghoulardi, the Ghoul, and then Son of Ghoul. Did you ever feel any pressure from that legacy?*

SS: I personally don't feel any pressure. Most of the horror hosts are my friends. They have always been very supportive and all bring unique styles to their shows.

BC: *Who will carry the torch, now that you've finished?*

SS: I'm sure there will always be creative people who enjoy horror and sci-fi and will want to share that with others.

BC: *Did you help write the show?*

SS: I did help with writing some of the show. The whole cast came up with ideas. Bob was also very big on improv. He would give us a rough outline and we would fill in the sketch. I provided occasional props such as the singing flowers, and the segments of *Suspira's Twisted Toy Shop*.

BC: *What's your day job?*

SS: I'm a nurse, and a singer in a rock band, Splattertude. Splattertude started when Bob, Louu the Xmas Devil and I did short musical segments at Ghastlee's Saturday night variety shows at the Cinema Wasteland Convention in Cleveland. All three of us had been involved with music and bands most of our lives. Our original band was called No Bad Kitty after my cat, who thought that was his name. Later we tried to find a band name that nobody had, which is difficult. We were doing a lot of underground goth-rock punk shows. So I put Splatter (horror) and 'tude (attitude) together and came up with Splattertude—a big mess with attitude! And even though we've added singers and musicians, we always end up with our three original members, but we make a *big* noise. Currently, we've started playing a lot of outdoor music festivals, which we really rock. We do mostly original music, but also some covers. Bob and I recently bought a huge house, with a huge basement which we're hoping to convert into a recording space.

BC: *Do you have any horror host role models?*

SS: I guess my horror host models would be Dr. Creep, Barry Hobart and of course vampires!

BC: *What are some of your fondest memories of the show?*

SS: My fondest memories are, of course, meeting Ghastlee, working with Dr. Creep, and being a crazy, dysfunctional family pushing the limits.

BC: *Funny you should say dysfunctional. Are there any especially dysfunctional memories of the show?*

SS: They were *all* dysfunctional; that's what we do best. Probably Louu the Xmas Devil catching his hair on fire from some flash powder during a show, Dr. Creep pinching our asses, and of course being stalked by Grimmsburger the doorman.

BC: *How did it feel to get married at a horror convention?*

SS: Having all of our horror host family together to share our special day. Grimm drove me up in a hearse; one of my bridesmaids, the Zombie Cheerleader, got caught in the rollers. Dr. Creep was being best man, Carpathian and Kuzibak handling the ceremony. And, of course, being carried off by Chucky.

HOST: *The Ghastlee Movie Show* (1988–2013), T-W Cable Channel 20, Dayton, Ohio

Tabitha

REAL NAME: Tabitha Halley, a.k.a. Tabitha Clutterbuck
BIRTHPLACE: Melbourne, Australia
HOST: *Graveyard Shift* (1997–1998), Arena Pay TV Channel, Melbourne, Australia
BIOGRAPHY: Tabitha Halley has been a TV presenter, voice artist and producer for almost 20 years. She's been involved with practically every TV network in Australia, and affiliated with the medium in over 20 other countries. Tabitha spent seven years as location producer for the series *The Great Outdoors*, one of her most fulfilling experiences. Harold Achatz, from Sydney, contributed this brief bit of info to E-Gor's Chamber (used with permission): "The show goes out each Friday from 8:30 p.m. to about 1 or 1:30 Saturday morning, and then is repeated from the start so it goes for the rest of the night."

Michael Monahan (Dr. Ghoulfinger) elaborates in E-Gor's Chamber (used with permission):

> For the last couple of years, Australians have been enjoying Tabitha, host of a Friday night double bill (and then some) called *Graveyard Shift*. They book theme nights: "Love in Vein" for *Return of the Vampire* and *Corridors of Blood*; "Frankly My Dear" for *Curse of Frankenstein* and *Frankenstein Must Be Destroyed*, etc. They also mix in documentaries, including the syndicated John McCarthy series *The Fearmakers*, with even the documentaries reflecting the night's theme. The "Frankly My Dear" evening screened the *Fearmakers* episode on Terence Fisher, for instance. A night of Ed Wood consisted of *Plan 9 from Outer Space, Night of the Ghouls* and *The Haunted World of Edward D. Wood*.
>
> Tabitha is a saucy little thing—sexy, slyly humorous, smart, and fearless. She has a tendency to get her movie facts wrong on occasion, but clearly loves the genre. She's developed quite a following, and has appeared in numerous magazine interview-photo essays. Tabitha has recently appeared, er, *au naturel* in a large format fashion-art magazine called *Black & White*. The theme for the magazine is "Heroes, Devils, and Angels," and it features models and actors and such in a wide variety of often mythical scenarios. While many present themselves as literal winged angels and demons, Tabitha pays tribute to Bettie Page.

Other Genre Credits—TELEVISION: *20 to 1*: "Adults Only 20 to 1—Movie Monsters," 2010 (Herself); *The Professor's Scary Movie Show*: *The Giant Gila Monster*, 2015 (Herself, in archive footage)

Tarantula Ghoul

REAL NAME: Suzanne Waldron (1932–1982)
BIRTHPLACE: Portland, Oregon
HOST: *House of Horror* (October 9, 1957—November 26, 1958), KPTV, Channel 12, Portland, Oregon

BIOGRAPHY: "Ever had that strangled feeling? Ever had your throat slit? Oh, well! Have a bang-up Fourth of July. Bet you're scared to hold a lighted firecracker. See you on *House of Horror*." So read the hilariously politically incorrect print ad for a show featuring another of the original women horror hosts, the alluring and mysterious Tarantula Ghoul. There are no known video records of her show; the only recordings of Tarantula are a couple of songs she recorded with her backing band, the Gravediggers (flip sides of a 45 RPM record). I could "scare up" very little biographical material on her at all.

Another local print ad read: "WE DARE YOU to watch *House of Horror* (You'll scream with terror)—Tarantula Ghoul presents *The Cat People*, RKO 1943... Wednesday 10:30 P.M. on KPTV, Channel 12 ... P.S.—Not recommended for children, sissies, or the weak-hearted. (Chicken if you don't)" Accompanying the ad was a *very* Charles Addams-ish drawing of Tarantula.

Here's the most substantial piece of info out there, part of an article ("TV's Nightmares") on horror hosts in the February 1959 issue of *TV Star Parade.* The section on her is called "Tarantula Ghoul pokes morbid fun at everything within range of Portland's KPTV"):

> Nobody, but nobody, is safe from the witty, but acid, tongue of Tarantula Ghoul, a cross between the Charles Addams woman and a "road company" Tallulah Bankhead, who welcomes viewers to her *House of Horror* in Portland, Oregon, on Wednesdays (10:30 P.M., KPTV). She attacks the Highway Commission for removing the few decent death traps left, assails the City Zoo Commission for not exhibiting prehistoric animals, and kids the D.A.R. (Daughters of the American Revolution) with her own organization, the D.S.W.T. (Daughters of the Salem Witchcraft Trials). She's active in the Black Cross, lectures on Second Aid, and keeps her finger in the political pie through her party, the Cemetarians (which boasts more ex-presidents than any other political group). With an occasional assist from Milton, a retired grave-robber turned gardener, Suzanne Waldron clowns up the Tarantula role enough to win family acceptance for the show. Taranch, as she's known off-camera, introduces the films either with a special set or from her "home"—a weirdly decorated room overlooking a rundown cemetery (which she refers to as "the neighborhood") and a patio where she and Milton "plant things." For *Frankenstein* pictures, the lab was recreated for her entrance from the operating table. For the *Mummy* films, she made her entrance from a mummy case. For *Murders in the Rue Morgue*, she did the show in French with English subtitles. *King Kong* was presented as a satire of *This Is Your Life*, with a large studio audience of costumed monsters paying tribute to a live chimp, Kenya, an alleged great, great grandson of Kong. A native of Portland, Suzanne describes herself as having been "depressingly tall, thin, and shy" during high school. But at Highland University in Las Vegas, New Mexico, she discovered the value of individualism—which she had. Ironically, her first dramatic appearance was as one of the witches in *Macbeth*. After college, stock and touring shows, she returned to Portland to do radio commercials. Since the horror show started in 1957, Suzanne's been carted around in coffins, appeared with gorillas, [and] held press parties in cemeteries, etc. Her most embarrassing moment—she fell asleep in a coffin and did NOT arise as scheduled for the half-time ceremonies of a nationally televised football game. Her most frightening time was appearing on stage with an 11-foot boa constrictor which, at the last minute, replaced the smaller, less-active snake that she was used to. In her free time, Suzanne reads, and listens to hi-fi in an apartment she shares with a Great Dane named Frankenstein. She likes people, all kinds of music (she made two R'n'R records—"King Kong" and "Graveyard Shift"), dancing, art, skiing, riding and surf-swimming. She still does commercials, and spoofs the Movie of the Month, looking ahead to the day the horror craze joins Davy Crockett, but the way things look now, that may be a long way off.

The only "things" this writer failed to mention were her "regular" snake's name (it was "Baby"), her rattlesnake and her tarantula, Sir Galahad.

Another interesting artifact comes in the form of a *faux* "Dear Abby"-type column-promo piece from a local publication:

> *Tell me Your Problems* (Watch the Tarantula Ghoul show—Wed. Nights at 10 p.m.—KPTV Channel 12): Dear Tarantula, I wish to thank you for the wonderful way you've helped my business. All sorts of talented people who want to get on TV are employing me to bump them off so they too can be ghosts and become TV stars. Fingers Malzone, Murder, Inc. Have gun, will murder.

Tarantula replied: "I am not a ghost. I'M a GHOUL! I am not in accord with such drastic measures being taken to get into television. So few of us in the veil beyond ever really make [*sic*]. It would be much simpler if people would just buy automobile dealerships, then they can ALL be on TV!—Tarantula"

Suzanne Waldron as the ultra-cool Tarantula Ghoul, along with The Hunchback of Notre Doom, 1957 (courtesy George "E-Gor" Chastain).

One intrepid fan contacted one of Suzanne's sons and discovered what happened to her: She got pregnant, and had no husband, she was removed from the air. She went on to act in the theater, and still did commercials in Portland, until the family moved to Omaha. There, just short of her 50th birthday, she died of cancer in 1982.

Terminal Stare

REAL NAME: Donna Rae
BIRTHPLACE: West Mifflin, Pennsylvania
HOST: *Chiller Theater* (1976–1984), WIIC-TV, Channel 11, Pittsburgh, Pennsylvania
BIOGRAPHY: Donna Rae played the unforgettable character Terminal Stare on Pittsburgh's *Chiller Theater,* and reprised her role for a couple of Chiller Reunion specials and *Chiller Theater* Halloween cruises on the Gateway Clipper. She never spoke once during the entire run of the show, the cruises or at conventions. There have been more than a few sidekicks who have played their parts mute, but none of them had her looks, or, more importantly, the *look....* Terminal Stare's stare seemed to burn holes through the camera. And although her character was "dumb," Rae was anything but. A reporter for Pittsburgh TV's *Evening Magazine,* she started the Pittsburgh New Works Festival, an annual event dedicated to fostering the development of original one-act plays, and was responsible for *Womenscene,* an evening of monologues and short scenes written for women and about women to benefit women, in 2008.

Donna Rae as Terminal Stare, one of the most popular members of Pittsburgh's *Chiller Theater* family, in an autographed photo from 1964.

Vampira (1922–2008)

REAL NAME: Maila Elizabeth Syrjaniemi, a.k.a. Maila Nurmi

BIRTHPLACE: Petsamo, Finland

HOST: *The Vampira Show* (April 30, 1954–May 2, 1955) (the pilot-preview was called "Dig Me Later, Vampira"), KABC-TV, Channel 7, Los Angeles, California; *Vampira Returns* (1956), KHJ-TV, Channel 9, Los Angeles, California

BIOGRAPHY: I thought that this entry would be easy to write. But as one delves deeper into the mystery that was Maila Nurmi, one thing becomes apparent: Aside from the few solid, documented facts, such as when her show aired, the magazine exposure and such, most of the information about her life, loves and what have you came from Maila. And when you asked her about, well, almost any aspect of her career ... and I apologize for using another Pittsburgh Steelers reference here, but I think it fits Maila Nurmi like a waist-cincher. Gary M. Pomerantz, in his monumental *Their Life's Work* (Simon & Schuster, 2013), described why Terry Bradshaw was popular with the Pittsburgh press corps, starting off with a quote from Bradshaw: "'Ten guys would talk to me, and ask me the same question, and they'd get ten different answers! I wanted everybody to have a scoop ... nothin' wrong with that.' For Bradshaw, an interview remains a performance, and he gives himself to his role completely." If you've been asked the same questions a thousand times, you're probably going to answer a little differently each time, if for no other reason than to keep yourself from getting bored. And I think it was the same for both Bradshaw and Nurmi; each interview was a performance, and they just wanted everyone to have a scoop. But it gives biographers fits when it comes to trying to nail down a definitive version of their life stories.

She was a hipster before the word was invented. She hung out with James Dean. She went to a Hollywood party in a costume inspired by Charles Addams' Morticia, and a short time later, a legend was born. A legendary character that was not only the first of its kind, but that she created. Vampira was an instant sensation, getting coverage in the national magazines *Newsweek*, *Life* and *TV Guide*. She was nominated for an Emmy. She left the original show after an argument with producer Hunt Stromberg, Jr. (he wanted the rights to the character, she refused to give them up). She went to rival station KHJ and carried on for another year. She didn't cash in the next year, when the "Shock Theater" package made the rounds. She also didn't cash in on the surely many attempts to merchandise the character, but then, she always marched to the beat of her own drummer.

To some of the women in this book, their stint as a horror host was merely a job; a way to pick up some extra money at the station or to help them through school (or, in Nurmi's case, maybe a vehicle to launch her career in evangelism). The new generation does it

The day the pumpkins cried. Vampira, the Godmother of Goth, 1954.

because they want to. Elvira is a multi-million dollar franchise. Their stories are never less than interesting, but virtually none of them contain the operatic peaks and valleys that are the story of Vampira.

The reason she didn't capitalize on Vampira is (I hope) explained below, but it must be said right here and now: a book that I read while researching this book, W. Scott Poole's *Vampira: Dark Goddess of Horror*, is a good book, but sometimes frustrating due to errors. These range from fairly minor (writing that *Abbott and Costello Meet Frankenstein* was made in 1943) to fairly major (he calls Vampirella co-creator Trina Robbins "Trina Roberts" and calls Forrest J Ackerman the publisher, not editor, of *Famous Monsters of Filmland*).

I still think it's a good book, but more for the ways he uses Vampira as a prime example of the overall neuroses, fear, obsessions and consumerism of the '50s and beyond, and what kind of threat her mere existence posed to those conditions. But sometimes Vampira is related to these theories only tangentially, and while one can see his point, it's at those points when it becomes more a case of the author projecting theories onto the character. I would call Poole's book "selectively well-researched." He also wrote that Maila Nurmi was as much of a creation as Vampira, with which I agree. So I will incorporate his research, and note it, but only when the facts differ significantly from the accepted storyline. Vampira fans are much better served by the documentaries *Vampira: The Movie* and, in particular, R.H. Greene's *Vampira and Me*. One of the best moments in the latter is a scene where Greene asks Maila what a cheesecake model is; the look she gives him is priceless (like she can't believe he doesn't know what one is), as is her answer to the question: "Aww ... it's a young bunny in a bikini," she giggles. "I was trying to be cute!"

But we're putting the bat before the hearse. Maila was born in Finland; her family moved to either Ohio (most sources) or Gloucester, Massachusetts (Nurmi), when she was two years old. Poole says that she was actually born in Gloucester, not Finland; he claims that she only said she was born in Finland so that she would have more of a connection to the Finnish poetess Maila Talvio. Of course, she need not have lived in Finland for her parents to name her that, if that were the reason. They lived there for 15 years before moving to Oregon; she moved on to the City of Angels after graduating high school. Nurmi says, in an interview quoted below, that her parents "gave her away." Poole claims she ran away. While she was still living at home, she said in *Vampira and Me*,

> One day I was in the tub. Still at home, 17 years old and Mother had the radio on in the other room. I heard a voice, jumped out of the tub, shrieking, forgetting my modesty, rushed into the bedroom, ran to the radio, threw my arms around it, and shrieked, "Mama, Mama, that radio announcer! That ordinary radio announcer is no ordinary radio announcer! He was talking about airplane wings or something ... he's a genius! That man is a genius! And he's my friend!" Oh, Mother was shocked. "Of course he's a genius! That's Orson Welles! He's a famous genius; everybody knows that! Don't you ever talk like that! He's not your friend! You're Maila Elizabeth Syrjaniemi and you work in a fish cannery in Astoria, Oregon, and don't you forget it! And don't you talk like that—people are gonna say you're crazy." Some months later in New York City, perhaps eight months later when I met Orson Welles and told him that story and he asked me to give my mother a message. "Tell her you are right. ... I am your friend, and tell your mother to have more faith in people."

Nurmi was later, for a short time, linked to Welles romantically, as she was to Marlon Brando.

She began her career, as many actresses do, by modeling; her early poses came for the likes of Alberto Vargas and Man Ray. She used what little money she made from this to finance a trip to New York, where she found work on the stage. In 1944 or 1945, she played a handmaiden to Mae West on Broadway in *Catherine Was Great*, but was fired (according to her) because West thought Nurmi was upstaging her. It was while she was on Broadway that Vampira was really born; although she didn't do the character in name or dress, a midnight show produced by Mike Todd, *Spook Scandals*, featured her screaming, fainting, lying in a coffin and sexily slinking around a graveyard set. Like Elvira, she was a showgirl in a chorus line (where she worked with the Romer Twins; see Moona Lisa).

While Nurmi was on Broadway, she caught the eye of movie director Howard Hawks. Some accounts say that he caught her act; some say he only read about her in *The Hollywood Reporter* or saw a picture. She moved back to Los Angeles. Hawks put her under personal contract for a filmed version of the Russian novel *Dreadful Hollow*, which was to have a screenplay by William Faulkner. Hollywood being Hollywood, the project immediately ran into obstacles (and continued to run into them for years; it never did get made). Nurmi was getting paid $75 a week for essentially doing nothing. Tired of the delays, Nurmi says that she tore up her contract and told Hawks where to put it. ("In one of his many wastebaskets," she recalled in *Vampira and Me*.) Hawks had visions, according to Maila, of turning her into "the new Lauren Bacall," but she considered Hawks "stupid." According to Nurmi, Hawks was, later in his life, a guest at a film school, and someone asked him about Maila, and Nurmi said that he said, "Ah, that's the one that got away."

She returned to supporting herself by doing pin-up photos for magazines, "the kind men like," and working in a cloakroom. In the introduction to Poole's book, Sheri Holman states a couple of times that she was also a bondage model, but no

A rare autographed still of Maila Nurmi as Vampira from 1954 (courtesy Paul Riggie).

record has been found. Nurmi gave her career years as a cheesecake model from 1948 to 1951; she never mentioned the earlier modeling sessions for Vargas and Ray, possibly because they would have to have been done when she was underage. Nurmi claims that she was one of the top ten cheesecake models of the time, and she had plenty of competition—including Bettie Page, something of a legend herself. Maila was certainly aware of Page, but she spoke of the style of some of her work rather dismissively. On the East Coast, Maila said, it was all lingerie, stockings and bondage, on the opposite coast, it was all sun and surf, girls in bikinis rather than bondage. I don't think that Nurmi is being quite fair to Bettie—Page did plenty of bikini shoots, and was even the centerfold in an early issue of *Playboy*. But I feel it was somewhat disingenuous to dismiss Bettie's more fetishistic work, as Maila admitted that the type of work was a major influence on the image of Vampira. What cannot be argued is that both women had a huge influence, not only on style and fashion but, more importantly, on the sexual mores of the time. Both of them were, in their own way, subversive; Vampira was a potent cocktail of sex, death and a dry wit that skewered typical American values of the day. Page, a girl-next-door type who just happened to be wearing stockings and have a ball-gag in her mouth, showed with a literal wink that similar "girls next door" engaged in similar practices, that it wasn't just the province of the decadent upper class or women that looked like they'd been rode hard and put away wet. The two icons also share one other thing in common: They were both re-discovered by the punk rock kids. Both had been virtually forgotten until the punks and succeeding generations helped to seal their status as cultural icons.

It was also during this time that she met and "married" ex-child star and screenwriter Dean Riesner, and the reason for the quotes is that they weren't legally married; it was a common-law cabin. Riesner was mainly a television writer, although he co-wrote the screenplay for *Dirty Harry*, but his most lasting contribution to pop culture was coming up with the name Vampira for his bride's television creation. And although Nurmi called Riesner "my own private teddy bear," the union didn't last long; by 1958, she was on her second husband, John Brinkley, and by 1961, Fabrizio Mioni, presumably by the same arrangement. None of the marriages produced any children.

Maila has said that the reason she created the character of Vampira was because she wanted to raise the money needed to become a traveling evangelist. Her father had been involved in church activities—despite being very much to the left of center in his politics—but Maila herself was not a regular attendee. She was also a committed non-conformist who refused to be bound by traditional values and how American society viewed women, so it is fair to wonder exactly what Nurmi might have preached from her pulpit.

The inspiration for the character that was to become Vampira proper came in 1953, when she attended choreographer Lester Horton's annual Halloween Bel Caribe costume ball. She had an idea for an "Addams Family" TV series for a few years, but not being in the Hollywood mainstream, it never went anywhere. So she decided to make herself up in the style of (the as-yet unnamed) Morticia Addams and went to the Ball, hoping to get discovered and sell the idea for the show to a studio. She got discovered, as related above, but still couldn't sell the idea of a show based on Addams' cartoon family. KABC, however, was more than willing to appropriate the character without permission; however, Maila refused. She told the station to give her a few days to see what she could come up with.

She kept the black wig and dress, but sexed it up considerably with a plunging neckline, a high-slit skirt, which revealed her shapely legs in a pair of fishnet hose, and platform shoes. She also sexed up the presentation; not in the obvious manner of Elvira, but a more subtle, sensuous approach (if a scream, which she used to begin her show after striding down a fog-filled hallway, could be called subtle). And yet it was, especially when followed by a smiling Vampira in her best sex-kitten voice, "Aaaaaah ... screaming relaxes me so." The America of the '50s was definitely not ready for this. "You know, I've often been asked why I don't light my attic with electricity ... isn't that ridiculous? Everybody knows electricity is for chairs.... Our little fairy-tale tonight is called *The Thirteenth Guest*. The *Thirteen* makes it timely, topical ... and terrifying. It's about a humorous fellow who dies ... telling a joke ... something of a deadpan comedian." In a *Cult Movies* #11 article (1994), Nurmi told author Robert Rees what went into the character:

> Vampira was not exactly derived from Morticia [Addams]. Here's how it went—at first, I did the Addams lady exactly at a masquerade ball. A TV studio asked me to portray the character without the consent of Charles Addams. So I kept the dress only (but slit the skirt way up).... Also, of course, I kept the fact that the lady was a Victorian vampire. ...Morticia was a matron, mother and head of a pedestrian household. Vampira was a vamp and a bachelor girl and distinctly adverse to things pedestrian. I wanted the job, but was unwilling to steal so broadly from a respected artist. I thought if I had brought the studio something visually similar, they would accept it. Here is the concoction as I wrote the recipe:
>
> 2 oz. Theda Bara (Vamp, vamp)
> 2 oz. Morticia (morbid Victoriana)
> 3 oz. Norma Desmond (*Sunset Blvd.*)
> 4 oz. Tallulah Bankhead (the voice, dah-ling)
> 2 oz. Marilyn Monroe (Demons are a ghoul's best friend)
> 3 oz. Katie Hepburn (Victorian English)
> 2 oz. Bette Davis (mama, baby)
> 3 oz. Billie Burke (dilettante insouciance)
> 3 oz. Marlene Dietrich (singing voice)
> 8 oz. *Bizarre Magazine* pin-up (big boobs, waist cincher, mesh hose, high shoes and long nails)
>
> Shake vigorously until steaming.

So Maila Nurmi played the character of Vampira, who in turn portrayed other characters in skits on the show, such as Groucho Marx. But she also, sometimes subtly and sometimes not, played, in Vampira, a character that was a parody of America's fixation with "cheesecake" and a parody of the American obsession with "family values." It was a very real example of female empowerment.

As was said, the character became an overnight sensation, and it seemed that Vampira was everywhere, except on store shelves; no Davy Crockett-style "Bat-Skin Caps," no nothing. She was nominated for an Emmy in 1954 for "Most Outstanding Television Personality." The show was only three weeks old when *Newsweek* came to call; six weeks later, a three-page spread in *Life* appeared. Vampira got coverage in the *New York Daily News* as well as international newspapers and magazines. It was exposure which was unheard of for a local television show. She got fan mail from around the world. "I was the number-one item around—for five minutes," she laughingly recalled in *Vampira and Me*. KABC provided an antique car for chaos-causing drives around town.

As Vampira and her show were being touted as flagship programming to potential advertisers, the station launched another hosted movie show, this one exploiting low-budget romances. Its host was the polar opposite of Vampira: Voluptua, the "Love Goddess." Where Vampira spun her web of sex and terror, Voluptua (Gloria Pall) just spun sex; where Vampira resided in a dark, spooky attic, Voluptua held court in her bedroom. "I'm not breathless from hurrying here for our date," she would coo, "I'm breathless because I know the date is with you ... welcome to my boudoir.... I want you to feel as if it's your special hideaway, so relax ... take off your shoes, loosen your tie ... together, you and I are going to be good friends." Pall shared Nurmi's background as a cheesecake model; but whereas Vampira subverted it, Voluptua exploited it to the limit. No clips of Voluptua are known to exist. Voluptua was also the subject of a three-page *Life* spread, and only photos exist of the woman who would often strip down behind a translucent screen into "something more comfortable." By the movie's end, she was often clad only in panties and a man's pajama shirt. Vampira slyly hinted at sex; Voluptua was one of Pall's male-magazine fantasies come to life. KABC promoted them as "the chill and charm girls." Vampira had 54 shows in her original run for the station, plus another 13 when she took the character to another station; Voluptua lasted for a mere seven weeks, her show a victim of outraged moralists. But their only rivalry was on-screen; when Nurmi was down and out (which was often), Pall would take her bags of groceries and hang them on Maila's door.

On August 7, 1954, there came the first in a string of nationally televised appearances (always as Vampira, never Maila Nurmi) on NBC's *Saturday Night Revue*. She next did a game show, *Place the Face*, sort of a combination of *This Is Your Life* and *What's My Line*, hosted by Bill Cullen. Cullen is announcing her appearance on the show, expressing his doubts that such a person even exists, when the stage behind him revolves to reveal a set uncannily like her show. Then she walks up behind him, and when she sees his face, she screams. Then she appeared on the top-rated *Red Skelton Show*, playing in a vampire sketch with Bela Lugosi, with whom she would later "reunite" in *Plan 9 from Outer Space*. She did *The George Gobel Show*, appearing in a lengthy skit with the flat-topped purveyor of po-faced humor.

When Vampira returned to the Skelton show, it wasn't Maila Nurmi. One of the skits was a parody of *The Honeymooners* with guest star Peter Lorre taking Jackie Gleason's role of Ralph, Skelton subbing for Art Carney as Norton, and Alice played by Vampira—at least, that's what it looked like at first glance. But upon closer inspection, Vampira wasn't being played by Maila. It wasn't the first time a TV show or film would appropriate her image, nor was it the last. A thousand questions surround the decision, especially with the real Vampira readily available, but it really all boils down to one: Why?

In 1956, Maila was the model for Maleficent, the evil witch of the classic animated Disney feature *Sleeping Beauty*, despite having undergone a horrific and traumatizing experience to start the year. In 1955, she had moved back to New York City, to get the taste of Hollywood out of her mouth and to get a fresh start, which she attempted by, literally, singing the blues in nightclubs. But on the morning of January 8, she cracked open her apartment door to a man asking for "Peggy." The man turned out to be serial rapist Ellis Barber, who forced the door open and attacked Maila with a straight razor. He told her, "You'll be dead by morning." She said that Barber dragged her up and down stairs; she fought him, by some accounts for close to two hours, and finally managed to escape, nearly nude and bloodied. Barber was captured, and his attack brought the usual throngs of paparazzi, for whom Maila posed for the most disturbing photographs of her career.

They are unsettling and sad; she struck a pin-up model pose, but the skin exposed was not soft and sunlit—it was bruised and battered. It wasn't the first time; a year earlier, there was an L.A. newspaper account of her being molested in public by a crazed fan. The attacker, John Fenwick, was arrested, but for some reason, the reporter who wrote the piece treated an attack upon a woman and her resultant trauma as a joke. "Clutching Hand Brings Screams from Vampira," the headline read, as though there was not a real human being under the makeup. She received the same treatment from the press around Christmas 1956 when her apartment caught on fire; an *L.A. Times* article said that when firemen arrived at the blaze, they expected to find "Vampira's funeral pyre," hinting at some sort of dark ritual, but much to their surprise, "it turned out to be an honest-to-gosh fire." Imagine that! Maila didn't help her case any when she did things like she did on Halloween of that year. She attended a party as a variation on Vampira; the same dress, but in a blond wig, topped off by a witch's hat. But accompanying her was an unidentified male wearing a red jacket, his face wrapped in bandages, who was supposed to be James Dean as accident victim. It was the blackest of humor, obviously instigated by someone who was still in shock over Dean's death. The gossip magazines ate it up.

It was strange that she created the television horror-movie host and then, when the "Monster Boom" hit in 1957–58, she was M.I.A. In 1954, it looked like the world was her oyster; by decade's end she was appearing in Grade-Z (but beloved) productions such as *Plan 9 from Outer Space*, *The Beat Generation* and *Sex Kittens Go to College*. *The Magic Sword* (1962) was the last Hollywood film for over 25 years. The main reason was that she was blacklisted by ABC. They wanted her to sign over her rights to the Vampira character, and when she refused, they began to turn down all offers for other work, even guest appearances on other shows. There has always been the question of whether she was officially blacklisted or if it was an unwritten "gentlemen's agreement." Either way, it worked. Some of the situation can be attributed to Nurmi's headstrong ways, but a lot of it was brought on by the death of James Dean and the scandal magazines' willingness to cast Maila as the "Black Madonna" who somehow had something to do with Dean's death by putting a curse on him with her "black magic" TV show. But, then again, if for nothing else, Hollywood is famous for chewin' 'em up and spittin' 'em out like that. By the mid 60s she was installing linoleum flooring and running an antique store, "Vampira's Attic." She was forced to close its doors because of lack of business; she claimed that people thought it was an antique museum, and rarely asked to buy anything. It only got worse. She was living in real poverty, sometimes working in restaurants in exchange for food, holed up in the back half of a garage with no place to sleep.

Plan 9 from Outer Space, known as "the worst movie ever made" thanks to the reprehensible Medved brothers and the patronizing "bad movie crowd" that followed in their wake, was both the literal blessing and the curse of Vampira's career. It's a curse for the above-stated reasons, but it's also a blessing: Since very little footage of her show exists, it's also the best opportunity to see her. Nurmi had her own, less-than-flattering take on the *Plan 9* experience, as she described it in *Vampira: The Movie*:

> The atom bomb had just been invented, and [Robert] Oppenheimer was much in the news shortly before *Plan 9* was being written [1956]—so Ed Wood's theories about nukes were logical deductions of a probable future. When I first heard about *Grave Robbers from Outer Space*, this is what I heard: [Ed] had 1) film footage of the Hollywood premiere of the first Liberace film, *Sincerely Yours*, 2) stock footage of "flying

saucers," 3) stock footage of tanks, 4) cutting room clips from 3 Lugosi movies, 5) backers who will put up $5,000 from a church group, and 6) the will to formulate a movie from this mismatched footage. It grew into *Plan 9 from Outer Space*. Little did I dream I would be a part of it. Under the cape was the by-then-deceased Bela's wife's chiropractor, not the chiropractor… Other than 15 minutes before his camera (in which I insisted on playing mute and I was paid $200.00. I did *not* work for Ed.

She certainly cared enough about her legacy to start giving extensive interviews as she got on in years, and she certainly cared enough about her "brand" to bring the infamous lawsuit against Elvira (Cassandra Peterson). When horror host Sinister Seymour died, KHJ decided to get a female to host *Fright Night*, Seymour's old show. Apparently, KHJ wanted to revive *The Vampira Show* (after a failed attempt to lure Moona Lisa back to the tube), but with someone else playing the role. One imagines that this was the station's idea, although, the author believes that even at 60, Nurmi could have essayed the role, especially since she said in that article that the Vampira persona was part Norma Desmond. All she would have had to do was play up the Norma Desmond part, and it would have been like old times. But the station said that Nurmi insisted on dancer Lola Folana as her replacement, and they were having none of that. They issued a casting call for a new horror hostess, and Cassandra prevailed. Since the station could no longer use the Vampira character, they left Peterson to her own devices, which led to Elvira, Mistress of the Dark. Now it all comes down to whose version of the story you believe: The only thing that the station and Nurmi could agree on was that she left the production due to that old saw "creative differences"; the station said she decamped early in the process, which left them scrambling and putting out the casting call, while Nurmi said that Peterson was the reason she walked out, because she had never approved her. Here's what Cassandra Peterson said in *Vampira: The Movie* about the lawsuit that was brought against her:

> [KHJ] said they were going to have a character named Vampira, and they wanted somebody who could do this character and host the late-night horror movies. So I agreed to do it, and they told me I needed to come up with a costume that looked spooky… Obviously, I didn't look that spooky … and so a friend of mine came up with a costume that was all sheer, pink, sort of gauzy, with long red curly hair, and a white face, white lips and big black circles under the eyes, and we took it in to them, and said, "How about this look?" and they said, "no, you have to have black hair, you have to have black clothes".... "We want you to look sexy." So my friend designed this costume… He took the wig after … Ronnie Spector … as an homage to her, did the makeup from a Kabuki makeup book, and he obviously sewed the tightest skin-baring dress he could possibly sew.... It's the first day of shooting, and they come running in and go, "You can't use the name Vampira, somebody owns it," and we're like, "Oh, okay, what are we gonna do now?" and they go, "Oh, we'll just pick another name," so everybody writes down a name, and we throw it in a coffee can, and then I pick "Elvira." I'm like, oh my God, it sounds like a country & western song, but, oh well.... I didn't think I'd be doing the job 25 years later, I thought it would be more like a week. Well, a few weeks went by, and I got a subpoena for a lawsuit that said we'd infringed on the character, and the character was too closely based on Vampira, and I was like, "Who the hell is Vampira?" They told me that Vampira was in *Plan 9 from Outer Space*, which … I had never seen. So I took a look at her and I said, yeah, it is similar … but when they tell you to dress in black, look spooky and look sexy, there's not much leeway. …She did sue me; it ended up just being thrown out of court, because she didn't show up at any of the [hearings]. She caused me quite a bit of anxiety and trouble … and a lot of money. Of course, when you get a lawsuit, whether you win or lose, you still have to hire a lawyer… But I didn't feel like I was a responsible party … it was a no-win situation for everybody … but there you go, at least we got a credit at the end of *Ed Wood*, by Tim Burton.

Nurmi waived the appeal, and in a document written by hand, she gave the reasons why: "I, Maila Nurmi, a.k.a. Vampira, Plaintiff, do regretfully declare that in view of lack of counsel, and further in lack of funds, I have no alternative but to discontinue this action." The similarities between the two characters are undeniable, as are the differences, and all the author will say is that he wishes it had never come to that; the readers are left to their own conclusions and opinions.

In 1959, the great Spike Jones released an album called *Spike Jones in Stereo*, a.k.a. *Spike Jones in Hi-Fi* and *A Spooktacular in Screaming Sound*. The Jim Jonson cover painting features monsters a-plenty, a maniacally grinning Jones dressed as a surgeon with a meat cleaver in his hand and, on his left, a female who looks very much like Vampira. In fact, Vampira is listed as one of the contributors. But it was not Maila Nurmi; it was an actress named Loulie Jean Norman impersonating her (and doing a fine job of it). She also did a promotional tour to support the album. A famous photo shows her at one of the tour stops, with Zacherley putting in an appearance.

And then there's James Dean. What is to be made of their relationship, and how close was it? It all depends on who you ask. If you'd asked vicious, Communist-naming gossip columnist Hedda Hopper, she would have said (and did in her 1962 book *The Whole Truth and Nothing But*), "We discussed the thin-cheeked actress who calls herself Vampira on television (and who cashed in, after Jimmy died, on the publicity she got from knowing him, and claimed she could talk to him "through the veil"). He said, 'I had studied the Golden Bough and the Marquis De Sade, and I was interested in finding out if this girl had been obsessed by a satanic force. She knew absolutely nothing. I found her void of any true interest except her Vampira makeup. She has no absolute.'" But, considering the sheer number of outright lies that Hopper published during her career, Hopper as a source must be taken with a salt-lick. Plus the fact that Hopper, of course, ignores the fact that she was one of the people cashing in on Dean's death by including a whole chapter on him in the above-mentioned book. In the 2010 radio documentary *Vampira and Me*, author-director R.H. Greene cites a production memo from the Warner Brothers archives that tells of a visit from "Vampira" made to Dean while he was filming *Rebel Without a Cause*. He also cites a Shelley Winters interview, conducted by Lawrence Frascella and Al Weisel (*Live Fast, Die Young: The Making of Rebel Without a Cause*; Simon & Schuster, 2006), in which she claimed that Dean interrupted an on-set argument with director Nicholas Ray so that Dean could watch *The Vampira Show*. And in the documentary, Nurmi tells Greene that Dean once appeared on her show, with Vampira as a librarian rapping Dean's knuckles with a ruler for "being a very naughty boy." In *Vampira: The Movie*, Nurmi said that Dean was "the closest person to me I've ever had in my life.... I didn't ever have to tell Jimmy what I was thinking, he didn't ever have to tell me what he was thinking, we knew instinctively."

Like Cassandra Peterson, she reportedly dated Elvis, although, like Cassandra, there is little documentation to support this supposition (numerous biographies on Elvis fail to mention either woman). Of course, a book on Elvis's paramours, flirtations and one-night stands would be a massive volume (or three) in and of itself, so perhaps this isn't a surprise. This particular affair, if you want to call it that, was only two or three weeks long, and it caught the two performers at different points in their careers; Elvis was on the way up, and Maila had already started her downwards slide on the slippery slope of success. Before Elvis became as identified with Las Vegas as the Rat Pack, he played an engagement there near the beginning of his career, when he was sending shock waves through the nation. Apparently, they didn't feel the tremors in Vegas; they booed him.

To be fair, the crowd of middle-aged businessmen was not Elvis's target audience (at least, not at that time), and they treated him as most other middle-aged businessmen did at the time—like a pox. Reportedly, it was after he had been booed off the stage that Nurmi met him, as he was dejectedly sitting outside the New Frontier casino. She herself was in Vegas as part of a Liberace revue; the members of the revue had been advised to attend as many of the town's entertainment offerings as possible. She was coy about what actually went on (although it's possible that she was still traumatized over the events at the beginning of the year), but apparently the two enjoyed each other's company for at least a couple of more weeks, attending other various Vegas shows and even being spotted playing bumper cars at the new Frontier's Western Village amusement park.

When the Punk and Goth scenes both found an icon in Vampira, she gained a whole new generation of fans. The Damned, the original horror-punk band, sang a song called "Plan 9, Channel 7" (the music video featured a Vampira lookalike), and practically every "Goth Girl" owes a little to Vampira, if only in spirit. Each and every female horror host owes her a lot more than that. The beautiful, very personable actress Lisa Marie made a spot-on Vampira in the wonderful Disney-Touchstone biopic *Ed Wood* (1994), recreating the real-life incident where Nurmi was so broke, she had to take a bus to the *Plan 9* studio, in full Vampira makeup and costume. It seems that Maila was as dubious about this incarnation of Ed Wood as she was the original; she thought that Disney was trying to steal the image from her in order to turn it into a merchandising bonanza. That never happened, but the movie did its part in helping to return her to the spotlight. The Misfits, the inheritors of the horror-punk mantle, immortalized her in the song "Vampira" (*Misfits Walk Among Us*), and on one of their tours met and posed for pictures with her. (Their original label was called "Plan 9.") Bobby Bare was there first; he recorded a corny country ditty called "Vampira" in 1958. Commander Cody and his Lost Planet Airmen also did a song called "Vampira" in 1978, about the time the Misfits recorded their first version of the song. In 2006, Devin Townsend recorded yet another "Vampira." Nurmi got into the act, doing guest vocals for the punk band Satan's Cheerleaders, on two singles.

Maila Nurmi is a legend, an iconoclast, a pioneer and an inspiration. She passed away from natural causes in 2008, and while people can die, legends live forever.

Other Genre Credits—FILMS: *Plan 9 from Outer Space*, Reynolds Pictures, 1959 (Vampire Girl); *The Magic Sword*, United Artists, 1962 (Hag/Sorceress); *I Woke Up Early the Day I Died*, Muse, 1999 (Woman in Lobby); TELEVISION: *The Red Skelton Hour*: "Dial 'B' for Brush," 1954 (Vampira); *Playhouse 90*: "The Jet-Propelled Couch," 1957 (Vampira); *The Incredibly Strange Films Show*: "Ed Wood, Jr.," 1989, (Herself); *E! Mysteries and Scandals*: "Bela Lugosi," 1998 (Herself), "Ed Wood," 1999 (Herself); GENRE DOCUMENTARIES: *Flying Saucers Over Hollywood—The* Plan 9 *Companion*, 1992; *Vampira: About Sex, Death and Taxes*, 1995; *The Haunted World of Edward D. Wood, Jr.*, 1995; *Schlock! The Secret History of American Movies*, 2001; *American Scary*, 2006; *Vampira—The Movie*, 2006; *Vampira and Me*, 2012

Vampira (2)

REAL NAME: Phyllis Child

HOST: *Shock!* (1958–1959), KUTV, Channel 2, Salt Lake City, Utah; *Mystery Mansion* (1964), KSL-TV, Channel 5, Salt Lake City, Utah

BIOGRAPHY: Roderick (Jack Whitaker) was host of Salt Lake City's edition of *Shock Theater* in 1958 and '59, and the "other" Vampira was his co-host. In 1964 Whitaker briefly returned to the role when he hosted *Mystery Mansion* on a rival station, KSL-TV; this time, there was no Vampira. Following Roderick's appearance on a children's Halloween makeup special, Whitaker stepped out of the spotlight for a return to teaching. Ten years ago, while doing the research for his website, E-Gor heard from one David Humes of Seattle, Washington, that a friend of his was one of Child's two daughters, and that he would be able to get in touch, through her, with Child. Phyllis responded, and Humes forwarded this information to E-Gor in August 2005 (used with permission).

When I started to work at Channel 2 in September 1958, I was going by my married name, Ranson. KUTV was an ABC station, but a year or so later, there was a big shakeup, and it became Salt Lake's NBC station. Channel 4, KTVT, became the ABC affiliate. It was a big deal to make it to NBC, and when the station went to color a few years earlier, they used "The Peacock" at every opportunity. Many people in the business played musical chairs between the three TV stations in Salt Lake City. I had several friends at KSL, which was only two or three doors down the street, and at the radio stations along Social Hall Avenue. Although working there was the most fun to be had while employed, I left my employment at Channel 2 at the end of 1960 to work for a newly elected Salt Lake County Commissioner.

Jack Whitaker ... worked mostly during the late afternoon show for children; he played the role of Kimbo the Clown. One day Jack mentioned that he had been assigned to host the lead-ins for the Saturday night horror movies, to be called *Shock Theater*. Jack planned to call himself Roderick for the show, and asked me to be Vampira, his girlfriend. I asked him what my role would involve, and he told me all I'd have to do was stand there and stare! I said I'd try it; it sounded like fun to me. I would have to furnish my own wardrobe for the show. I asked him what would be appropriate. He said a long, white dress would be the best choice. The only item in my closet that was long and white was my wedding dress, which, I'm sorry to admit, had no sentimental value to me. I couldn't afford to buy a dress or even fabric to make one, so my wedding dress had its second life as a costume for a spook show! Late every Saturday night for the next several months, I went to the station and appeared as Vampira at midnight. It was terrific fun and often so hilarious I had difficulty not breaking up. There was no script as such; it was a seat-of-the-pants type thing. Jack led us and we followed. The other "supporting actors" were station prop boys, Jerry and Ollie Hunter. Jerry played the part of Igor and Ollie was a big hulk who merely wandered around in the background The music came from opera or classical selections, and Jack handled that, too. Usually, at the beginning of the movie, Vampira would be put into a coffin, and Jack would close the lid and the movie would begin; in a subsequent break he directed Jerry and Ollie to raise the lid of the coffin and assist me in my exit. We only had one and a half minutes for the break—oh, the joys of early TV!—so there was no pre-planning at all. During other breaks I got out and stood staring, just as he promised I would. The hardest part was keeping my eyes steady and trying not to laugh! We seldom had a clue of what was expected of us. His instructions for my appearances came willy-nilly. One night I was caught in mid-question just as the red light went on—indicating that we were on the air. "What am I to be doing?" I was asking, and Roderick replied, "Just stare, my dear, just stare!" When the light went off to indicate the movie was rolling, the guys in the control room were yukking it up hilariously!

Nearly every Saturday night, [my daughters] Paula and Cindy begged to stay awake so they could watch me on television; when I finally gave permission for them to do so, they fell asleep before midnight! I don't think they ever saw me as Vampira, and, to my regret, no photos exist that I know of. My friends then didn't accompany me to my gigs. Jack and I—I to a much lesser extent than he—achieved a minor fame around town. That Halloween night—probably 1959—Roderick pushed the coffin containing Vampira for a block. I was "driven" all the way down State Street from Social Hall Avenue and into the lobby of the Lyric Theatre, where I ascended from the coffin and we made a personal appearance prior to the movie. An unruly thong of teenagers and a few adults was gathered at the Lyric to applaud us, and a big cheer went up as I exited the coffin. I felt like a bona fide celebrity!

Veronique Von Venom
REAL NAME: Mindy Robinson (1980–)
BIRTHPLACE: Fall River, Massachusetts

HOST: *Veronique Von Venom—Horror Hostess Hottie* (2012–2013)

BIOGRAPHY: Mindy Robinson graduated from Bristol County Agricultural High School in 1998. She then moved to California, where she attended California State University and graduated in 2006 with a Bachelor of Arts degree in American History. Robinson made her screen debut in the short *Sexy and I Know It* (2011) and since then, the arrow has only pointed up for this very busy actress. Perusing her filmography, it seems that she appears in a movie or television show at least once a month, if not more! The films and shows listed below are only the tip of the iceberg. In 2012, after already having appeared in seven films, she made her first genre effort, *The Haunting of Whaley House*. Later that year, she debuted as Veronique Von Venom in the 13-episode TV series *Veronique Von Venom—Horror Hostess Hottie*. She differed from the usual horror hosts in that her show didn't consist of bumpers wrapped around horror movies; it had a continuing plot, and was as much about her misadventures as it was horror. A typical episode was "Backstabbing Bitches Must Die!" Miss V, as she was referred to on the show, was joined by her "backstabbing bitch friend" Clarisse Starling (Giselle Marie), who reviews the erotic horror novel *Phantom*. They also review (they did a lot of reviews on the show) a DVD boxed set called *When Horror Came to Shochiku*, which includes *The Living Skeleton* and *Goke, Body Snatcher from Hell*. The rest of the show consisted of Miss V finding out that Clarisse was dating Miss V's old boyfriend.

"Personally, I want to be the female Vincent Price," she declared in her first episode. "I wanna be in more horror movies than anyone, and I'm pretty sure I can make that happen." At the rate she's going, she just might make it.

Other Genre Credits—FILMS: *The Haunting of Whaley House*, Asylum, 2012 (Candy Galore); *Killjoy Goes to Hell*, Full Moon Features, 2012 (Red Devil Girl); *Captain Battle—Legacy War*, Saint James Films, 2013 (Anna); *V/H/S/2*, Collective Digital Studios, 2013 (Tabitha); *Bounty Killer*, Just Chorizo Productions, 2013 (Estelle); *Iron Man 3*, Paramount Pictures, 2013 (Girl in Bikini); *Fork You*, Creepersin Films, 2013 (Sandy); *Lizzie Borden's Revenge*, Saint James Films, 2013 (Ashley); *Gingerdead Man versus Evil Bong*, Full Moon Features, 2013 (Phoebe); *Dracula—The Impaler*, Flawless Production, 2013 (Ivina); *Bloodsucka Jones*, N/A, 2013 (Vega); *After School Massacre*, Frolic Pictures, 2014 (Linda); *The Coed and the Zombie Stoner*, Asylum, 2014 (Nurse Escandalo); *Burying the Ex*, Voltage Pictures, 2014 (Mindy); *The Oatmeal Man*, Colossal Theatre, 2014 (Danielle); *Our Way*, Romane Simon Film Production, 2014 (Tory); *Club Lingerie*, Frolic Pictures, 2014 (Trisha); *A Blood Story*, Hollow Films, 2015 (Madison Sheffield); *Mansion of Blood*, Elusive Entertainment, 2015 (Shirley); *Ballet of Blood*, Frolic Pictures, 2015 (Sylvie); *Book of Fire*, Tommy Frazier Productions, 2015 (Lucilla); *Less Than a Whisper*, Metropolis Pictures Entertainment, 2015 (Mrs. Sandra); *White Zombie*, Creepersin Films, 2016 (Madame Pierrette); *The Kirkbride Project*, Fire Born Films, 2016 (Nancy); *The Doll*, Sahara Vision Productions, 2016 (Leslie); *Ted Bundy Had a Son*, Mad Sin Cinema, 2016 (Grace); *Rhonda Rides to Hell*, Seven Devils Productions, 2016 (Kimi); *7 Faces of Jack the Ripper*, Sky Entertainment Group, 2016 (Catherine); *Range 15*, Street Justice Films, 2016 (Eliza); *Hallucinogen*, Sahara Vision Productions, 2016 (Amanda); *Evil Bong—High 5*, Full Moon Features, 2016 (Phoebe); *Bloody Island*, A Shadow in the Dark Productions, 2016 (Daisy); TELEVISION: *Horror Haiku*: "It's Only a Game," 2013 (Sarah).

Bibliography

Books

Burns, Bob. *Bob Burns' Monster Kid Memories: The Revised Edition*. Duncan, Oklahoma: BearManor Media, 2013.
Counelis, Paul. *11:59 and Counting: Horror Hosting in the 21st Century*. Flint, Michigan: Hallow Harvest Books, 2014.
Fetters, James M. *Creatures of the Night that We Loved So Sell: TV Horror Hosts of Southern California*. Boise, Idaho: Sabre Enterprises, LLC, 2011.
Glut, Donald. *Shock Theatre: Chicago Style*. Jefferson, North Carolina: McFarland, 2012.
Keesey, Pam. *Vamps: An Illustrated History of the Femme Fatale*. San Francisco: Cleis Press Inc., 1997.
Monahan, Michael. *Shock It To Me: Golden Ghouls of the Golden Gate*. San Francisco, California: UHF Nocturne, 2011.
Monahan, Michael. *American Scary—Conversations with the Kings, Queens, and Jesters of Late-Night Horror TV*. Baltimore: Midnight Marquee Press, 2011.
Okuda, Ted, and Mark Yurkiw. *From Shock Theatre to Svengoolie: Chicago TV Horror Movie Shows*. Chicago: Lake Claremont Press, 2007.
Poole, W Scott. *Vampira: Dark Goddess of Horror*. Berkeley, California: Soft Skull Press, 2014.
Ross, Jonathan. *The Incredibly Strange Film Book*. London: Simon & Schuster, 1995.
Watson, Elena. *Television Horror Movie Hosts*. Jefferson, North Carolina: McFarland, 1991.

Periodicals

Draculina #24, 1995
Fangoria #334, 2015
Femme Fatales vol. 5 #7, vol. 6 #7, vol. 7 #7, vol. 10 #5
Filmfax #13 (December, 1988)
Midnight Marquee #46
Scary Monsters #5, 8, 10, 27, 43, 50, 56, *Monster Memories Yearbook* (1994), *Monster Memories Yearbook* (2005)

Websites

Chicago Television History—http://www.chicagotelevision.com/
E-Gor's Chamber of TV Horror Hosts—http://myweb.wvnet.edu/e-gor/tvhorrorhosts/hostsm.html

Index

Numbers in ***bold italics*** refer to pages with photographs.

Aunt Gertie 7

Barney, Bonnie Sue 43–44; *see also* Georgette, the Fudge-Maker
Bennett, Joy 24–26; *see also* Dear
Bernhard, Sandra 7, ***8***, 9
Blaidonella 9–10
Brewton, Catherine 95–98; *see also* Misty Brew III
Brooks, Nichole 129–132; *see also* Sally, the Zombie Cheerleader
Brown, Kathy 143–145; *see also* Suspira Sheridan
Bubbles 10, ***11***, 12
Bunny Galore 12–13
Burns, Bob 80–84; *see also* Miss Shock
Burns, Kathy 80–84; *see also* Miss Shock

Cardille, "Chilly Billy" 43–44, 136, 147–148
Cherry Payne 13
Child, Phyllis 158–159; *see also* Vampira II
Clark, Lisa 99–106; *see also* Moona Lisa
Coppock, Brandi Lynn 123–124; *see also* Ravena, Goddess of Stonehenge
Cosmosina 13–14
Countess Lutzika 14
Countess Vampula 14–15
Countess Von Stauffenberger 15
Crematia Mortem 15–19, ***16***

Darcinia, Duchess of Darkness 19–20
Daughter of Ghoul 20–24, ***23***
Dear 24, ***25***, 26
Decay, Janet 20–24; *see also* Daughter of Ghoul
Denney, Nora ***68***; *see also* Marilyn the Witch
Dick, Karen ***51***; *see also* Grizelda MacCabre
Die Wilde Hilde 26–27
Dix, Nancy Lee 107; *see also* Mrs. Lucifer
Dixie Dellamorto ***27***–31

Earp, Rose Marie 116; *see also* Penny Dreadful I
Edwards, Jami 55–60; *see also* Jami Deadly
Elvira 32–42, ***34***, ***37***
Ends, Barbara 75–77; *see also* Millicent B. Ghastly
Erickson, Neils 67–68; *see also* Margali
Esmeralda 42
Evilun 42–43

Feverita 43

Gelehrter, Danielle 116–123; *see also* Penny Dreadful II
Georgette, the Fudge-Maker 43–44
Ghoulda ***44***–45
Ghoulia-Goolya 45–48, ***47***
Ghoulita 48–50
Gilbert, Glori-Anne 106–107; *see also* Morella
Grannell, Joshua 113; *see also* Peaches Christ
Grant, Rachel 111; *see also* Nina III
Grizelda MacCabre ***51***

Hagen, Nina 109–110; *see also* Nina I
Halley, Tabitha 145; *see also* Tabitha
Halloween Jacqueline 51–53
Harvey, Lietta 48–50; *see also* Ghoulita
Hayslett, Carmela 124–129; *see also* Roxsy Tyler
Hazel Witch 53
Herman, Eleanor 15; *see also* Countess Von Stauffenberger
Hildebrandt, Erika 124; *see also* Robyn Graves

Inge, Anna 53; *see also* Hazel Witch
Ione 53–54
Isobel-My Dear 54–55
Ivonna Cadaver 55

Jami Deadly 55–60, ***56***

Katarina 60–61
Klara Kackel 61

Lucretia 63

Macabra 63, ***64***, 65
Madame Cadaver 65
Madame Mortem 65–66
Malena Teves 66–67
Margali Morwentari 67–68
Marilyn the Witch ***68***
Marlena Midnite 68–72, ***69***, ***71***
McPherson, Julianna 123–124; *see also* Ravena, Goddess of Stonehenge
Medusa 72–73
Metzger, Marlena 68–72; *see also* Marlena Midnite
Midnight 73–***75***
Millicent B. Ghastly 75–77
Miss Misery 77–80, ***78***
Miss Shock 80–84, ***83***
Misty Brew I 84–90
Misty Brew II 90–95, ***92***
Misty Brew III 95–***98***
Moana 98–99
Moona Lisa 99–106, ***101***, ***102***, ***103***
Morella 106–107
Mrs. Lucifer 107
Ms. Monster ***108***–109
Mummy (and the Monkey) 109; *see also* Daughter of Ghoul

Nesmith, Ottola 111–113; *see also* The Old Lady
Newman, Laraine 61–63
Nina I ***109***–110
Nina II 110–111
Nina III 111
Nocturna 111
Norris, Kim 98–99; *see also* Moana
Nurmi, Maila 148–158; *see also* Vampira

The Old Lady 111, ***112***, 113
Ozmum, Patricia 65; *see also* Madame Cadaver

Peaches Christ 113
Penny Dreadful I 116

Penny Dreadful II 116–123, *118*, *120*
Peterson, Cassandra 32–42; see also Elvira
Popovich, Natalie 55; see also Ivonna Cadaver

Rae, Donna 147–*148*; see also Terminal Stare
Ramirez, Samantha 65–66; see also Madame Mortem
Ravena, Goddess of Stonehenge 123–124
Redgrave, Lynn 73–75; see also Midnight
Richards, Jennifer 72–73; see also Medusa
Roberts, Geri *44*–45; see also Ghoulda
Robinson, Mindy 159–160; see also Veronique Von Venom
Robyn Graves 124
Rolnick, Ione 53–54; see also Ione
Romer, Jeanne 99–106; see also Moona Lisa
Rowan, Jo 139–143; see also Stella Lugosi
Roxsy Tyler 124–129, *125*, *127*

Sally, the Zombie Cheerleader 129–132, *130*
Scarticia 132–133
Schlitt, Caroline 13
Scioli, Karen 136–139; see also Stella
Scott, Peg 113–116, *114*
Selman, Shirley 45–48; see also Ghoulia-Goolya
Shear, Rhonda 133–136, *134*
Sister Susie 136
Skully MacCabre 136
Smith, A.K. *108*–109; see also Ms. Monster
Solomon, Roberta 15–19; see also Crematia Mortem
Sprayberry, Ruth 42–43; see also Evilun
Stella 136–*137*, 138–*139*
Stella Lugosi 139–143
Sterling, Joyce 136; see also Sister Suzie
Suspira Sheridan *143*–145

Tabitha 145
Tarantula Ghoul 146–*147*
Terminal Stare 147–*148*

Vampira 148–158, *149*, *151*

Vampira II 158–159
Varma, Indira 110–111; see also Nina II
Veronique Von Venom 159–160
Voight, John 42; see also Esmeralda
Von Hoene, Dick 7; see also Aunt Gertie

Waldron, Suzanne 146–*147*; see also Tarantula Ghoul
Ward, Faye Fisher 84–90; see also Misty Brew I
Waters, Katarina 60–61; see also Katarina

Young, Reyna 77–80; see also Miss Misery

Zacherley 7, 54–55, 137, 138
Zawislak, Doreen 10–12; see also Bubbles

www.ingramcontent.com/pod-product-compliance
Ingram Content Group UK Ltd.
Pitfield, Milton Keynes, MK11 3LW, UK
UKHW050523150426
5217IPUK00026B/1765